A Stephen Birnbaum Travel Guide

Birnbaum's
TORONTO
1993

Alexandra Mayes Birnbaum
EDITOR

Lois Spritzer
EXECUTIVE EDITOR

Laura L. Brengelman
Managing Editor

D0066814

Mary Callahan
Jill Kadetsky
Susan McClung
Beth Schlau
Dana Margaret Schwartz
Associate Editors

Gene Gold
Assistant Editor

 HarperPerennial
A Division of HarperCollins*Publishers*

To Stephen, who merely made all this possible.

FIRST EDITION

ISSN 0749-2561 (Stephen Birnbaum Travel Guides)
ISSN 1061-5393 (Toronto)
ISBN 0-06-278062-X (pbk.)

93 94 95 96 97 CC/WP 10 9 8 7 6 5 4 3 2 1

"No other guide has as much to offer . . . these books are a pleasure to read." Gene Shalit on the *Today Show*

". . . Excellently organized for the casual traveler who is looking for a mix of recreation and cultural insight."
Washington Post

★ ★ ★ ★ ★ (5-star rating) "Crisply written and remarkably personable. Cleverly organized so you can pluck out the minutest fact in a moment. Satisfyingly thorough."
Réalités

"The information they offer is up-to-date, crisply presented but far from exhaustive, the judgments knowledgeable but not opinionated." *New York Times*

"The individual volumes are compact, the prose succinct, and the coverage up-to-date and knowledgeable . . . The format is portable and the index admirably detailed."
John Barkham Syndicate

". . . An abundance of excellent directions, diversions, and facts, including perspectives and getting-ready-to-go advice — succinct, detailed, and well organized in an easy-to-follow style." *Los Angeles Times*

"They contain an amount of information that is truly staggering, besides being surprisingly current."
Detroit News

"These guides address themselves to the needs of the modern traveler demanding precise, qualitative information . . . Upbeat, slick, and well put together."
Dallas Morning News

". . . Attractive to look at, refreshingly easy to read, and generously packed with information." *Miami Herald*

"These guides are as good as any published, and much better than most." *Louisville* (Kentucky) *Times*

Stephen Birnbaum Travel Guides

CONTRIBUTING EDITORS

Douglas Armour
S. E. Barber
George Bryant

SYMBOLS Gloria McKeown
MAPS Mark Stein Studios

Contents

GETTING READY TO GO

All the practical travel data you need to plan your vacation down to the final detail.

When and How to Go

Preparing

On the Road

Sources and Resources

THE CITY

A thorough, qualitative guide to Toronto. Each section offers a comprehensive report on the city's most compelling attractions and amenities, designed to be used on the spot.

DIVERSIONS

A selective guide to active and cerebral vacation themes, including the best places to pursue them.

DIRECTIONS

Five of the best walks in and around Toronto.

A Word from the Editor

Although Toronto may be just a hop, skip, and very broad jump away from the US border, make no mistake — it's Canadian through and through. For far too long, the capital of Ontario has been better known to business travelers than to vacationers. The rest of you don't know what you're missing. For whether meandering along Yonge Street, holder of the title "longest street in the world," or prowling around Yorkville, that up-to-the-minute rendering of the best of affluent young life in the Dominion, I am an ardent fan of Canada's no longer second city.

In its very own north-of-the-border way, this city is Canada's largest melting pot, with a helping of just about every ethnic group imaginable. My husband Steve Birnbaum and I found no better way to spend a Toronto Saturday than sampling Greek, Polish, Portuguese, or Ukrainian specialties at *Kensington Market,* and today's resident recipe has added ingredients from all over Asia and has been spiced up by Caribbean communities, too. (Try to time a visit in late June, to coincide with *Caravan,* the city's celebration of its ethnic exuberance.)

Foreign, yet familiar, Toronto needs no translation: I still remember laughing 'til my sides ached at the *Second City,* the comedy training ground for Martin Short, John Candy, and Andrea Martin (okay, some of the humor was very "inside," but those of us from the lower forty-eight found it hilarious).

With its streamlined skyline, sophisticated dining spots, and elegant *Eaton Centre,* Toronto is a city that has all too often been overlooked. We hope this book remedies that.

My own evolution as a traveler (which happily continues) is mirrored by the evolution of our guidebook series. When we began our series of modern travel guides, we logically began with "area" books, attempting to publish guides that would include the widest possible number of attractive destinations. When the public seemed to accept our new way of delivering travel data, we added titles covering only a single country, and when these became popular Steve and I began our newest expansion phase, which centers on a group of books that deal with only a single city. Now we can not only highlight our favorite urban destinations, but really describe how to get the very most out of a visit.

Such treatment of travel information only mirrors an increasingly pervasive trend among travelers — the frequent return to a treasured travel spot. Once upon a time, even the most dedicated travelers would visit distant parts of the world no more than once in a lifetime — usually as part of that fabled Grand Tour. But greater numbers of would-be sojourners are now availing themselves of the opportunity to visit a favored part of the world over and over again.

So where once it was routine to say you'd "seen" a particular city or country after a very superficial, once-over-lightly encounter, the more perceptive travelers of today recognize that it's entirely possible to have only skimmed the surface of a specific travel destination even after having visited that place more than a dozen times. Similarly, repeated visits to a single site permit true exploration of special interests, whether they be sporting, artistic, or intellectual.

For those of us who now have spent the last several years working out the special system under which we present information in this series, the luxury of being able to devote nearly as much space as we'd like to just a single city is as close to paradise for guide writers and editors as any of us expects to come. But clearly this is not the first guide to Toronto — one suspects that guides of one sort or another have existed since the 18th century, when fur traders built a fort in this uncharted land — so a traveler might logically ask why a new one is suddenly necessary.

Our answer is that the nature of travel to Toronto — and even of the travelers who now routinely make the trip — has changed dramatically of late. For the past 200 years or so, travel to even a town within our own country was considered an elaborate undertaking, one that required extensive advance planning. But with the advent of jet air travel in the late 1950s and of increased-capacity, wide-body aircraft during the late 1960s, travel to and around once distant destinations became extremely common. Attitudes as well as costs have changed significantly in the last couple of decades.

Obviously, any new guidebook to Toronto must keep pace with and answer the real needs of today's travelers. That's why we've tried to create a guide that's specifically organized, written, and edited for the more demanding modern traveler, one for whom qualitative information is infinitely more desirable than mere quantities of unappraised data. We think that this book, along with all the other guides in our series, represents a new generation of travel guides — one that is especially responsive to modern needs and interests.

But I should, I think, apologize for at least one indulgence in this text that is baldly chauvinistic, and that is our reference to citizens of the US as "Americans." Strictly speaking, Canadian citizens are just as much residents of the North American continent as US citizens, and we apologize for any slight our Canadian readers may feel about our having appropriated this terminology. It was done strictly in an effort to simplify the narrative, rather than an attempt to appropriate a common continental distinction.

For years, dating back as far as Herr Baedeker, travel guides have tended to be encyclopedic, seemingly much more concerned with demonstrating expertise in geography and history than with a real analysis of the sorts of things that actually concern a typical modern tourist. But today, when it is hardly necessary to tell a traveler where Toronto is (in many cases, the traveler has been there nearly as often as the guidebook editors), it becomes the responsibility of those editors to provide new perspectives and to suggest new directions in order to make the guide genuinely valuable.

That's exactly what we've tried to do in this series. I think you'll notice a different, more contemporary tone to the text, as well as an organization and focus that are distinctive and more functional. And even a random reading of what follows will demonstrate a substantial departure from the standard guidebook orientation, for we've not only attempted to provide information of a more compelling sort, but we also have tried to present the data in a format that makes it particularly accessible.

Needless to say, it's difficult to decide just what to include in a guidebook of this size — and what to omit. Early on, we realized that giving up the encyclopedic approach precluded our listing every single route and restaurant, a realization that helped define our overall editorial focus. Similarly, when we discussed the possibility of presenting certain information in other than strict geographic order, we found that the new format enabled us to arrange data in a way that we feel best answers the questions travelers typically ask.

Large numbers of specific questions have provided the real editorial skeleton for this book. The volume of mail we regularly receive emphasizes that modern travelers want very precise information, so we've tried to organize our material in the most responsive way possible. Readers who want to know the best restaurants or the best places to shop for furs in Toronto will have no trouble extracting that data from this guide.

Travel guides are, understandably, reflections of personal taste, and putting one's name on a title page obviously puts one's preferences on the line. But I think I ought to amplify just what "personal" means. Like Steve, I don't believe in the sort of personal guidebook that's a palpable misrepresentation on its face. It is, for example, hardly possible for any single travel writer to visit thousands of restaurants (and nearly as many hotels) in any given year and provide accurate appraisals of each. And even if it were physically possible for one human being to survive such an itinerary, it would of necessity have to be done at a dead sprint, and the perceptions derived therefrom would probably be less valid than those of any other intelligent individual visiting the same establishments. It is, therefore, impossible (especially in a large, annually revised and updated guidebook *series* such as we offer) to have only one person provide all the data on the entire world.

I also happen to think that such individual orientation is of substantially less value to readers. Visiting a single hotel for just one night or eating one hasty meal in a random restaurant hardly equips anyone to provide appraisals that are of more than passing interest. No amount of doggedly alliterative or oppressively onomatopoeic text can camouflage a technique that is essentially specious. We have, therefore, chosen what I like to describe as the "thee and me" approach to restaurant and hotel evaluation and, to a somewhat more limited degree, to the sites and sights we have included in the other sections of our text. What this really reflects is a personal sampling tempered by intelligent counsel from informed local sources, and these additional friends-of-the-editor are almost always residents of the city and/or area about which they are consulted.

Despite the presence of several editors, writers, researchers, and local contributors, very precise editing and tailoring keep our text fiercely subjective. So what follows is the gospel according to Birnbaum, and it represents as much of our own taste and instincts as we can manage. It is probable, therefore, that if you like your cities stylish and prefer small hotels with personality to huge high-rise anonymities, we're likely to have a long and meaningful relationship. Readers with dissimilar tastes may be less enraptured.

I also should point out something about the person to whom this guidebook is directed. Above all, he or she is a "visitor." This means that such elements as restaurants have been specifically picked to provide the visitor with a representative, enlightening, stimulating, and above all pleasant experience. Since so many extraneous considerations can affect the reception and service accorded a regular restaurant patron, our choices can in no way be construed as an exhaustive guide to resident dining. We think we've listed all the best places, in various price ranges, but they were chosen with a visitor's enjoyment in mind.

Other evidence of how we've tried to tailor our text to reflect modern travel habits is most apparent in the section we call DIVERSIONS. Where once it was common for travelers to spend an urban visit in a determinedly passive state, the emphasis is far more active today. So we've organized every activity we could reasonably evaluate and arranged the material in a way that is especially accessible to activists of either athletic or cerebral bent. It is no longer necessary, therefore, to wade through a pound or two of superfluous prose just to find the most elegant hostelry or the most dramatic ski slopes within a reasonable distance of the city.

If there is a single thing that best characterizes the revolution in and evolution of current holiday habits, it is that most travelers now consider travel a right rather than a privilege. No longer is a family trip to the far corners of the world necessarily a once-in-a-lifetime thing; nor is the idea of visiting exotic, faraway places in the least worrisome. Travel today translates as the enthusiastic desire to sample all of the world's opportunities, to find that elusive quality of experience that is not only enriching but comfortable. For that reason, we've tried to make what follows not only helpful and enlightening, but the sort of welcome companion of which every traveler dreams.

Finally, I also should point out that every good travel guide is a living enterprise; that is, no part of this text is carved in stone. In our annual revisions, we refine, expand, and further hone all our material to serve your travel needs better. To this end, no contribution is of greater value to us than your personal reaction to what we have written, as well as information reflecting your own experiences while using the book. We earnestly and enthusiastically solicit your comments about this guide *and* your opinions and perceptions about places you have recently visited. In this way, we will be able to provide the most current information — including the actual experiences of recent travelers — and to make those experiences more readily available to others. Please write to us at 10 E. 53rd St., New York, NY 10022.

We sincerely hope to hear from you.

ALEXANDRA MAYES BIRNBAUM

How to Use This Guide

? A great deal of care has gone into the special organization of this guidebook, and we believe it represents a real breakthrough in the presentation of travel material. Our aim is to create a new, more modern generation of travel books, and to make this guide the most useful and practical travel tool available today.

Our text is divided into four basic sections in order to present information in the best way on every possible aspect of a vacation to Toronto. This organization itself should alert you to the vast and varied opportunities available, as well as indicate all the specific data necessary to plan a successful visit. You won't find much of the conventional "swaying palms and shimmering sands" text here; we've chosen instead to deliver more useful and practical information. Prospective itineraries tend to speak for themselves, and with so many diverse travel opportunities, we feel our main job is to highlight what's where and to provide basic information — how, when, where, how much, and what's best — to assist you in making the most intelligent choices possible.

Here is a brief summary of the four basic sections of this book, and what you can expect to find in each. We believe that you will find both your travel planning and en route enjoyment enhanced by having this book at your side.

GETTING READY TO GO

This mini-encyclopedia of practical travel facts is a sort of know-it-all companion with all the precise information necessary to create a successful trip to Toronto. There are entries on more than 25 separate topics, including how to get where you're going, what preparations to make before leaving, what to expect, what your trip is likely to cost, and how to avoid prospective problems. The individual entries are specific, realistic, and, where appropriate, cost-oriented. Except where noted, all prices in this book are in US dollars.

We expect you to use this section most in the course of planning your trip, for its ideas and suggestions are intended to simplify this often confusing period. Entries are intentionally concise, in an effort to get to the meat of the matter with the least extraneous prose. These entries are augmented by extensive lists of specific sources from which to obtain even more specialized data, plus some suggestions for obtaining travel information on your own.

THE CITY

The individual report on Toronto has been prepared with the assistance of researchers, contributors, professional journalists, and other experts who live in the city. Although useful at the planning stage, THE CITY is really designed to be taken along and used on the spot. The report offers a short-stay guide, including an essay introducing the city as a historic entity and as a contemporary place to visit. *At-a-Glance* material is actually a site-by-site survey of the most important, interesting, and sometimes most eclectic sights to see and things to do. *Sources and Resources* is a concise listing of pertinent tourist information meant to answer myriad potentially pressing questions as they arise — from simple things such as the address of the local tourism office, how to get around, which sightseeing tours to take, and when special events occur, to something more difficult, like where to find the best nightspot or hail a taxi, which are the chic places to shop and where to find the more irresistible bargains, and where the best museums and theaters are to be found. *Best in Town* lists our cost-and-quality choices of the best places to eat and sleep on a variety of budgets.

DIVERSIONS

This section is designed to help travelers find the best places in which to pursue a wide range of physical and cerebral activities, without having to wade through endless pages of unrelated text. This very selective guide lists the broadest possible range of activities, including all the best places to pursue them.

We start with a list of special places to stay and eat, and move to activities that require some perspiration — sports preferences and other rigorous pursuits — and go on to report on a number of more spiritual vacation opportunities. In every case, our suggestion of a particular location — and often our recommendation of a specific hotel — is intended to guide you to that special place where the quality of experience is likely to be highest. Whether you seek a historic hotel or museum or the best place to shop or ski, each category is the equivalent of a comprehensive checklist of the absolute best in Toronto.

DIRECTIONS

Here are five walks that cover the city, along its main thoroughfares and side streets, past its most spectacular landmarks and splendid greenspaces. This is the only section of the book that is organized geographically; itineraries can be "connected" for longer sojourns, or used individually for short, intensive explorations.

Although each of this book's sections has a distinct format and a special function, they have all been designed to be used together to provide a complete inventory of travel information. To use this book to full advantage, take a few minutes to read the table of contents and random entries in each section to get a firsthand feel for how it all fits together.

Pick and choose needed information. Assume, for example, that you always wanted to visit Toronto, experience its colorful food markets, and enjoy its broad range of ethnic cuisines, but never really knew how to organize it or where to go. Choose specific restaurants from the selections offered in "Eating Out" in THE CITY, add some of those noted in each walking tour in DIREC-

TIONS, and cross-reference with those in the roundup of the best in the cities in the *Toronto's Top Restaurants* section in DIVERSIONS.

In other words, the sections of this book are building blocks designed to help you put together the best possible trip. Use them selectively as a tool, a source of ideas, a reference work for accurate facts, and a guidebook to the best buys, the most exciting sights, the most pleasant accommodations, the tastiest food — *the best travel experience* that you can possibly have.

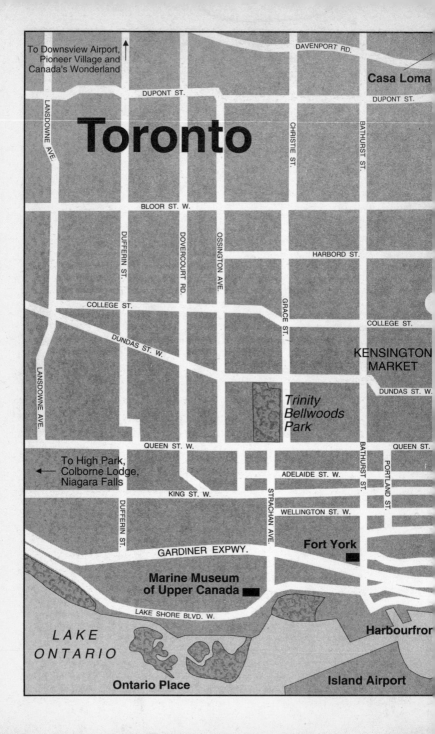

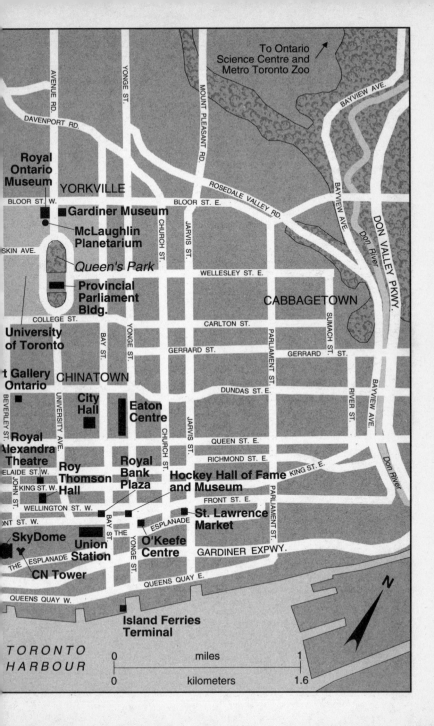

GETTING READY TO GO

When and How to Go

When to Go

 Though there really isn't a "best" time to visit Toronto, the months of May through September traditionally have been the most popular vacation time. However, more and more travelers who have the choice are enjoying the substantial advantages of off-season, or "shoulder" season travel. Though some tourist attractions may close during the slower seasons, the majority remain open and tend to be less crowded. What's more, while winter sports such as skiing are in full swing in surrounding areas, travel to and from Toronto and environs during these seasons generally is less expensive.

For some, the most convincing argument in favor of off-season travel is the economic one. Getting there and staying there is more affordable during less popular travel periods, as airfares, hotel rooms, and car rental rates go down and less expensive package tours become available; the independent traveler can go farther on less, too.

A definite bonus to visiting during the off-season is that even the most basic services are performed more efficiently. In theory, off-season service is identical to that offered during high season, but the fact is that the absence of demanding crowds inevitably begets much more thoughtful and personal attention.

Even during the off-season, high-season rates also may prevail because of an important local event. Particularly in Toronto, special events and major trade shows or conferences held at the time of your visit also are sure to affect not only the availability of discounts on accommodations, but the basic availabilty of a place to stay.

In short, like many other popular places in Canada, the vacation appeal of Toronto has become multi-seasonal. But the noted exceptions notwithstanding, most travel destinations are decidedly less heavily trafficked and less expensive during the winter.

WEATHER: While there's no getting around Toronto's cold and snowy winters, its summers seem to make up for them, delivering pleasantly warm temperatures averaging 83F (25C). June and September evenings can be cooler, however. Spring temperatures average about 53F (12C) and in fall drop to 45F (7C). December through March ushers in frigid temperatures — the low averaging about 18F (-8C), the high about 30F (-1C) — and a fair amount of snow.

Travelers can get current readings and extended forecasts through the *Weather Channel Connection*, the worldwide weather report center of the *Weather Channel*, a cable television station. By dialing 900-WEATHER and punching in either the first four letters of the city name or area code for over 600 US cities, an up-to-date recording will provide such information as current temperature, barometric pressure, relative humidity, and wind speed, as well as a general 2-day forecast. Boating and highway reports are also provided for some locations. Weather information for over 225 international destinations can be obtained by punching in the first 4 letters of the city name. To hear the weather report for TORONTO, punch in TORO. (To find out which cities or locations in a given country are covered, enter the first four letters of the *country* name.) Callers also can access information on the weather patterns for any time of the year in the area requested, as well as international travel information such as visa requirements, US State Department travel advisories, tipping, and voltage requirements. This 24-hour service can be accessed from any touch-tone phone in the US, and costs 95¢ per minute. The charge will show up on your phone bill. For additional information, contact the *Weather Channel Connection,* 2600 Cumberland Pkwy., Atlanta, GA 30339 (phone: 404-434-6800).

SPECIAL EVENTS: Spring in Toronto finds baseball fans cheering the *Blue Jays* to another spectacular season. In May it's the *International Children's Festival,* which features jugglers, mimes, and entertainment for all. *Du Maurier Downtown Jazz Festival* offers many free concerts around town during June. Summer also presents the *Benson & Hedges International Fireworks Festival,* which lasts 2 weeks and brings together the most talented pyrotechnicians from around the world. Toronto plays host in July to the *Molson Indy* auto championship, where for one day race cars weave through the city streets. The *Festival of Festivals* screens more than 300 international films in September. And in October, the *Royal Agricultural Winter Fair,* billed as the largest agricultural fair under one roof, runs for 10 days.

Traveling by Plane

Flying usually is the quickest and most efficient way to get to Toronto. When all costs are taken into account for traveling any substantial distance, plane travel usually is less expensive per mile than traveling by car. It also is the most economical way to go in terms of time. Although touring by car, bus, or train certainly are more scenic ways to travel, air travel is far faster and more direct — the less time spent in transit, the more time spent at your destination.

Despite recent attempts at price simplification by a number of major US carriers, the airlines offering flights to Toronto continue to sell seats at a variety of prices under a vast spectrum of requirements and restrictions. Since you probably will spend more for your airfare than for any other single item in your travel budget, try to take advantage of the lowest available fare. You should know what kinds of flights are available, the rules and regulations pertaining to air travel, and all the special package options.

SCHEDULED FLIGHTS: Air service to Toronto is provided by three Canadian airlines and a number of US carriers. *Air Canada* flies from Baltimore, Boston, Chicago, Cleveland, Hartford (CT), Los Angeles, Miami, New York, San Francisco, and Tampa (FL). *Air Ontario* provides service from Baltimore, Cleveland, Hartford, and New York (Newark). *Canadian Airlines International* flies from Allentown (PA), Columbus (OH), Dayton (OH), Harrisburg (PA), Indianapolis, and Pittsburgh (PA). *Alaska Airlines* flies only from Los Angeles and San Diego. *American* provides service from Chicago, Dallas/Ft. Worth, Nashville, and New York. *Atlantic Coast Airlines* flies from Newburgh (NY). *Delta* has flights from Albany (NY), Atlanta, Boston, Buffalo (NY), Cincinnati, Miami/Ft. Lauderdale, Orlando, Pittsburgh, Syracuse (NY), and Washington, DC. *Northwest* flies from Detroit, Milwaukee, and Minneapolis. *United* has flights from Chicago and Seattle. *USAir* has flights from Buffalo, Charlotte (NC), Cleveland, Indianapolis, Philadelphia, Pittsburgh, and Rochester (NY).

Tickets – When traveling on one of the many regularly scheduled flights, a full-fare ticket provides maximum travel flexibility (although at considerable expense), because there are no advance booking requirements. A prospective passenger can buy a ticket for a flight right up to the minute of takeoff — if a seat is available. If your ticket is for a round trip, you can make the return reservation whenever you wish — months before you leave, or the day before you return. Assuming the foreign immigration requirements are met, you can stay at your destination for as long as you like. (Tickets generally are good for a year and can be renewed if not used.) On some airlines, you also may be able to cancel your flight at any time without penalty; on others, cancellation — even of a full-fare ticket — may be subject to a variety of restrictions. It pays to check with the individual carrier *before* booking your flight. In addition, while it is true that this category of ticket can be purchased at the last minute, it is advisable to reserve well in advance during popular vacation periods and around holiday times.

Fares – Airfares continue to change so rapidly that even the experts find it difficult to keep up with them. This ever-changing situation is due to a number of factors, including airline deregulation (in both the US and Canada), volatile labor relations, increasing fuel costs, and vastly increased competition.

Perhaps the most common misconception about fares on scheduled airlines is that the cost of the ticket determines how much service will be provided on the flight. This is true only to a certain extent. A far more realistic rule of thumb is that the less you pay for your ticket, the more restrictions and qualifications are likely to come into play before you board the plane (as well as after you get off). These qualifying aspects relate to the months (and the days of the week) during which you must travel, how far in advance you must purchase your ticket, the minimum and maximum amount of time you may or must remain away, your willingness to decide on a return date at the time of booking — and your ability to stick to that decision. It is not uncommon for passengers sitting side by side on the same wide-body jet to have paid fares varying by hundreds of dollars, and all too often the traveler paying more would have been equally willing (and able) to accept the terms of the far less expensive ticket.

In general, the great variety of US domestic fares, Canadian domestic fares, and fares between the two countries can be reduced to four basic categories, including first class, coach (also called economy or tourist class), and excursion or discount fares. A fourth category, called business class, has been added by many airlines in recent years. In addition, Advance Purchase Excursion (APEX) fares offer savings under certain conditions.

A **first class** ticket is your admission to the special section of the aircraft, with larger seats, more legroom, sleeperette seating on some wide-body aircraft, better (or, at least, more elaborately served) food, free drinks and headsets for movies and music channels, and, above all, personal attention. First class fares are about twice those of full-fare economy, although both first class passengers and those paying full economy fares are entitled to reserve seats and are sold tickets on an open reservation system. Sometimes, a first class ticket offers the additional advantage of allowing travelers to schedule any number of stops en route to or from their most distant destination — provided that certain set, but generous, restrictions regarding maximum mileage limits and flight schedules are respected.

Not too long ago, there were only two classes of air travel, first class and all the rest, usually called economy or tourist. Then **business class** came into being — one of the most successful recent airline innovations. At first, business class passengers were merely curtained off from the other economy passengers. Now a separate cabin or cabins — usually toward the front of the plane — is the norm. While standards of comfort and service are not as high as in first class, they represent a considerable improvement over conditions in the rear of the plane, with roomier seats, more leg and shoulder space between passengers, and fewer seats abreast. Free liquor and headsets, a choice of meal entrées, and a separate counter for speedier check-in are other inducements. As in first class, a business class passenger may travel on any scheduled flight he or she wishes, buy a one-way or round-trip ticket, and have the ticket remain valid for a year. There are no minimum or maximum stay requirements, no advance booking requirements, and sometimes (depending on the carrier), no cancellation penalties. If the particular airline allows first class passengers unlimited free stopovers, this privilege generally also is extended to those flying business class. Though airlines often have their own names for their business class service, such as Executive Class on *Air Canada* or Medallion Class on *Delta, Canadian Airlines International* simply refers to it as business class.

The terms of the **coach** or **economy** fare may vary slightly from airline to airline, and in fact from time to time airlines may be selling more than one type of economy fare. Coach or economy passengers sit more snugly, as many as 10 in a single row on a wide-body jet, behind the first class and business class sections. Normally, alcoholic drinks are not free, nor are the headsets. If there are two economy fares on the books, one (often called "regular economy") still may include a number of free stopovers. The other, less expensive fare (often called "special economy") may limit stopovers to one or two, with a charge (typically $25) for each one.

Like first class passengers, however, passengers paying the full coach fare are subject to none of the restrictions that usually are attached to less expensive excursion and discount fares. There are no advance booking requirements, no minimum stay requirements, and often no cancellation penalties — but beware, the rules regarding cancellation vary from carrier to carrier. Tickets are sold on an open reservation system: They can be bought for a flight right up to the minute of takeoff (if seats are available), and if the ticket is round trip, the return reservation can be made anytime you wish. Both first class and coach tickets generally are good for a year, after which they can be renewed if not used, and if you ultimately decide not to fly at all, your money may be refunded (again, policies vary). The cost of economy and business class tickets between the US and Canada does not change much in the course of the year, though on some routes they vary from a basic (low-season) price in effect most of the year to a peak (high-season) price — these seasonal demarcations vary according to the destination.

Excursion and other **discount** fares are the airlines' equivalent of a special sale and usually apply to round-trip bookings only. These fares generally differ according to the season and the number of travel days permitted. They are only a bit less flexible than full-fare economy tickets, and are, therefore, often useful for both business and holiday travelers. Most round-trip excursion tickets include strict minimum and maximum stay requirements and reservations can be changed only within the specified time limits. So don't count on extending a ticket beyond the prescribed time of return or staying less time than required. Again, different airlines may have different regulations concerning stopover privileges and sometimes excursion fares are less expensive midweek. The availability of these reduced-rate seats is most limited at busy times such as holidays. Discount or excursion fare ticket holders sit with the coach passengers and, for all intents and purposes, are indistinguishable from them. They receive all the same basic services, even though they may have paid anywhere between 30% and 55% less for the trip. Obviously, it's wise to make plans early enough to qualify for this less expensive transportation if possible.

These discount or excursion fares may masquerade under a variety of names, and they may vary from city to city (from the East Coast to the West Coast, especially), but they invariably have strings attached. A common requirement is that the ticket be purchased a certain number of days — usually between 7 and 21 days — in advance of departure, though it may be booked weeks or months in advance (it has to be "ticketed," or paid for, shortly after booking, however). The return reservation usually has to be made at the time of the original ticketing and often cannot be changed later than a certain number of days (again, usually 7 to 21 days) before the return flight. If events force a change in the return reservation after the date allowed, the passenger may have to pay the difference between the round-trip excursion rate and the round-trip coach rate, although some carriers permit such scheduling changes for a nominal fee. In addition, some airlines also may allow passengers to use their discounted fares by standing by for an empty seat, even if they don't otherwise have standby fares. Another common condition is a minimum and maximum stay requirement: for example 1 to 6 days or 6 to 14 days (but including at least a Saturday night). Last, cancellation penalties of up to 50% of the full price of the ticket have been assessed — if a refund is offered at all — so careful planning is imperative. Check the specific penalty in effect when you purchase your discount/excursion ticket.

On some airlines, the ticket bearing the lowest price of all the current discount fares is the ticket where no change at all in departure and/or return flights is permitted, and where the ticket price is totally nonrefundable. If you do buy such a nonrefundable ticket, you should be aware of a policy followed by *some* airlines that may make it easier to change your plans if necessary. For a fee — set by each airline and payable at the airport when checking in — you *may* be able to change the time or date of a return flight on a nonrefundable ticket. However, if the nonrefundable ticket price for the replacement flight is higher than that of the original (as often is the case when trading in a weekday for a weekend flight), you will have to pay the difference. Any such change must be made a certain number of days in advance — in some cases as little as 2 days — of either the original or the replacement flight, whichever is earlier; restrictions are set by the individual carrier. (Travelers holding a nonrefundable or other restricted ticket who must change their plans due to a family emergency should know that some carriers may make special allowances in such situations; for further information, see *Staying Healthy*, in this section.)

■ **Note:** Due to recent changes in many US airlines' policies, nonrefundable tickets are now available that carry none of the above restrictions. Although passengers still may *not* be able to obtain a refund for the price paid, the time or date of a departing or return flight may be changed at any time (assuming seats are available) for a nominal service charge.

There also is a newer, often less expensive type of excursion fare, the **APEX**, or **Advance Purchase Excursion**, fare. As with traditional excursion fares, passengers paying an APEX fare sit with and receive the same basic services as any other coach or economy passengers, even though they may have paid up to 50% less for their seats. In return, they are subject to certain restrictions. In the case of flights to Canada, the ticket usually is good for a minimum of approximately 4 days away (spanning at least 1 weekend), and a maximum, currently, of 1 month to 1 year (depending on the airline and the destination); and as its name implies, it must be "ticketed," or paid for in its entirety, a certain period of time before departure — usually between 7 and 21 days.

The drawback to some APEX fares is that they penalize travelers who change their minds — and travel plans. Usually, the return reservation must be made at the time of the original ticketing, and if for some reason you change your schedule, you will have to pay a penalty of $100 or 10% of the ticket value, whichever is greater, as long as you travel within the validity period of your ticket. More flexible APEX fares recently have been introduced that allow travelers to make changes in the date or time of their flights for a nominal charge (as low as $25).

With either type of APEX fare, if you change your return to a date less than the minimum stay or more than the maximum stay, the difference between the round-trip APEX fare and the full round-trip coach rate will have to be paid. There also is a penalty of anywhere from $50 to $100 or more for canceling or changing a reservation *before* travel begins — check the specific penalty in effect when you purchase your ticket. No stopovers are allowed on an APEX ticket. Depending on the destination, APEX tickets to Canada may be sold at basic and peak rates (the peak season will vary) and may include surcharges for weekend flights.

Standby fares, at one time the rock-bottom price at which a traveler could fly to Canada, have become elusive. At the time of this writing, most major scheduled airlines did not regularly offer standby fares on direct flights to Canada. Because airline fares and their conditions constantly change, however, bargain hunters should not hesitate to ask if such a fare exists at the time they plan to travel.

While the definition of standby varies somewhat from airline to airline, it generally means that you make yourself available to buy a ticket for a flight (usually no sooner than the day of departure), then literally stand by on the chance that a seat will be empty. Once aboard, however, a standby passenger has the same meal service and frills (or lack of them) enjoyed by others in the economy class compartment.

Something else to check is the possibility of qualifying for a **GIT** (Group Inclusive Travel) fare, which requires that a specific dollar amount of ground arrangements be purchased, in advance, along with the ticket. The requirements vary as to number of travel days and stopovers permitted, and the minimum number of passengers required for a group. The actual fares also vary, but the cost will be spelled out in brochures distributed by the tour operators handling the ground arrangements. In the past, GIT fares were among the least expensive available from the established carriers, but the prevalence of discount fares has caused group fares to all but disappear from some air routes. Travelers reading brochures on group package tours to Canada will find that, in almost all cases, the applicable airfare given as a sample (to be added to the price of the land package to obtain the total tour price) is an APEX fare, the same discount fare available to the independent traveler.

The major airlines serving Canada from the US also may offer individual fare excursion rates similar to GIT fares, which are sold in conjunction with ground accommodation packages. Previously called ITX and sometimes referred to as individual tour-basing fares, these fares generally are offered as part of "air/hotel/car/transfer packages," and can reduce the cost of an economy fare by more than a third. The packages are booked for a specific amount of time, with return dates specified; rescheduling and cancellation restrictions and penalties vary from carrier to carrier. At the time of this writing, these fares were offered to popular destinations throughout Canada by *Air Canada, American, Canadian Airlines International, Delta,* and *USAir.* Note that their offerings may or may not represent substantial savings over standard economy fares, so check at the time you plan to travel. (For further information on package options, see *Package Tours,* in this section.)

Travelers looking for the least expensive possible airfares should, finally, scan the pages of their hometown newspapers (especially the Sunday travel section) for announcements of special promotional fares. Most airlines offer their most attractive special fares to encourage travel during slow seasons and to inaugurate and publicize new routes. Even if none of these factors applies, prospective passengers can be fairly sure that the number of discount seats per flight at the lowest price is strictly limited, or that the fare offering includes a set expiration date — which means it's absolutely necessary to move fast to enjoy the lowest possible price.

Among other special airline promotional deals for which you should be on the lookout are discount or upgrade coupons sometimes offered by the major carriers and found in mail-order merchandise catalogues. For instance, airlines sometimes issue coupons that typically cost around $25 each and are good for a percentage discount or an upgrade on an international airline ticket — including flights to Canada. The only requirement beyond the fee generally is that a coupon purchaser must buy at least one item from the catalogue. There usually are some minimum airfare restrictions before the coupon is redeemable, but in general these are worthwhile offers. Restrictions often include certain blackout days (when the coupon cannot be used at all), usually imposed during peak travel periods. These coupons are particularly valuable to business travelers who tend to buy full-fare tickets, and while the coupons are issued in the buyer's name, they can be used by others who are traveling on the same itinerary.

It's always wise to ask about discount or promotional fares and about any conditions that might restrict booking, payment, cancellation, and changes in plans. Check the prices from neighboring cities. A special rate may be offered in a nearby city but not in yours, and it may be enough of a bargain to warrant your leaving from that city. Ask if there is a difference in price for midweek versus weekend travel, or if there is a further discount for traveling early in the morning or late at night. Also be sure to investigate package deals, which are offered by virtually every airline. These may include car rental, accommodations, and dining and/or sightseeing features, in addition to the basic airfare, and the combined cost of packaged elements usually is considerably less than the cost of the identical elements when purchased separately.

If in the course of your research you come across a deal that seems too good to be true, keep in mind that logic may not be a component of deeply discounted airfares — there's not always any sane relationship between miles to be flown and the price to get there. More often than not, the level of competition on a given route dictates the degree of discount, and don't be dissuaded from accepting an offer that sounds irresistible just because it also sounds illogical. Better to buy that inexpensive fare while it's being offered and worry about the sense — or absence thereof — while you're flying to your desired destination.

When you're satisfied that you've found the lowest possible price for which you can conveniently qualify (you may have to call the airline more than once, because different airline reservations clerks have been known to quote different prices), make your booking. Then, to protect yourself against fare increases, purchase and pay for your ticket as soon as possible after you've received a confirmed reservation. Airlines generally will honor their tickets, even if the operative price at the time of your flight is higher than the price you paid; if fares go up between the time you *reserve* a flight and the time you *pay* for it, you likely will be out of luck. Finally, with excursion or discount fares, it is important to remember that when a reservations clerk says that you must purchase a ticket by a specific date, this is an absolute deadline. Miss the deadline and the airline may automatically cancel your reservation without telling you.

■ **Note:** Another wrinkle in the airfare scene is that if the fares go *down* after you purchase your ticket, you *may* be entitled to a refund of the difference. However, this is only possible in certain situations — availability and advance purchase restrictions pertaining to the lower rate are set by the airline. If you suspect that you may be able to qualify for such a refund, check with your travel agent or the airline.

Frequent Flyers – The leading carriers serving Toronto from the US — *Air Canada, American, Canadian Airlines International, Delta, Northwest, United,* and *USAir* — offer a bonus system to frequent travelers. After the first 10,000 miles, for example, a passenger might be eligible for a first class seat for the coach fare; after another 10,000 miles, he or she might receive a discount on his or her next ticket purchase. The value of the bonuses continues to increase as more miles are logged.

Bonus miles also may be earned by patronizing affiliated car rental companies or hotel chains, or by using one of the credit cards that now offer this reward. In deciding whether to accept such a credit card from one of the issuing organizations that tempt you with frequent flyer mileage bonuses on a specific airline, first determine whether the interest rate charged on the unpaid balance is the same as (or less than) possible alternate credit cards, and whether the annual "membership" fee also is equal or lower. If these charges are slightly higher than those of competing cards, weigh the difference against the potential value in airfare savings. Also ask about any bonus miles awarded just for signing up — 1,000 is common, 5,000 generally the maximum.

For the most up-to-date information on frequent flyer bonus options, you may want to send for the monthly newsletter *Frequent*. Issued by Frequent Publications, it provides current information about frequent flyer plans in general, as well as specific data about promotions, awards, and combination deals to help you keep track of the profusion — and confusion — of current and upcoming availabilities. For a year's subscription, send $33 to Frequent Publications, 4715-C Town Center Dr., Colorado Springs, CO 80916 (phone: 800-333-5937).

There also is a monthly magazine called *Frequent Flyer,* but unlike the newsletter mentioned above, its focus is primarily on newsy articles of interest to business travelers and other frequent flyers. Published by Official Airline Guides (PO Box 58543, Boulder, CO 80322-8543; phone: 800-323-3537), *Frequent Flyer* is available for $24 for a 1-year subscription.

Low-Fare Airlines – Increasingly, the stimulus for special fares is the appearance of airlines associated with bargain rates. On these airlines, all seats on any given flight generally sell for the same price, which tends to be somewhat below the lowest discount fare offered by the larger, more established airlines. It is important to note that tickets offered by these smaller companies frequently are not subject to the same restrictions as some of the discounted fares offered by the more established carriers. They may not require advance purchase or minimum and maximum stays, may involve no cancellation penalties, and may be available one way or round trip. A disadvantage to some low-fare airlines, however, is that when something goes wrong, such as delayed baggage or a flight cancellation due to equipment breakdown, their smaller fleets and fewer flights mean that passengers may have to wait longer for a solution than they would on one of the equipment-rich major carriers.

Taxes and Other Fees – Travelers who have shopped for the best possible flight at the lowest possible price should be warned that a number of extras will be added to that price and collected by the airline or travel agent who issues the ticket. For instance, the $6 International Air Transportation Tax is a departure tax paid by all passengers flying from the US to a foreign destination.

Still another fee is charged by some airlines to cover more stringent security procedures, prompted by recent terrorist incidents. The 10% federal US Transportation Tax applies to travel within the US or US territories. It does not apply to passengers flying between US cities or territories en route to a foreign destination, unless the trip includes a stopover of more than 12 hours at a US point. Someone flying from Los Angeles to New York and stopping in New York for more than 12 hours before boarding a flight to Canada, for instance, would pay the 10% tax on the domestic portion of the trip. When flying from Canada back to the US, a Canadian Departure Tax also is charged; this amounts to 5% of the ticket cost, plus CN$4, the total of which may not exceed CN$19. Note that these taxes *usually* (but not always) are included in advertised fares and in the prices quoted by airline reservation clerks.

Reservations – For those who don't have the time or patience to investigate personally all possible air departures and connections for a proposed trip, a travel agent can be of inestimable help. A good agent should have all the information on which flights go where and when, and which categories of tickets are available on each. Most have computerized reservation links with the major carriers, so that a seat can be reserved and confirmed in minutes. An increasing number of agents also possess fare-comparison computer programs, so they often are very reliable sources of detailed competitive price data. (For more information, see *How to Use a Travel Agent,* in this section.)

When making plane reservations through a travel agent, ask the agent to give the airline your home phone number, as well as your daytime business phone number. All too often the agent uses the agency number as the official contact for changes in flight plans. Especially during the winter, weather conditions hundreds or even thousands of miles away can wreak havoc with flight schedules. Aircraft are constantly in use, and a plane delayed in the Orient or on the West Coast can miss its scheduled flight from the East Coast the next morning. The airlines are fairly reliable about getting this sort of information to passengers if they can reach them; diligence does little good at 10 PM if the airline has only the agency's or an office number.

Reconfirmation is strongly recommended for all international flights (though it is not usually required on US domestic flights) and, in the case of flights to Canada, it is essential to confirm your round-trip reservations — especially the return leg — as well as any point-to-point flights within the country. Some (though increasingly fewer) reservations to and from international destinations are automatically canceled after a required reconfirmation period (typically 72 hours) has passed — even if you have a confirmed, fully paid ticket in hand. It always is wise to call ahead to make sure that the airline did not slip up in entering your original reservations, or in registering any changes you may have made since, and that it has your seat reservation and/or special meal request in the computer. If you look at the printed information on your ticket, you'll see the airline's reconfirmation policy stated explicitly. Don't be lulled into a false sense of security by the "OK" on your ticket next to the number and time of the flight. This only means that a reservation has been entered; a reconfirmation still may be necessary. If in doubt — call.

If you plan not to take a flight on which you hold a confirmed reservation, by all means inform the airline. Because the problem of "no-shows" is a constant expense for airlines, they are allowed to overbook flights, a practice that often contributes to the threat of denied boarding for a certain number of passengers (see "Getting Bumped," below).

Seating – For most types of tickets, airline seats usually are assigned on a first-come, first-served basis at check-in, although some airlines make it possible to reserve a seat at the time of ticket purchase. Always check in early for your flight, even with advance seat assignments. A good rule of thumb for international flights is to arrive at the airport *at least* 2 hours before the scheduled departure to give yourself plenty of time in case there are long lines.

Most airlines furnish seating charts, which make choosing a seat much easier, but there are a few basics to consider. You must decide whether you prefer a window, aisle, or middle seat. On flights where smoking is permitted, you also should indicate if you prefer the smoking or nonsmoking section.

The amount of legroom provided (as well as chest room, especially when the seat in front of you is in a reclining position) is determined by something called "pitch," a measure of the distance between the back of the seat in front of you and the front of the back of your seat. The amount of pitch is a matter of airline policy, not the type of plane you fly. First class and business class seats have the greatest pitch, a fact that figures prominently in airline advertising. In economy class or coach, the standard pitch ranges from 33 to as little as 31 inches — downright cramped.

The number of seats abreast, another factor determining comfort, depends on a combination of airline policy and airplane dimensions. First class and business class have the fewest seats per row. Economy generally has 9 seats per row on a DC-10 or an L-1011, making either one slightly more comfortable than a 747, on which there normally are 10 seats per row. Charter flights on DC-10s and L-1011s, however, often have 10 seats per row and can be noticeably more cramped than 747 charters, on which the seating normally remains at 10 per row. A 727 has 6 seats across.

Airline representatives claim that most aircraft are more stable toward the front and midsection, while seats farthest from the engines are quietest. Passengers who have long legs and are traveling on a wide-body aircraft might request a seat directly behind a door or emergency exit, since these seats often have greater than average pitch, or a seat in the first row of a given section, which offers extra legroom — although these seats are increasingly being reserved for passengers who are willing (and able) to perform certain tasks in the event of emergency evacuation. It often is impossible, however, to see the movie from these seats, which are directly behind the plane's exits.

Be aware that seats in the first row of the economy section (called "bulkhead" seats) on a conventional aircraft (not a widebody) do *not* offer extra legroom, since the fixed partition will not permit passengers to slide their feet under it, and that watching a movie from these first-row seats can be difficult and uncomfortable. These bulkhead seats do, however, provide ample room to use a bassinet or safety seat and often are reserved for families traveling with children.

Despite all these rules of thumb, finding out which specific rows are near emergency exits or at the front of a wide-body cabin can be difficult because seating arrangements on two otherwise identical planes vary from airline to airline. There is, however, a quarterly publication called the *Airline Seating Guide* that publishes seating charts for most major US airlines and many foreign carriers as well. Your travel agent should have a copy, or you can buy the US edition for $39.95 per year and the international edition for $44.95. Order from Carlson Publishing Co., Box 888, Los Alamitos, CA 90720 (phone: 800-728-4877 or 213-493-4877).

Simply reserving an airline seat in advance, however, actually may guarantee very little. Most airlines require that passengers arrive at the departure gate at least 45 minutes (sometimes more) ahead of time to hold a seat reservation. *Air Canada,* for example, may cancel seat assignments and may not honor reservations of passengers who have not checked in some period of time — usually around 20 to 30 minutes, depending on the airport — before the scheduled departure time, and they *ask* travelers to check in at least 1 hour before all domestic flights and 2 hours before international flights. It pays to read the fine print on your ticket carefully and plan ahead.

A far better strategy is to visit an airline ticket office (or one of a select group of travel agents) to secure an actual boarding pass for your specific flight. Once this has been issued, airline computers show you as checked in, and you effectively own the seat you have selected (although some carriers may not honor boarding passes of passengers arriving at the gate less than 10 minutes before departure). This also is good — but not foolproof — insurance against getting bumped from an overbooked flight and is, therefore, an especially valuable tactic at peak travel times.

Smoking – One decision regarding choosing a seat has been taken out of the hands of many travelers who smoke. Effective February 25, 1990, the US government imposed a ban that prohibits smoking on all flights scheduled for 6 hours or less within the US and its territories. The new regulation applies to both domestic and international carriers serving these routes.

In the case of flights to Canada, by law these rules do not apply to nonstop flights from the US to destinations in Canada, or those with a *continuous* flight time of over 6 hours between stops in the US or its territories. As we went to press, however, all major carriers flying from the US to Canada included such flights in their "domestic" category in terms of nonsmoking rules, and no smoking was allowed on flights between the US and Canada with a continuous flight time of under 6 hours. (Note that there is no smoking on any *Air Canada* flight or any *Canadian Airlines International* flight.)

For a wallet-size guide, which notes in detail the rights of nonsmokers according to these regulations, send a self-addressed, stamped envelope to *ASH (Action on Smoking and Health)*, Airline Card, 2013 H St. NW, Washington, DC 20006 (phone: 202-659-4310).

Meals – If you have specific dietary requirements, be sure to let the airline know well before departure time. The available meals include vegetarian, seafood, kosher, Muslim, Hindu, high-protein, low-calorie, low-cholesterol, low-fat, low-sodium, diabetic, bland, and children's menus (not all of these may be available on every carrier). There is no extra charge for this option. It usually is necessary to request special meals when you make your reservations — check-in time is too late. It's also wise to reconfirm that your request for a special meal has made its way into the airline's computer — the time to do this is 24 hours before departure. (Note that special meals generally are not available on intra-Canadian flights on small local carriers. If this poses a problem, try to eat before you board, or bring a snack with you.)

Baggage – Travelers from the US face two different kinds of rules. When you fly in on a US airline or on a major international carrier, US baggage regulations will be in effect. Though airline baggage allowances vary slightly, in general all passengers are allowed to carry on board, without charge, one piece of luggage that will fit easily under a seat of the plane or in an overhead bin and whose combined dimensions (length, width, and depth) do not exceed 45 inches. A reasonable amount of reading material, camera equipment, and a handbag also are allowed. In addition, all passengers are allowed to check two bags in the cargo hold: one usually not to exceed 62 inches when length, width, and depth are combined, the other not to exceed 55 inches in combined dimensions. Generally no single bag may weigh more than 70 pounds.

In general, baggage allowances follow these guidelines in Canada, but care should be exercised on regional and local airlines. If you are flying from the US to Canada and connecting to a domestic flight, you generally will be allowed the same amount of baggage as on the international flight. If you break your trip and then take a domestic flight, the local carrier's weight restrictions apply. Particularly if traveling to remote outposts, be aware that the smaller aircraft used by carriers serving these routes often have limited luggage capacity and also may have to carry mail and freight. When booking flights off the routes of major trunk carriers, always verify baggage allowances.

Charges for additional, oversize, or overweight bags usually are made at a flat rate; the actual dollar amount varies from carrier to carrier. If you plan to travel with any special equipment or sporting gear, be sure to check with the airline beforehand. Most have specific procedures for handling such baggage, and you may have to pay for transport regardless of how much other baggage you have checked. Golf clubs and skis may be checked through as luggage (most airlines are accustomed to handling them), but tennis rackets should be carried onto the plane. Some airlines require that bicycles be partially dismantled and packaged.

To reduce the chances of your luggage going astray, remove all airline tags from previous trips, label each bag inside and out — with your business address rather than your home address on the outside, to prevent thieves from knowing whose house might be unguarded. Lock everything and double-check the tag that the airline attaches to make sure that it is coded correctly for your destination: YYZ for Lester B. Pearson International Airport; YTZ for Toronto Island Airport.

If your bags are not in the baggage claim area after your flight, or if they're damaged, report the problem to airline personnel immediately. Keep in mind that policies regarding the specific time limit within which you have to make your claim vary from carrier to carrier. Fill out a report form on your lost or damaged luggage and keep a copy of it and your original baggage claim check. If you must surrender the check to claim a damaged bag, get a receipt for it to prove that you did, indeed, check your baggage on the flight. If luggage is missing, be sure to give the airline your destination and/or a telephone number where you can be reached. Also take the name and number of the person in charge of recovering lost luggage.

Most airlines have emergency funds for passengers stranded away from home without their luggage, but if it turns out your bags are truly lost and not simply delayed, do not then and there sign any paper indicating you'll accept an offered settlement. Since the airline is responsible for the value of your bags within certain statutory limits ($1,250 per passenger for lost baggage on a US domestic flight; $9.07 per pound or $20 per kilo for checked baggage, and up to $400 per passenger for unchecked baggage on an international flight), you should take some time to assess the extent of your loss (see *Insurance,* in this section). It's a good idea to keep records indicating the value of the contents of your luggage. A wise alternative is to take a Polaroid picture of the most valuable of your packed items just after putting them in your suitcase.

Considering the increased incidence of damage to baggage, it's now more than ever a good idea to keep the sales slips that confirm how much you paid for your bags. These are invaluable in establishing the value of damaged luggage and eliminate any arguments. A better way to protect your precious gear from the luggage-eating conveyers is to try to carry it on board wherever possible.

Airline Clubs – Some US and foreign carriers often have clubs for travelers who pay for membership. These clubs are not solely for first class passengers, although a first class ticket *may* entitle a passenger to lounge privileges. Membership entitles the traveler to use the private lounges at airports along their route, to refreshments served in those lounges, and to check-cashing privileges at most of their counters. Extras include special telephone numbers for individual reservations, embossed luggage tags, and a membership card for identification. Airlines serving Toronto that offer membership in such clubs include the following:

American: The *Admiral's Club.* Single yearly membership $225 for the first year; $125 yearly thereafter; spouse an additional $70 per year.

Delta: The *Crown Club.* Single yearly membership $150; spouse an additional $50 per year; 3-year and lifetime memberships also available.

Northwest: The *World Club.* Single yearly membership $140 (plus a onetime $50 initiation fee); spouse an additional $50 per year; 3-year and lifetime memberships also available.

United: The *Red Carpet Club.* Single yearly membership $225 for the first year (spouse an additional $70); $125 per year thereafter; 3-year and lifetime memberships also available.

USAir: The *USAir Club.* Single yearly membership $125; spouse an additional $25 per year; 3-year and lifetime memberships also available.

In addition, *very* frequent travelers who have flown over 60,000 miles on *Air Canada* and are members of the carrier's frequent flyer program — called *Aeroplan* (membership costs about CN$28) — may use the carrier's *Maple Leaf Lounges* at major airports across Canada. Club members with an *Aeroplan Elite* card also may bring a guest.

Note that the companies above do not have club facilities in all airports. Other airlines also may offer a variety of special services in many airports.

Getting Bumped – A special air travel problem is the possibility that an airline will accept more reservations (and sell more tickets) than there are seats on a given flight. This is entirely legal and is done to make up for "no-shows," passengers who don't show up for a flight for which they have made reservations and bought tickets. If the airline has oversold the flight and everyone does show up, there simply aren't enough seats. When this happens, the airline is subject to stringent rules designed to protect travelers.

In such cases, the airline first seeks ticket holders willing to give up their seats voluntarily in return for a negotiable sum of money or some other inducement, such as an offer of upgraded seating on the next flight or a voucher for a free trip at some other time. If there are not enough volunteers, the airline may bump passengers against their wishes.

Anyone inconvenienced in this way, however, is entitled to an explanation of the criteria used to determine who does and does not get on the flight, as well as compensation if the resulting delay exceeds certain limits. If the airline can put the bumped passengers on an alternate flight that is *scheduled to arrive* at their original destination within 1 hour of their originally scheduled arrival time, no compensation is owed. If the delay is more than 1 hour but less than 2 hours on a domestic US flight, they must be paid denied-boarding compensation equivalent to the one-way fare to their destination (but not more than $200). If the delay is more than 2 hours beyond the original arrival time on a domestic flight or more than 4 hours on an international flight, the compensation must be doubled (not more than $400). The airline also may offer bumped travelers a voucher for a free flight instead of the denied-boarding compensation. The passenger may be given the choice of either the money or the voucher, the dollar value of which may be no less than the monetary compensation to which the passenger would be entitled. The voucher is not a substitute for the bumped passenger's original ticket; the airline continues to honor that as well.

Keep in mind that the above regulations and policies are only for flights leaving the US, and do *not* apply to charters or to inbound flights originating abroad, even on US carriers.

To protect yourself as best you can against getting bumped, arrive at the airport early, allowing plenty of time to check in and get to the gate. If the flight is oversold, ask immediately for the written statement explaining the airline's policy on denied-boarding compensation and its boarding priorities. If the airline refuses to give you this information, or if you feel it has not handled the situation properly, file a complaint with both the airline and the appropriate government agency.

Delays and Cancellations – The above compensation rules also do not apply if the flight is canceled or delayed, or if a smaller aircraft is substituted due to mechanical problems. Each airline has its own policy for assisting passengers whose flights are delayed or canceled or who must wait for another flight because their original one was overbooked. Most airline personnel will make new travel arrangements if necessary. If the delay is longer than 4 hours, the airline may pay for a phone call or telegram, a meal, and, in some cases, a hotel room and transportation to it.

■ **Caution:** If you are bumped or miss a flight, be sure to ask the airline to notify other airlines on which you have reservations or connecting flights. When your name is taken off the passenger list of your initial flight, the computer usually cancels all of your reservations automatically, unless *you* take steps to preserve them.

CHARTER FLIGHTS: By booking a block of seats on a specially arranged flight, charter tour operators offer travelers air transportation for a substantial reduction over the full coach or economy fare. These operators may offer air-only charters (selling transportation alone) or charter packages (the flight plus a combination of land arrangements such as accommodations, meals, tours, or car rentals). Charters are especially attractive to people living in smaller cities or out-of-the-way places, because they frequently take off from nearby airports, saving travelers the inconvenience and expense of getting to a major gateway.

From the consumer's standpoint, charters differ from scheduled airlines in two main respects: You generally need to book and pay in advance, and you can't change the itinerary or the departure and return dates once you've booked the flight. In practice, however, these restrictions don't always apply. Today, although most charter flights still require advance reservations, some permit last-minute bookings (when there are unsold seats available), and some even offer seats on a standby basis.

Some things to keep in mind about the charter game are:

1. It cannot be repeated often enough that if you are forced to cancel your trip, you can lose much (and possibly all) of your money unless you have cancellation insurance, which is a *must* (see *Insurance,* in this section). Frequently, if the cancellation occurs far enough in advance (often 6 weeks or more), you may forfeit only a $25 or $50 penalty. If you cancel only 2 or 3 weeks before the flight, there may be no refund at all unless you or the operator can provide a substitute passenger.

2. Charter flights may be canceled by the operator up to 10 days before departure for any reason, usually underbooking. Your money is returned in this event, but there may be too little time for you to make new arrangements.

3. Most charters have little of the flexibility of regularly scheduled flights regarding refunds and the changing of flight dates; if you book a return flight, you must be on it or lose your money.

4. Charter operators are permitted to assess a surcharge, if fuel or other costs warrant it, of up to 10% of the airfare up to 10 days before departure.

5. Because of the economics of charter flights, your plane almost always will be full, so you will be crowded, though not necessarily uncomfortable. (There is, however, a new movement among charter airlines to provide flight accommodations that are more comfort-oriented, so this situation may change in the near future.)

To avoid problems, *always* choose charter flights with care. When you consider a charter, ask your travel agent who runs it and carefully check the company. The Better Business Bureau in the company's home city can report on how many complaints, if any, have been lodged against it in the past. Protect yourself with trip cancellation and interruption insurance, which can help safeguard your investment if you, or a traveling companion, are unable to make the trip and must cancel too late to receive a full refund from the company providing your travel services. (This is advisable whether you're buying a charter flight alone or a tour package for which the airfare is provided by charter or scheduled flight.)

Booking – If you do fly on a charter, read the contract's fine print carefully and pay particular attention to the following:

Instructions concerning the payment of the deposit and its balance and to whom the check is to be made payable. Ordinarily, checks are made out to an escrow account, which means the charter company can't spend your money until your flight has safely returned. This provides some protection for you. To ensure the safe handling of your money, make out your check to the escrow account, the number of which must appear by law on the brochure, though all too often it is on the back in fine print. Write the details of the charter, including the destination and dates, on the face of the check; on the back, print "For Deposit Only." Your travel agent may prefer that you make out your check to the agency, saying that it will then pay the tour operator the fee minus commission. It is perfectly legal to write the check as we suggest, however, and if your agent objects too vociferously (he or she should trust the tour operator to send the proper commission), consider taking your business elsewhere. If you don't make your check out to the escrow account, you lose the protection of that escrow should the trip be canceled. Furthermore, recent bankruptcies in the travel industry have served to point out that even the protection of escrow may not be enough to safeguard a traveler's investment. More and more, insurance is becoming a necessity. The charter company should be bonded (usually by an insurance company), and if you want to file a claim against it, the claim should be sent to the bonding agent. The contract will set a time limit within which a claim must be filed.

Specific stipulations and penalties for cancellations. Most charters allow you to cancel up to 45 days in advance without major penalty, but some cancellation dates are 50 to 60 days before departure.

Stipulations regarding cancellation and major changes made by the charterer. US rules say that charter flights may not be canceled within 10 days of departure except when circumstances — such as natural disasters or political upheavals — make it physically impossible to fly. Charterers may make "major changes," however, such as in the date or place of departure or return, but you are entitled to cancel and receive a full refund if you don't wish to accept these changes. A price increase of more than 10% at any time up to 10 days before departure is considered a major change; no price increase at all is allowed during the last 10 days immediately before departure.

Canadian Airlines International offers charter flights through its subsidiary *Canadian Holidays* (191 The West Mall, Etobicoke, Ontario M9C 5K8, Canada; phone: 800-237-0314 from the US; call local offices in Canada), both within Canada and to foreign destinations. Bookings can be made through *Canadian Airlines International* or through a travel agent. *Travel Charter* (1120 E. Longlake Rd., Detroit, MI 48098; phone: 313-528-3570) also sometimes offers charters to Canada. Also *Air Canada* (phone: 800-776-3000) offers charter flights to Toronto during the winter months from Florida.

You also may want to subscribe to the travel newsletter *Jax Fax*, which regularly features a list of charter companies and packagers offering seats on charter flights and may be a source for other charter flights to and within Canada. For a year's subscription send a check or money order for $12 to *Jax Fax*, 397 Post Rd., Darien, CT 06820 (phone: 203-655-8746).

DISCOUNTS ON SCHEDULED FLIGHTS: Promotional fares often are called discount fares because they cost less than what used to be the standard airline fare — full-fare economy. Nevertheless, they cost the traveler the same whether they are bought through a travel agent or directly from the airline. Tickets that cost less if bought from some outlet other than the airline do exist, however. While it is likely that the vast majority of travelers flying to Canada in the near future will be doing so on a promotional fare or charter rather than on a "discount" air ticket of this sort, it still is a good idea for cost-conscious consumers to be aware of the latest developments in the budget airfare scene. Note that the following discussion makes clear-cut distinctions among the types of discounts available based on how they reach the consumer; in actual practice, the distinctions are not nearly so precise.

Net Fare Sources – The newest notion for reducing the costs of travel services comes from travel agents who offer individual travelers "net" fares. Defined simply, a net fare is the bare minimum amount at which an airline or tour operator will carry a prospective traveler. It doesn't include the amount that normally would be paid to the travel agent as a commission. Traditionally, such commissions amount to about 10% on domestic fares and from 10% to 20% on international fares — not counting significant additions to these commission levels that are paid retroactively when agents sell more than a specific volume of tickets or trips for a single supplier. At press time, at least one travel agency in the US was offering travelers the opportunity to purchase tickets and/or tours for a net price. Instead of earning its income from individual commissions, this agency assesses a fixed fee that may or may not provide a bargain for travelers; it requires a little arithmetic to determine whether to use the services of a net travel agent or those of one who accepts conventional commissions. One of the potential drawbacks of buying from agencies selling travel services at net fares is that some airlines refuse to do business with them, thus possibly limiting your flight options.

Travel Avenue is a fee-based agency that rebates its ordinary agency commission to the customer. For domestic flights, they will find the lowest retail fare, then rebate 7% to 10% (depending on the airline selected) of that price minus a $10 ticket-writing charge. The rebate percentage for international flights varies from 5% to 16% (again depending on the airline), and the ticket-writing fee is $25. The ticket-writing charge is imposed per ticket; if the ticket includes more than eight separate flights, an additional $10 or $25 fee is charged. Customers using free flight coupons pay the ticket-writing charge, plus an additional $5 coupon-processing fee.

Travel Avenue will rebate its commissions on all tickets, including heavily discounted fares and senior citizen passes. Available 7 days a week, reservations should be made far enough in advance to allow the tickets to be sent by first class mail, since extra charges accrue for special handling. It's possible to economize further by making your own airline reservation, then asking *Travel Avenue* only to write/issue your ticket. For travelers outside the Chicago area, business may be transacted by phone and purchases charged to a credit card. For information, contact *Travel Avenue* at 641 W. Lake St., Suite 201, Chicago, IL 60606-1012 (phone: 312-876-1116 in Illinois; 800-333-3335 elsewhere in the US).

Consolidators and Bucket Shops – Other vendors of travel services can afford to sell tickets to their customers at an even greater discount because the airline has sold the tickets to them at a substantial discount (usually accomplished by sharply increasing commissions to that vendor), a practice in which many airlines indulge, albeit discreetly, preferring that the general public not know they are undercutting their own "list" prices. Airlines anticipating a slow period on a particular route sometimes sell off a certain portion of their capacity at a very great discount to a wholesaler, or consolidator. The wholesaler sometimes is a charter operator who resells the seats to the public as though they were charter seats, which is why prospective travelers perusing the brochures of charter operators with large programs frequently see a number of flights designated as "scheduled service." As often as not, however, the consolidator, in turn, sells the seats to a travel agency specializing in discounting. Airlines also can sell seats directly to such an agency, which thus acts as its own consolidator. The airline offers the seats either at a net wholesale price, but without the volume-purchase requirement that would be difficult for a modest retail travel agency to fulfill, or at the standard price, but with a commission override large enough (as high as 50%) to allow both a profit and a price reduction to the public.

Travel agencies specializing in discounting sometimes are called "bucket shops," a term once fraught with connotations of unreliability in this country. But in today's highly competitive travel marketplace, more and more conventional travel agencies are selling consolidator-supplied tickets, and the old bucket shops' image is becoming respectable. Agencies that specialize in discounted tickets exist in most large cities, and usually can be found by studying the smaller ads in the travel sections of Sunday newspapers.

Before buying a discounted ticket, whether from a bucket shop or a conventional, full-service travel agency, keep the following considerations in mind: To be in a position to judge how much you'll be saving, first find out the "list" prices of tickets to your destination. Then do some comparison shopping among agencies. Also bear in mind that a ticket that may not differ much in price from one available directly from the airline may, however, allow the circumvention of such things as the advance-purchase requirement. If your plans are less than final, be sure to find out about any other restrictions, such as penalties for canceling a flight or changing a reservation. Most discount tickets are non-endorsable, meaning they can be used only on the airline that issued them, and they usually are marked "nonrefundable" to prevent their being cashed in for a list price refund.

A great many bucket shops are small businesses operating on a thin margin, so it's a good idea to check the local Better Business Bureau for any complaints registered against the one with which you're dealing — before parting with any money. If you still do not feel reassured, consider buying discounted tickets only through a conventional travel agency, which can be expected to have found its own reliable source of consolidator tickets — some of the largest consolidators, in fact, sell only to travel agencies.

A few bucket shops require payment in cash — we strongly advise *against* this — or by certified check or money order, but if credit cards are accepted, use that option. Note, however, if buying from a charter operator selling both scheduled and charter flights, that the scheduled seats are not protected by the regulations — including the use of escrow accounts — governing the charter seats. Well-established charter operators, nevertheless, may extend the same protection to their scheduled flights and, when this is the case, consumers should be sure that the payment option selected directs their money into the escrow account.

Following is a list of companies active in the North American market. Although, at press time, none offered discount fares to Canada, it might prove useful to call when planning your trip to see if Toronto is among the destinations served at the time.

Bargain Air (655 Deep Valley Dr., Suite 355, Rolling Hills, CA 90274; phone: 800-347-2345 or 213-377-2919).

Council Charter (205 E. 42nd St., New York, NY 10017; phone: 800-800-8222 or 212-661-0311).

TFI Tours International (34 W. 32nd St., 12th Floor, New York, NY 10001; phone: 212-736-1140).

Travac Tours and Charters (989 Ave. of the Americas, New York, NY 10018; phone: 800-TRAV-800 or 212-563-3303).

25 West Tours (2490 Coral Way, Miami, FL 33145; phone: 305-856-0810 in Florida; 800-925-0250 elsewhere in the US).

Unitravel (1177 N. Warson Rd., St. Louis, MO 63132; phone: 314-569-2501 in Missouri; 800-325-2222 elsewhere in the US).

■**Note:** Although rebating and discounting are becoming increasingly common, there is some legal ambiguity concerning them. Strictly speaking, it is legal to discount domestic tickets, but not international tickets. On the other hand, the law that prohibits discounting, the Federal Aviation Act of 1958, consistently is ignored these days, in part because consumers benefit from the practice and in part because many illegal arrangements are indistinguishable from legal ones. Since the line separating the two is so fine that even the authorities can't always tell the difference, it is unlikely that most consumers would be able to do so, and in fact it is not illegal to *buy* a discounted ticket. If the issue of legality bothers you, ask the agency whether any ticket you're about to buy would be permissible under the above-mentioned act.

Last-Minute Travel Clubs – Still another way to take advantage of bargain airfares is open to those who have a flexible schedule. A number of organizations, usually set up as last-minute travel clubs and functioning on a membership basis, routinely keep in touch with travel suppliers to help them dispose of unsold inventory at discounts of between 15% and 60%. A great deal of the inventory consists of complete package tours and cruises, but some clubs offer air-only charter seats and, occasionally, seats on scheduled flights.

Members pay an annual fee and receive a toll-free hotline telephone number to call for information on imminent trips. In some cases, they also receive periodic mailings with information on bargain travel opportunities for which there is more advance notice. Despite the suggestive names of the clubs providing these services, last-minute travel does not necessarily mean that you cannot make plans until literally the last minute. Trips can be announced as little as a few days or as much as 2 months before departure, but the average is from 1 to 4 weeks' notice.

Among the organizations regularly offering such discounted travel opportunities to Canada are the following:

Discount Travel International (152 W. 72nd St., Suite 223, New York, NY 10023; phone: 212-362-3636). Annual fee: $45 per household.

Encore/Short Notice (4501 Forbes Blvd., Lanham, MD 20706; phone: 410-459-8020; 800-638-0930 for customer service). Annual fee: $36 per family for its Short Notice program only; $48 per family to join the Encore program, which provides additional travel services.

Last Minute Travel (1249 Boylston St., Boston MA 02215; phone: 800-LAST-MIN or 617-267-9800). No fee.

Moment's Notice (425 Madison Ave., New York, NY 10017; phone: 212-486-0500). Annual fee: $45 per family.

Spur-of-the-Moment Tours and Cruises (10780 Jefferson Blvd., Culver City, CA 90230; phone: 310-839-2418 in Southern California; 800-343-1991 elsewhere in the US). No fee.

Traveler's Advantage (3033 S. Parker Rd., Suite 1000, Aurora, CO 80014; phone: 800-835-8747). Annual fee: $49 per family.

Vacations to Go (1502 Augusta Dr., Suite 215, Houston, TX 77057; phone: 800-338-4962). Annual fee: $19.95 per family.

Worldwide Discount Travel Club (1674 Meridian Ave., Miami Beach, FL 33139; phone: 305-534-2082). Annual fee: $40 per person; $50 per family.

■**Note:** For additional information on last-minute travel discounts, a new "900" number telephone service called *Last Minute Travel Connection* (phone: 900-446-8292) provides recorded advertisements (including contact information) for discount offerings on airfares, package tours, cruises, and other travel opportunities. Since companies update their advertisements as often as every hour, listings are current. This 24-hour service is available to callers using touch-tone phones; the cost is $1 per minute (the charge will show up on your phone bill). For more information, contact *La Onda, Ltd.,* 601 Skokie Blvd., Suite 224, Northbrook, IL 60062 (phone: 708-498-9216).

Generic Air Travel – Organizations that apply the same flexible-schedule idea to air travel only and sell tickets at literally the last minute also exist. Their service sometimes is known as "generic" air travel, and it operates somewhat like an ordinary airline standby service except that the organizations running it offer seats on not one but several scheduled and charter airlines.

One pioneer of generic flights is *Airhitch* (2790 Broadway, Suite 100, New York, NY 10025; phone: 212-864-2000). Prospective travelers stipulate a range of at least five consecutive departure dates and their desired destination, along with alternate choices, and pay the fare in advance. They are then sent a voucher good for travel *on a space-available basis* on flights to their destination *region* (i.e., not necessarily the specific destination requested) during this time period. The week before this range of departure dates begins, travelers must contact *Airhitch* for specific information about flights that will probably be available and instructions on how to proceed for check-in. (Return flights are arranged in the same manner as the outbound flights — a specified period of travel is decided upon, and a few days before this date range begins, prospective passengers contact *Airhitch* for details about flights that may be available.) If the client does not accept any of the suggested flights or cancels his or her travel plans after selecting a flight, the amount paid can be applied toward a future fare or the flight arrangements can be transferred to another individual (although, in both cases, an additional fee may be charged). No refunds are offered unless the prospective passenger does not ultimately get on any flight in the specified date range; in such a case, the full fare is refunded. (Note that *Airhitch*'s slightly more expensive "Target" program, which provides confirmed reservations on specific dates to specific destinations, offers passengers greater — but not guaranteed — certainty regarding flight arrangements.) At the time of this writing, *Airhitch* did not offer flights between the US and Canada, but do check at the time you plan to travel.

Bartered Travel Sources – Suppose a hotel buys advertising space in a newspaper. As payment, the hotel gives the publishing company the use of a number of hotel rooms in lieu of cash. This is barter, a common means of exchange among hotels, airlines, car rental companies, cruise lines, tour operators, restaurants, and other travel service companies. When a bartering company finds itself with empty airline seats (or excess hotel rooms, or cruise ship cabin space, and so on) and offers them to the public, considerable savings can be enjoyed.

Bartered travel clubs often offer discounts of up to 50% to members, who pay an annual fee (approximately $50 at press time) that entitles them to select from the flights, cruises, hotel rooms, or other travel services that the club obtained by barter. Members usually present a voucher, club credit card, or scrip (a dollar-denomination voucher negotiable only for the bartered product) to the hotel, which in turn subtracts the dollar amount from the bartering company's account.

Selling bartered travel is a perfectly legitimate means of retailing. One advantage to club members is that they don't have to wait until the last minute to obtain flight or room reservations.

Among the companies specializing in bartered travel, two that offer members travel services to and in Canada are *IGT (In Good Taste) Services* (1111 Lincoln Rd., 4th Floor, Miami Beach, FL 33139; phone: 800-444-8872 or 305-534-7900), with an annual fee of $48 per family, and *Travel Guild* (18210 Redmond Way, Redmond, WA 98052; phone: 206-861-1900), which charges $48 per family per year.

OTHER DISCOUNT TRAVEL SOURCES: An excellent source of information on economical travel opportunities is the *Consumer Reports Travel Letter,* published monthly by Consumers Union. It keeps abreast of the scene on a wide variety of fronts, including package tours, rental cars, insurance, and more, but it is especially helpful for its comprehensive coverage of airfares, offering guidance on all the options from scheduled flights on major or low-fare airlines to charters and discount sources. For a year's subscription, send $37 ($57 for 2 years) to *Consumer Reports Travel Letter* (PO Box 53629, Boulder, CO 80322-3629; phone: 800-234-1970). For information on other travel newsletters, see *Books, Magazines, and Newsletters,* in this section.

On Arrival

 FROM THE AIRPORT TO THE CITY: Toronto's airports for both international and domestic flights are Lester B. Pearson International Airport, located about 20 miles (32 km) northwest of metropolitan Toronto, and Toronto Island Airport, on the western tip of Toronto Island, approximately 2 miles (3 km) from downtown.

Taxi – From Lester B. Pearson International Airport, it's about a half-hour drive to the city; the fare is CN$30. Only taxis with the letters TIA on their license plates are authorized to transport passengers from Pearson International Airport to downtown areas.

Public Transportation – The most convenient way to get from Lester B. Pearson International Airport to downtown is to use *Gray Coach Lines* (phone: 416-351-3311), which has daily scheduled service leaving every 20 minutes. Depending upon the departure point from the airport, the ride takes about 45 minutes; it costs CN$10.75 (children under 11 ride free). From Toronto Island Airport, passengers are advised to take the ferry, which departs every 15 minutes (it's free if you hold a airline ticket). The ride takes approximately 10 minutes, and leaves passengers at the foot of Bathurst Street. From there, take a taxi to downtown (about CN$4).

CAR RENTAL: Unless planning to drive round-trip from home, most travelers who want to drive while on vacation simply rent a car.

Renting a car in Canada is not inexpensive, but it is possible to economize by determining your own needs and then shopping around among the car rental companies until you find the best deal. Ask about special rates or promotional deals, such as weekend or weekly rates, bonus coupons for airline tickets, or 24-hour rates that include gas and unlimited mileage.

Renting from the US – Travel agents can arrange foreign rentals for clients, but it is just as easy to call and rent a car yourself. Listed below are some of the major international rental companies that have representation in Toronto and have information and reservations numbers that can be dialed toll-free from the US:

Avis (phone: 800-331-1084 throughout the US; 800-387-7600 in Quebec; 800-268-2310 elsewhere in Canada). Has representatives at Pearson International Airport and 7 other locations in Toronto.

Budget (phone: 800-527-0700 in the US; 800-268-8900 in Canada). Has representatives at both airports and 8 city locations.

Hertz (phone: 800-654-3001 in the US; 800-263-0600 in Canada). Has representatives at Pearson International Airport and 7 city locations.

National Car Rental (phone: 800-CAR-RENT throughout the US and Canada). Has representatives at Pearson International Airport and 3 other locations in Toronto.

Sears Rent-A-Car (phone: 800-527-0770 in the US; 800-268-8900 in Canada). Has a representative at Pearson International Airport.

Thrifty Rent-A-Car (phone: 800-367-2277 in the US and Canada). Has representatives at Pearson International Airport and 5 city locations.

Tilden Rent-A-Car System: Largest Canadian firm, affiliated with *National* in the US; for *National,* or reservations through them with *Tilden* in Canada, call 800-CAR-RENT throughout the US and Canada.

It also is possible to rent a car before you go by contacting any number of smaller or less well known US companies that do not operate worldwide. These organizations may specialize in North American auto travel, including leasing and car purchase in addition to car rental, or may actually be tour operators with a well-established Canadian car rental program.

Requirements – Whether you decide to rent a car in advance from a large international rental company with Canadian branches or wait to rent from a local company, you should know that renting a car is rarely as simple as signing on the dotted line and roaring off into the night. To drive in Toronto, you need certain documents (see below), and will have to convince the renting agency that (1) you are personally creditworthy, and (2) you will bring the car back at the stated time. This will be easy if you have a major credit card; most rental companies accept credit cards in lieu of a cash deposit, as well as for payment of your final bill. If you prefer to pay in cash, leave your credit card imprint as a "deposit," then pay your bill in cash when you return the car.

If you are planning to rent a car once you're in Canada, *Avis, Budget, Hertz,* and other US rental companies usually *will* rent to travelers paying in cash and leaving either a credit card imprint or a substantial amount of cash as a deposit. This is not necessarily standard policy, however, as some of the other international chains and a number of local and regional Canadian companies will *not* rent to an individual who doesn't have a valid credit card. In this case, you will have to call around to find a company that accepts cash.

Also keep in mind that although the minimum age to drive a car in Canada is 16 years, the minimum age to rent a car is set by the rental company. (Restrictions vary from company to company, as well as at different locations.) Many firms have a minimum age requirement of 21 years, some raise that to between 23 and 25 years, and for some models of cars it rises to 30 years. The upper age limit at many companies is between 69 and 75; others have no upper limit or may make drivers above a certain age subject to special conditions.

Don't forget that all car rentals in the province of Ontario are subject to an 8% province tax, as well as the Canadian Goods and Services Tax (GST) of 7%. This tax rarely is included in the rental price that's advertised or quoted, but it always must be paid — whether you pay in advance in the US or pay it when you drop off the car.

Driving Documents – A valid driver's license from his or her own state of residence is required for a US citizen to drive in Canada. Proof of liability also is required and is a standard part of any car rental contract. Car rental companies also make provisions for breakdowns, emergency service, and assistance; ask for a number to call when you pick up the vehicle.

Rules of the Road – Driving in Canada is on the right side of the road, as in the US. Passing is on the left; the left turn signal must be flashing before and while passing, and the right indicator must be used when pulling back to the right.

According to law, those coming from the right at intersections have the right of way, as in the US, and pedestrians, provided they are in marked crosswalks, have priority over all vehicles.

In the city, speed limits usually are 50 kmh (about 30 mph). Outside the city, the speed limit is 100 kmh (about 60 mph) on freeways and 80 kmh (about 50 mph) on highways.

Parking is plentiful; however, motorists are asked to heed signs designating appropriate parking areas and times. Public parking facilities are available throughout Toronto.

Gasoline – The major oil companies have stations in Canada: *Chevron, Exxon, Gulf, Shell, Sunoco,* and *Texaco.* Even more common are Canadian companies, like *Petro-Canada.* Gas is sold by the liter, which is slightly more than 1 quart; approximately 3.8 liters equal 1 US gallon. As in the US, regular, leaded, and diesel gas generally are available in several grades, and self-service (where you do the pumping) often is less expensive than full service. Similarly, gas paid for in cash often costs less that when you pay for it with a credit card.

Package Tours

If the mere thought of buying a package for your visit to Toronto conjures up visions of a trip marching in lockstep with a horde of frazzled fellow travelers, remember that packages have come a long way. For one thing, not all packages necessarily are escorted tours, and the one you buy does not have to include any organized touring at all — nor will it necessarily include traveling companions. If it does, however, you'll find that people of all sorts — many just like yourself — are taking advantage of packages today because they are economical and convenient, and save you an immense amount of planning time. Given the high cost of travel these days, packages have emerged as a particularly wise buy.

In essence, a package is just an amalgam of travel services that can be purchased in a single transaction. A Toronto package (tour or otherwise) may include any or all of the following: round-trip transportation, local transportation (and/or car rentals), accommodations, some or all meals, sightseeing, entertainment, transfers to and from the hotel, taxes, tips, escort service, and a variety of incidental features that might be offered as options at additional cost. In other words, a package can be any combination of travel elements, from a fully escorted tour offered at an all-inclusive price to a simple fly/drive booking that allows you to move about totally on your own. Its principal advantage is that it saves money: The cost of the combined arrangements invariably is well below the price of all of the same elements if bought separately, and, particularly if transportation is provided by discount flight, the whole package could cost less than just a round-trip economy airline ticket on a regularly scheduled flight. A package provides more than economy and convenience: It releases the traveler from having to make individual arrangements for each separate element of a trip.

Tour programs generally can be divided into two categories — "escorted" (or locally hosted) and "independent." An escorted tour means that a guide will accompany the group from the beginning of the tour through to the return flight; a locally hosted tour means that the group will be met upon arrival at each location by a different local host. On independent tours, there generally is a choice of hotels, meal plans, and sightseeing trips, as well as a variety of special excursions. The independent plan is for travelers who do not want a totally set itinerary, but who do prefer confirmed hotel reservations. Whether you choose an escorted or an independent tour, always bring along complete contact information for your tour operator in case a problem arises, although US tour operators often have local affiliates who can give additional assistance or make other arrangements on the spot.

To determine whether a package — or more specifically, *which* package — fits your travel plans, start by evaluating your interests and needs, deciding how much and what you want to spend, see, and do. Gather brochures on Toronto tours. Be sure that you take the time to read each brochure *carefully* to determine precisely what is included. Keep in mind that they are written to entice you into signing up for a package tour. Often the language is deceptive and devious. For example, a brochure may quote the lowest prices for a package tour based on facilities that are unavailable during the off-season, undesirable at any season, or just plain nonexistent. Information such as "breakfast included" (as it often is in packages to Canada) or "plus tax" (which can add up) should be taken into account. Note, too, that the prices quoted in brochures almost always are based on double occupancy: The rate listed is for each of two people sharing a double room, and if you travel alone, the supplement for single accommodations can raise the price considerably (see *Hints for Single Travelers,* in this section).

In this age of erratic airfares, the brochure most often will *not* include the price of an airline ticket in the price of the package, though sample fares from various gateway cities usually will be listed separately, as extras to be added to the price of the ground arrangements. Before figuring your actual costs, check the latest fares with the airlines, because the samples invariably are out of date by the time you read them. If the brochure gives more than one category of sample fares per gateway city — such as an individual tour-basing fare, a group fare, an excursion, APEX, or other discount ticket — your travel agent or airline tour desk will be able to tell you which one applies to the package you choose, depending on when you travel, how far in advance you book, and other factors. (An individual tour-basing fare is a fare computed as part of a package that includes land arrangements, thereby entitling a carrier to reduce the air portion almost to the absolute minimum. Though it always represents a saving over full-fare coach or economy, lately the individual tour-basing fare has not been as inexpensive as the excursion and other discount fares that also are available to individuals. The group fare usually is the least expensive fare, and it is the tour operator, not you, who makes up the group.) When the brochure does include round-trip transportation in the package price, don't forget to add the cost of round-trip transportation from your home city to the departure city to come up with the total cost of the package.

Finally, read the general information regarding terms and conditions and the responsibility clause (usually in fine print at the end of the descriptive literature) to determine the precise elements for which the tour operator is — and is not — liable. Here the tour operator frequently expresses the right to change services or schedules as long as equivalent arrangements are offered. This clause also absolves the operator of responsibility for circumstances beyond human control, such as floods, avalanches, earthquakes, or injury to you or your property. While reading, ask the following questions:

1. Does the tour include airfare or other transportation, sightseeing, meals, transfers, taxes, baggage handling, tips, or any other services? Do you want all these services?
2. If the brochure indicates that "some meals" are included, does this mean a welcoming and farewell dinner, two breakfasts, or every evening meal?
3. What classes of hotels are offered? If you will be traveling alone, what is the single supplement?
4. Does the tour itinerary or price vary according to the season?

5. Are the prices guaranteed; that is, if costs increase between the time you book and the time you depart, can surcharges unilaterally be added?
6. Do you get a full refund if you cancel? If not, be sure to obtain cancellation insurance.
7. Can the operator cancel if too few people join? At what point?

One of the consumer's biggest problems is finding enough information to judge the reliability of a tour packager, since individual travelers seldom have direct contact with the firm putting the package together. Usually, a retail travel agent is interposed between customer and tour operator, and much depends on his or her candor and cooperation. So ask a number of questions about the tour you are considering. For example:

● Has the travel agent ever used a package provided by this tour operator?
● How long has the tour operator been in business? Check the Better Business Bureau in the area where the tour operator is based to see if any complaints have been filed against it.
● Is the tour operator a member of the *United States Tour Operators Association?* (*USTOA;* 211 E. 51st St., Suite 12B, New York, NY 10022; phone: 212-944-5727)? *USTOA* will provide a list of its members on request; it also offers a useful brochure called *How to Select a Package Tour.*
● How many and which companies are involved in the package?
● If air travel is by charter flight, is there an escrow account in which deposits will be held; if so, what is the name of the bank?

This last question is very important. US law requires that tour operators deposit every charter passenger's deposit and subsequent payment in a proper escrow account (see "Charter Flights," above).

■**A word of advice:** Purchasers of vacation packages who feel they're not getting their money's worth are more likely to get a refund if they complain in writing to the operator — and bail out of the whole package immediately. Alert the tour operator to the fact that you are dissatisfied, that you will be leaving for home as soon as transportation can be arranged, and that you expect a refund. They may have forms to fill out detailing your complaint; otherwise, state your case in a letter. Even if difficulty in arranging immediate transportation home detains you, your dated, written complaint should help in procuring a refund from the operator.

SAMPLE PACKAGES IN TORONTO: As discussed above, a typical package tour to Toronto might include round-trip transportation, accommodations, a sightseeing tour, and several meals. Although some packages just cover arrangements at a specific hotel, others offer more extensive arrangements and may be built around activities such as fishing, hunting, or skiing, or special interests such as history or nature exploration.

Following is a list of some of the major tour operators that offer packages to Toronto. Most tour operators offer several departure dates, depending on the length of the tour and areas visited. As indicated, some operators are wholesalers only, and will deal only with a travel agent.

Adventure Tours (9818 Liberty Rd., Randallstown, MD 21133; phone: 410-922-7000 in Baltimore; 800-638-9040 elsewhere in the US). Offers 2- to 4-night city packages to Toronto; extensions also available. This tour operator is a wholesaler, so use a travel agent.

American Express Travel Related Services (offices throughout the US; phone:

800-241-1700 for information and local branch offices). Offers city packages to Toronto, as well as an 11-day Eastern Highlights tour that includes stops in US and Canadian cities. The tour operator is a wholesaler, so use a travel agent.

Brenden Tours (15137 Califa St., Van Nuys, CA 91411-3021; phone: 818-785-9696 or 800-421-8446). Offers a 10-day French Canada and Ontario tour that includes stays in Toronto.

Cartan Tours (1304 Parkview Ave., Suite 210, Manhattan Beach, CA 90266; phone: 800-422-7826). Offers a variety of Canada packages that include stays in Toronto.

Collette Tours (162 Middle St., Pawtucket, RI 02860; phone: 800-752-2655 in Rhode Island, 800-832-4656 elsewhere in the US). Offers 7- to 11-day city packages that include stays in Toronto.

Maupintour (PO Box 807, Lawrence, KS 66044; phone: 800-255-4266). Offers 1- to 2-week escorted tours throughout Canada, including several packages that include Toronto. The operator is a wholesaler, so use a travel agent.

Tauck Tours (PO Box 5027, Westport, CT 06881-5027; phone: 800-451-4708 in Connecticut, 800-468-2825 elsewhere in the US). Offers several tours of Canada, including city packages to Toronto.

■ **Note:** Frequently, the best city packages are offered by the hotels, which are trying to attract guests during the weekends, when business travel drops off, and during other off-periods. These packages are sometimes advertised in local newspapers and in the Sunday travel sections of major metropolitan papers, such as *The New York Times,* which has a national edition available in most parts of the US. It's worthwhile asking about packages, especially family and special-occasion offerings, when you call to make a hotel reservation. Calling several hotels can garner you a variety of options from which to choose.

Preparing

How to Use a Travel Agent

 A reliable travel agent remains the best source of service and information for planning a trip, whether you have a specific itinerary and require an agent only to make reservations or you need extensive help in sorting through the maze of airfares, tour offerings, hotel packages, and the scores of other arrangements that may be involved in a trip to Canada.

Know what you want from a travel agent so that you can evaluate what you are getting. It is perfectly reasonable to expect your travel agent to be a thoroughly knowledgeable travel specialist, with information about your destination and, even more crucial, a command of current airfares, ground arrangements, and other wrinkles in the travel scene.

Most travel agents work through computer reservations systems (CRS). These are used to assess the availability and cost of flights, hotels, and car rental, and through them they can book reservations. Despite reports of "computer bias," in which a computer may favor one airline over another, the CRS should provide agents with the entire spectrum of flights available to a given destination, and the complete range of fares, in considerably less time than it takes to telephone the airlines individually — and at no extra cost to the client.

Make the most intelligent use of a travel agent's time and expertise; understand the economics of the industry. As a client, traditionally you pay nothing for the agent's services; with few exceptions, it's all free, from hotel bookings to advice on package tours. Any money the travel agent makes on the time spent arranging your itinerary — booking hotels, resorts, or flights, or suggesting activities — comes from commissions paid by the suppliers of these services — the airlines, hotels, and so on. These commissions generally run from 10% to 15% of the total cost of the service, although suppliers often reward agencies that sell their services in volume with an increased commission called an override.

A conventional travel agent sometimes may charge a fee for special services. These chargeable items may include long-distance telephone costs incurred in making a booking, for reserving a room in a place that does not pay a commission (such as a small, out-of-the-way hotel), or for special attention such as planning a highly personalized itinerary. A fee also may be assessed in instances of deeply discounted airfares.

Choose a travel agent with the same care with which you would choose a doctor or lawyer. You will be spending a good deal of money on the basis of the agent's judgment, so you have a right to expect that judgment to be mature, informed, and interested. At the moment, unfortunately, there aren't many standards within the travel agent industry to help you gauge competence, and the quality of individual agents varies enormously.

At present, only nine states have registration, licensing, or other form of travel agent–related legislation on their books. Rhode Island licenses travel agents; Florida, Hawaii, Iowa, and Ohio register them; and California, Illinois, Oregon, and Washington have laws governing the sale of transportation or related services. While state licensing of agents cannot absolutely guarantee competence, it can at least ensure that an agent has met some minimum requirements.

Perhaps the best way to find a travel agent is by word of mouth. If the agent (or agency) has done a good job for your friends over a period of time, it probably indicates a certain level of commitment and competence. Always ask for the name of the company *and* the name of the specific agent with whom your friends dealt, for it is that individual who will serve you, and quality can vary widely within a single agency.

Entry Requirements and Documents

ENTRY REQUIREMENTS: The only requirement for citizens and legal residents of the US crossing the US-Canada border in either direction is that they present one form of identification. For native US citizens, this can be a valid passport or a driver's license, original or certified birth certificate, baptismal certificate, voter registration card or draft card, or other identification that officially verifies their US citizenship. Proof of current residency also may be required. Naturalized US citizens should carry their naturalization certificate or some other evidence of citizenship. Permanent residents of the US who are not American citizens should have Alien Registration Receipt cards (US Form I-151 or Form I-551). Visitors under 18 years of age not accompanied by an adult should carry a letter from a parent or guardian giving them permission to travel to Canada.

Any visitor to Canada who is not a US citizen or a permanent resident of the US must have a valid passport from some other nation. In addition, a visa may be required of visitors other than British citizens. Foreign visitors to the US who cross into Canada and then return to the US should check with the US Immigration and Naturalization Service to make sure that they have all the papers they need for re-entry into the US.

DUTY AND CUSTOMS: As a general rule, the requirements for bringing the majority of items *into Canada* is that they must be in quantities small enough not to imply commercial import.

Among the items that each person may take into Canada duty-free are 50 cigars, 200 cigarettes, and 2.2 pounds (1 kilo) of manufactured tobacco, as well as 40 ounces (1.1 liters) of liquor or wine or 24 12-ounce cans or bottles of beer or ale. Personal effects and sports equipment appropriate for a pleasure trip also are allowed.

If you are bringing along a computer, camera, or other electronic equipment for your own use that you will be taking back to the US, you should register the item with the US Customs Service to avoid paying duty both entering and returning from Canada. (Also see *Customs and Returning to the US,* in this section.) For information on this procedure, as well as for a variety of pamphlets on US customs regulations, contact the local office of the US Customs Service or the central office, PO Box 7474, Washington, DC 20044 (phone: 202-566-8195).

■ **One rule to follow:** When passing through customs, it is illegal not to declare dutiable items; penalties range from stiff fines and seizure of goods to prison terms. So don't try to sneak anything through — it just isn't worth it.

Insurance

It is unfortunate that most decisions to buy travel insurance are impulsive and usually are made without any real consideration of the traveler's existing policies. Therefore, the first person with whom you should discuss travel insurance is your own insurance broker, not a travel agent or the clerk behind the airport insurance counter. You may discover that the insurance you already carry — homeowner's policies and/or accident, health, and life insurance — protects you adequately while you travel and that your real needs are in the more mundane areas of excess value insurance for baggage or trip cancellation insurance.

TYPES OF INSURANCE: To make insurance decisions intelligently, however, you first should understand the basic categories of travel insurance and what they cover. Then you can decide what you should have in the broader context of your personal insurance needs, and you can choose the most economical way of getting the desired protection: through riders on existing policies; with onetime, short-term policies; through a special program put together for the frequent traveler; through coverage that's part of a travel club's benefits; or with a combination policy sold by insurance companies through brokers, automobile clubs, tour operators, and travel agents.

There are seven basic categories of travel insurance:

1. Baggage and personal effects insurance
2. Personal accident and sickness insurance
3. Trip cancellation and interruption insurance
4. Default and/or bankruptcy insurance
5. Flight insurance (to cover injury or death)
6. Automobile insurance (for driving your own or a rented car)
7. Combination policies

Baggage and Personal Effects Insurance – Ask your insurance agent if baggage and personal effects are included in your current homeowner's policy, or if you will need a special floater to cover you for the duration of a trip. The object is to protect your bags and their contents in case of damage or theft any time during your travels, not just while you're in flight, where only limited protection is provided by the airline. Baggage liability varies from carrier to carrier, but generally speaking, on domestic flights, luggage usually is insured to $1,250 — that's per passenger, not per bag. For most international flights, including domestic portions of international flights, the airline's liability limit is approximately $9.07 per pound or $20 per kilo (which comes to about $360 per 40-pound suitcase) for checked baggage and up to $400 per passenger for unchecked baggage. Canadian airlines insure baggage for up to a maximum of $750 on domestic flights and $640 on flights originating in the US that cross the Canadian border only. These limits should be specified on your airline ticket, but to be awarded the specified amount, you'll have to provide an itemized list of lost property, and if you're including new and/or expensive items, be prepared for a request that you back up your claim with sales receipts or other proofs of purchase.

If you are carrying goods worth more than the maximum protection offered by the airline, consider excess value insurance. Additional coverage is available from airlines at an average, currently, of $1 to $2 per $100 worth of coverage, up to a maximum of $5,000. This insurance can be purchased at the airline counter when you check in, though you should arrive early enough to fill out the necessary forms and avoid holding up other passengers.

Major credit card companies provide coverage for lost or delayed baggage — and this coverage often also is over and above what the airline will pay. The basic coverage usually is automatic for all cardholders who use the credit card to purchase tickets, but to qualify for additional coverage, cardholders generally must enroll.

Additional baggage and personal effects insurance also is included in certain of the combination travel insurance policies discussed below.

■**A note of warning:** Be sure to read the fine print of any excess value insurance policy; there often are specific exclusions, such as cash, tickets, furs, gold and silver objects, art, and antiques. Insurance companies ordinarily will pay only the depreciated value of the goods rather than their replacement value. The best way to protect your property is to take photos of your valuables, and keep a record of the serial numbers of such items as cameras, typewriters, laptop computers, radios, and so on. If an airline loses your luggage, you will be asked to fill out a Property Irregularity Report before you leave the airport. Also, report the loss to the police (since the insurance company will check with the police when processing your claim).

Personal Accident and Sickness Insurance – This covers you in case of illness during your trip or death in an accident. Most policies insure you for hospital and doctors' expenses, lost income, and so on. In most cases, it is a standard part of existing health insurance policies, though you should check with your insurance broker to be sure of the conditions for which your policy will pay. If your coverage is insufficient, take out a separate vacation accident policy or an entire vacation insurance policy that includes health and life coverage.

Two examples of such comprehensive health and life insurance coverage are the travel insurance packages offered by *Wallach & Co.:*

HealthCare Abroad: This program is available to individuals up to age 75. For $3 per day (minimum 10 days, maximum 90 days), policy holders receive $100,000 medical insurance and a $25,000 death benefit.

HealthCare Global: This insurance package, which can be purchased for periods of 10 to 180 days, is offered for two age groups: Men and women up to age 75 receive $25,000 medical insurance and a $50,000 death benefit; those from age 75 to 84 are eligible for $12,500 medical insurance and a $25,000 death benefit. For either policy, the cost for a 10-day period is $25, with decreasing rates up to 75 days, after which the rate is $1.50 per day.

Both of these basic programs also may be bought in combination with trip cancellation and baggage insurance at extra cost. For further information, write to *Wallach & Co.,* 107 W. Federal St., Box 480, Middleburg, VA 22117-0480 (phone: 703-687-3166 in Virginia; 800-237-6615 elsewhere in the US).

Trip Cancellation and Interruption Insurance – Most package tour passengers pay for their travel well before departure. The disappointment of having to miss a vacation because of illness or any other reason pales before the awful prospect that not all (and sometimes none) of the money paid in advance might be returned. So cancellation insurance for any package tour is a must.

Although cancellation penalties vary (they are listed in the fine print in every tour brochure, and before you purchase a package tour you should know exactly what they are), rarely will a passenger get more than 50% of this money back if forced to cancel within a few weeks of scheduled departure. Therefore, if you book a package tour, you should have trip cancellation insurance to guarantee full reimbursement or refund should you, a traveling companion, or a member of your immediate family get sick, forcing you to cancel your trip or *return home early.*

The key here is *not* to buy just enough insurance to guarantee full reimbursement for the cost of the package in case of cancellation. The proper amount of coverage should be sufficient to reimburse you for the cost of having to catch up with a tour after its departure or having to travel home at the full economy airfare if you have to forgo the return flight tied to the package. There usually is quite a discrepancy between an excursion or other special fare and the amount charged to travel the same distance on a regularly scheduled flight at full economy fare.

Trip cancellation insurance is available from travel agents and tour operators in two forms: as part of a short-term, all-purpose travel insurance package (sold by the travel agent); or as specific cancellation insurance designed by the tour operator for a specific charter tour. Generally, tour operators' policies are less expensive, but also less inclusive. Cancellation insurance also is available directly from insurance companies or their agents as part of a short-term, all-inclusive travel insurance policy.

Before you decide on a policy, read each one carefully. (Either type can be purchased from a travel agent when you book the charter or package tour.) Be sure to check the fine print for stipulations concerning "family members" and "pre-existing medical conditions," as well as allowances for living expenses if you must delay your return due to injury or illness.

Default and/or Bankruptcy Insurance – Although trip cancellation insurance usually protects you if *you* are unable to complete — or begin — your trip, a fairly recent innovation is coverage in the event of default and/or bankruptcy on the part of the tour operator, airline, or other travel supplier. In some travel insurance packages, this contingency is included in the trip cancellation portion of the coverage; in others, it is a separate feature. Either way, it is becoming increasingly important. Whereas sophisticated travelers have long known to beware of the possibility of default or bankruptcy when buying a tour package, in recent years more than a few respected airlines unexpectedly have revealed their shaky financial condition, sometimes leaving hordes of stranded ticket holders in their wake. While default/bankruptcy insurance will not ordinarily result in reimbursement in time to pay for new arrangements, it can ensure that you will get your money back, and even independent travelers buying no more than an airplane ticket may want to consider it.

Flight Insurance – Airlines have carefully established limits of liability for injury to or the death of passengers on international flights. For all international flights to, from, or with a stopover in the US, all carriers are liable for up to $75,000 per passenger. For all other international flights, the liability is based on where you purchase the ticket: If booked in advance in the US, the maximum liability is $75,000; if arrangements are made abroad, the liability is $10,000. But remember, these liabilities are not the same thing as insurance policies; every penny that an airline eventually pays in the case of death or injury may be subject to a legal battle.

But before you buy last-minute flight insurance from an airport vending machine, consider the purchase in light of your total existing insurance coverage. A careful review of your current policies may reveal that you already are amply covered for accidental death. Be aware that airport insurance, the kind typically bought at a counter or from a vending machine, is among the most expensive forms of life insurance coverage, and that even within a single airport, rates for approximately the same coverage vary widely.

If you buy your plane ticket with a major credit card, you generally receive automatic insurance coverage at no extra cost. Additional coverage usually can be obtained at extremely reasonable prices, but a cardholder must sign up for it in advance.

Automobile Insurance – All drivers in Canada are required by law to have automobile insurance for their car. The minimum coverage is determined by provincial law, but this minimum usually is too low for adequate protection. Your insurance agent can advise you on the proper amount of insurance necessary. There are several kinds of coverage you should have in Canada:

1. *Liability Insurance:* This provides protection if you are sued for injuring someone or his or her property. US motorists driving in Canada should obtain a Canadian Non-Resident Inter-Province Motor Vehicle Liability Insurance Card, which provides evidence of financial responsibility by a valid automobile liability insurance policy. This card is available only through insurance agents in the US. (There usually is no charge for this card.) All provinces in Canada require visiting motorists to produce evidence of financial responsibility should they be involved

in an accident. Minimum liability requirements vary from CN$50,000 to as much as CN$200,000 in some provinces. Information and advice regarding auto insurance may be obtained from the *Insurance Bureau of Canada,* 181 University Ave., Toronto, Ontario M5H 3M7, Canada (phone: 416-362-2031).

2. *Accident Insurance:* This protects against payments for death or bodily injury and includes loss of pay, medical expenses, and so on. These policies also include coverage against uninsured motorists.

3. *Comprehensive and Collision Insurance:* This protects against loss of or damage to your car. There usually is a deductible amount indicated for this coverage; it either is paid by the policy holder toward the cost of repairs or deducted from the loss settlement.

When you rent a car, the rental company is required to provide you with collision protection. In your car rental contract, you'll see that for about $10 to $13 a day, you may buy optional collision damage waiver (CDW) protection.

If you do not accept the CDW coverage, you may be liable for as much as the full retail value of the rental car; by paying for the CDW you are relieved of all responsibility for any damage to the car. Before agreeing to this coverage, however, check with your own broker about your own existing personal automobile insurance policy. It very well may cover your entire liability exposure without any additional cost, or you automatically may be covered by the credit card company to which you are charging the cost of your rental. To find out the amount of rental car insurance provided by major credit cards, contact the issuing institutions.

You also should know that an increasing number of the major international car rental companies automatically are including the cost of the CDW in their basic rates. Car rental prices have increased to include this coverage, although rental company ad campaigns may promote this as a new, improved rental package "benefit." The disadvantage of this inclusion is that you may not have the option to turn down the CDW — even if you already are adequately covered by your own insurance policy or through a credit card company.

Combination Policies – Short-term insurance policies, which may include a combination of any or all of the types of insurance discussed above, are available through retail insurance agencies, automobile clubs, and many travel agents. These combination policies are designed to cover you for the duration of a single trip.

Companies offering policies of this type include the following:

Access America International (PO Box 90310, Richmond, VA 23230; phone: 800-424-3391 or 804-215-3300).

Carefree Travel Insurance (Arm Coverage, 120 Mineola Blvd., Mineola, NY 11501; phone: 800-645-2424 or 516-294-0220).

NEAR Services (450 Prairie Ave., Suite 101, Calumet City, IL 60409; phone: 708-868-6700 in the Chicago area; 800-654-6700 elsewhere in the US and Canada).

Tele-Trip (3201 Farnam St., Omaha, NE 68131; phone: 402-345-2400 in Nebraska; 800-228-9792 elsewhere in the US).

Travel Assistance International (1133 15th St. NW, Suite 400, Washington, DC 20005; phone: 202-331-1609 in Washington, DC; 800-821-2828 elsewhere in the US).

Travel Guard International (1145 Clark St., Stevens Point, WI 54481; phone: 715-345-0505 in Wisconsin; 800-826-1300 elsewhere in the US).

Travel Insurance PAK c/o The Travelers Companies (Travelers Insurance Company, Travel Insurance Division 10NB, One Tower Sq., Hartford, CT 06183-5040; phone: 203-277-2319 in Connecticut; 800-243-3174 elsewhere in the US).

Hints for Handicapped Travelers

 From 40 to 50 million people in the US alone have some sort of disability, and over half this number are physically handicapped. Like everyone else today, they — and the uncounted disabled millions around the world — are on the move. More than ever before, they are demanding facilities they can use comfortably, and they are being heard.

With the 1990 passage of the Americans with Disabilities Act, the physically handicapped increasingly will be finding better access to places and services throughout the US. The provisions of the act relating to public accommodations and transportation, which took effect in January 1992, mandate that means of access be provided except where the cost would be prohibitive, and creative alternatives are being encouraged. As the impact of the law spreads across the country, previous barriers to travel in the US should be somewhat ameliorated.

PLANNING: Make your travel arrangements well in advance and specify to all services involved the exact nature of your condition or restricted mobility. The best way to find out if your intended destination can accommodate a handicapped traveler is to write or call the local tourist authority or hotel and ask specific questions.

It is also advisable to call the hotel you are considering and ask specific questions. If you require a corridor of a certain width to maneuver a wheelchair or if you need handles on the bathroom walls for support, ask the hotel manager (many large hotels have rooms designed for the handicapped). A travel agent or the local chapter or national office of the organization that deals with your particular disability — for example, the *American Foundation for the Blind* or the *American Heart Association* — will supply the most up-to-date information on the subject.

The following organizations offer general information on access:

ACCENT on Living (PO Box 700, Bloomington, IL 61702; phone: 309-378-2961). This information service for persons with disabilities provides a free list of travel agencies specializing in arranging trips for the disabled; for a copy send a self-addressed, stamped envelope. It also offers a wide range of publications, including a quarterly magazine ($10 per year, $17.50 for 2 years, $25 for 3 years) for persons with disabilities.

Canadian Paraplegic Association (520 Sutherland Dr., Toronto, Ontario M4G 3V9, Canada; phone: 416-422-5644) is a good source of information on travel for the mobility-disabled. The association has a comprehensive library, offers accessibility information, and provides referral services.

Community Information Centre of Metro Toronto (590 Jarvis St., 5th Floor, Toronto, Ontario M4Y 2J4, Canada; phone: 416-392-0505) provides informational pamphlets for the disabled on traveling in and around Toronto.

Information Center for Individuals with Disabilities (27-43 Wormwood St., Ft. Point Pl., 1st Floor, Boston, MA 02210; phone: 800-462-5015 in Massachusetts; 617-727-5540/1 elsewhere in the US; both numbers provide voice and TDD — telecommunications device for the deaf). The center offers information and referral services on disability-related issues, publishes fact sheets on travel agents, tour operators, and other travel resources, and can help you research your trip.

Mobility International USA (*MIUSA;* PO Box 3551, Eugene, OR 97403; phone: 503-343-1284; both voice and TDD). This US branch of *Mobility International* (the main office is at 228 Borough High St., London SE1 1JX, England; phone: 011-44-71-403-5688), a nonprofit British organization with affiliates worldwide, offers members advice and assistance — including information on accommodations and other travel services, and publications applicable to the traveler's disability. *Mobility International* also offers a quarterly newsletter and a comprehensive sourcebook, *A World of Options for the 90s: A Guide to International Education Exchange, Community Service and Travel for Persons with Disabilities* ($14 for members; $16 for non-members). Membership includes the newsletter and is $20 a year; subscription to the newsletter alone is $10 annually.

National Rehabilitation Information Center (*NRIC;* 8455 Colesville Rd., Suite 935, Silver Spring, MD 20910; phone: 301-588-9284). A general information, resource, research, and referral service.

Paralyzed Veterans of America (*PVA;* PVA/ATTS Program, 801 18th St. NW, Washington, DC 20006; phone: 202-416-7708 in Washington, DC, 800-424-8200 elsewhere in the US). The members of this national service organization all are veterans who have suffered spinal-cord injuries, but it offers advocacy services and information to all persons with a disability. *PVA* also sponsors Access to the Skies (ATTS), a program that coordinates the efforts of the national and international air travel industry in providing airport and airplane access for the disabled. Members receive several helpful publications, as well as regular notification of conferences on subjects of interest to the disabled traveler.

Royal Association for Disability and Rehabilitation (*RADAR;* 25 Mortimer St., London W1N 8AB, England; phone: 011-44-71-637-5400). Offers a number of publications for the handicapped, including *Holidays and Travel Abroad 1993/94 — A Guide for Disabled People,* a comprehensive guidebook focusing on international travel. This publication can be ordered by sending payment in British pounds to *RADAR.* As we went to press, it cost just over £3; call for current pricing before ordering.

Society for the Advancement of Travel for the Handicapped (*SATH;* 347 Fifth Ave., Suite 610, New York, NY 10016; phone: 212-447-7284). To keep abreast of developments in travel for the handicapped as they occur, you may want to join *SATH,* a nonprofit organization whose members include consumers as well as travel service professionals who have experience (or an interest) in travel for the handicapped. For an annual fee of $45 ($25 for students and travelers who are 65 and older) members receive a quarterly newsletter and have access to extensive information and referral services. *SATH* also offers two useful publications: *Travel Tips for the Handicapped* (a series of informative fact sheets) and *The United States Welcomes Handicapped Visitors* (a 48-page guide covering domestic transportation and accommodations, as well as useful hints for travelers with disabilities abroad); to order, send a self-addressed, #10 envelope and $1 per title for postage.

Travel Information Service (Moss Rehabilitation Hospital, 1200 W. Tabor Rd., Philadelphia, PA 19141-3099; phone: 215-456-9600 for voice; 215-456-9602 for TDD). This service assists physically handicapped people in planning trips and supplies detailed information on accessibility for a nominal fee.

Blind travelers should contact the *American Foundation for the Blind* (15 W. 16th St., New York, NY 10011; phone: 212-620-2147 or 800-829-0500) and *The Seeing Eye* (PO Box 375, Morristown, NJ 07963-0375; phone: 201-539-4425); both provide useful information on resources for the visually impaired. *Note:* Seeing Eye dogs accompanied by their owners may enter Canada without certification or other restrictions.

The American Society for the Prevention of Cruelty to Animals (*ASPCA;* Education Dept., 424 E. 92nd St., New York, NY 10128; phone: 212-876-7700) offers a useful booklet, *Traveling With Your Pet,* which lists inoculation and other requirements by country and territory. It is available for $5 (including postage and handling).

In addition, there are a number of publications — from travel guides to magazines — of interest to handicapped travelers. Among these are the following:

Access to the World, by Louise Weiss, offers sound tips for the disabled traveler. Published by Facts on File (460 Park Ave. S., New York, NY 10016; phone: 212-683-2244 in New York State; 800-322-8755 elsewhere in the US; 800-443-8323 in Canada), it costs $16.95. Check with your local bookstore; it also can be ordered by phone with a credit card.

The Diabetic Traveler (PO Box 8223 RW, Stamford, CT 06905; phone: 203-327-5832) is a useful quarterly newsletter for travelers with diabetes. Each issue highlights a single destination or type of travel and includes information on general resources and hints for diabetics. A 1-year subscription costs $18.95. When subscribing, ask for the free fact sheet including an index of special articles; back issues are available for $4 each.

Guide to Traveling with Arthritis, a free brochure available by writing to the Upjohn Company (PO Box 307-B, Coventry, CT 06238), provides lots of good, commonsense tips on planning your trip and how to be as comfortable as possible when traveling by car, bus, train, cruise ship, or plane.

Handicapped Travel Newsletter is regarded as one of the best sources of information for the disabled traveler. It is edited by wheelchair-bound Vietnam veteran Michael Quigley, who has traveled to 93 countries around the world. Issued every 2 months (plus special issues), a subscription is $10 per year. Write to *Handicapped Travel Newsletter,* PO Box 269, Athens, TX 75751 (phone: 903-677-1260).

Handi-Travel: A Resource Book for Disabled and Elderly Travellers, by Cinnie Noble, is a comprehensive travel guide full of practical tips for those with disabilities affecting mobility, hearing, or sight. To order this book, send $12.95, plus shipping and handling, to the *Canadian Rehabilitation Council for the Disabled,* 45 Sheppard Ave. E., Suite 801, Toronto, Ontario M2N 5W9, Canada (phone: 416-250-7490; both voice and TDD).

The Itinerary (PO Box 2012, Bayonne, NJ 07002-2012; phone: 201-858-3400). This quarterly travel magazine for people with disabilities includes information on accessibility, listings of tours, news of adaptive devices, travel aids, and special services, as well as numerous general travel hints. A subscription costs $10 a year.

The Physically Disabled Traveler's Guide, by Rod W. Durgin and Norene Lindsay, rates accessibility of a number of travel services and includes a list of organizations specializing in travel for the disabled. It is available for $9.95, plus $2 shipping and handling, from Resource Directories, 3361 Executive Pkwy., Suite 302, Toledo, OH 43606 (phone: 419-536-5353 in the Toledo area; 800-274-8515 elsewhere in the US).

Ticket to Safe Travel offers useful information for travelers with diabetes. A reprint of this article is available free from local chapters of the *American Diabetes Association.* For the nearest branch, contact the central office at 1660 Duke St., Alexandria, VA 22314 (phone: 800-232-3472 or 703-549-1500).

Travel for the Patient with Chronic Obstructive Pulmonary Disease, a publication of the George Washington University Medical Center, provides some sound practical suggestions for those with emphysema, chronic bronchitis, asthma, or other lung ailments. To order, send $2 to Dr. Harold Silver, 1601 18th St. NW, Washington, DC 20009 (phone: 202-667-0134).

Traveling Like Everybody Else: A Practical Guide for Disabled Travelers, by Jacqueline Freedman and Susan Gersten, offers the disabled tips on traveling by car, cruise ship, and plane, as well as lists of accessible accommodations, tour operators specializing in tours for disabled travelers, and other resources. It is available for $11.95, plus postage and handling, from Modan Publishing, PO Box 1202, Bellmore, NY 11710 (phone: 516-679-1380).

Travel Tips for Hearing-Impaired People, a free pamphlet for deaf and hearing-impaired travelers, is available from the *American Academy of Otolaryngology* (One Prince St., Alexandria, VA 22314; phone: 703-836-4444). For a copy, send a self-addressed, stamped, business-size envelope to the academy.

Travel Tips for People with Arthritis, a 31-page booklet published by the *Arthritis Foundation,* provides helpful information regarding travel by car, bus, train, cruise ship, or plane, planning your trip, medical considerations, and ways to conserve your energy while traveling, and includes listings of helpful resources, such as associations and travel agencies that operate tours for disabled travelers. For a copy, contact your local *Arthritis Foundation* chapter, or send $1 to the national office, 1314 Spring St. NW, Atlanta, GA 30309 (phone: 404-872-7100 or 800-283-7800).

A few more basic resources to look for are *Travel for the Disabled,* by Helen Hecker ($19.95) and, by the same author, *Directory of Travel Agencies for the Disabled* ($19.95). *Wheelchair Vagabond,* by John G. Nelson, is another useful guide for travelers confined to a wheelchair (hardcover, $14.95; paperback, $9.95). All three titles are published by Twin Peaks Press (PO Box 129, Vancouver, WA 98666; phone: 800-637-CALM or 206-694-2462). For $2, the publisher also will send you a catalogue of 26 books on travel for the disabled.

PLANE: The US Department of Transportation (DOT) has ruled that US airlines must accept all passengers with disabilities. As a matter of course, US airlines were pretty good about accommodating handicapped passengers even before the ruling, although each airline has somewhat different procedures. Canadian airlines also are good about accommodating the disabled traveler, but, again, policies may vary somewhat from carrier to carrier. Ask for specifics when you book your flight.

Disabled passengers always should make reservations well in advance, and should provide the airline with all relevant details of their conditions. These details include information on mobility and equipment that you will need the airline to supply — such as a wheelchair for boarding or portable oxygen for in-flight use. Be sure that the person to whom you speak fully understands the degree of your disability — the more details provided, the more effective help the airline can give you.

On the day before the flight, call back to make sure that all arrangements have been prepared, and arrive early on the day of the flight so that you can board before the rest of the passengers. It's a good idea to bring a medical certificate with you, stating your specific disability or the need to carry particular medicine.

Because most airports have jetways (corridors connecting the terminal with the door of the plane), a disabled passenger usually can be taken as far as the plane, and sometimes right onto it, in a wheelchair. If not, a narrow boarding chair may be used to take you to your seat. Your own wheelchair, which will be folded and put in the baggage compartment, should be tagged as escort luggage to assure that it's available at planeside upon landing rather than in the baggage claim area. Travel is not quite as simple if your wheelchair is battery-operated: Unless it has non-spillable batteries, it might not be accepted on board, and you will have to check with the airline ahead of time to find out how the batteries and the chair should be packaged for the flight. Usually people in wheelchairs are asked to wait until other passengers have disembarked. If you are making a tight connection, be sure to tell the attendant.

Passengers who use oxygen may not use their personal supply in the cabin, though it may be carried on the plane as cargo when properly packed and labeled (the tank must be emptied). If you will need oxygen during the flight, the airline will supply it to you (there is a charge) provided you have given advance notice — 24 hours to a few days, depending on the carrier.

Useful information on every stage of air travel, from planning to arrival, is provided in the booklet *Incapacitated Passengers Air Travel Guide*. To receive a free copy, write to the *International Air Transport Association* (Publications Sales Department, 2000 Peel St., Montreal, Quebec H3A 2R4, Canada; phone: 514-844-6311). Another helpful publication is *Air Transportation of Handicapped Persons*, which explains the general guidelines that govern air carrier policies. For a copy of this free booklet, write to the US Department of Transportation (Distribution Unit, Publications Section, M-443-2, Washington, DC 20590) and ask for "Free Advisory Circular #AC-120-32." *Access Travel: A Guide to the Accessibility of Airport Terminals*, a free publication of the *Airport Operators Council International*, provides information on more than 500 airports worldwide — including major airports in Canada — and offers ratings of 70 features, such as wheelchair accessibility to bathrooms, corridor width, and parking spaces. For a copy, contact the Consumer Information Center, Dept. 563W, Pueblo, CO 81009 (phone: 719-948-3334).

Among the major carriers serving Canada, the following airlines have TDD toll-free lines for the hearing-impaired:

Air Canada: 800-361-8071 only in Canada.
American: 800-582-1573 in Ohio; 800-543-1586 elsewhere in the US.
Canadian Airlines International: 800-465-3611 only in Canada.
Delta: 800-831-4488 throughout the US.
Northwest: 800-328-2298 throughout the US.
USAir: 800-245-2966 throughout the US.

GROUND TRANSPORTATION: Perhaps the simplest solution to getting around is to travel with an able-bodied companion who can drive. If you are accustomed to driving your own hand-controlled car and want to rent one, you may be in luck. Some rental car companies will fit cars with hand controls. *Avis* (phone: 800-331-1084) can convert a car to hand controls with 48 hours' notice, though it's a good idea to make arrangements more than one day in advance. *Hertz* (phone: 800-654-3001) can also convert a car to hand controls. Neither company charges extra for hand controls, but will fit them only on full-size cars. Both companies request that you present to them a handicapped driver's permit. Other car rental companies provide hand-control cars at some locations; however, as there usually are only a limited number available, call well in advance.

The *American Automobile Association (AAA)* publishes a useful book, *The Handicapped Driver's Mobility Guide*. Contact the central office of your local *AAA* club for availability and pricing, which may vary at different branch offices.

TOURS: Programs designed for the physically impaired are run by specialists who have researched hotels, restaurants, and sites to be sure they present no insurmountable obstacles. The following travel agencies and tour operators specialize in making group and individual arrangements for travelers with physical or other disabilities.

Access: The Foundation for Accessibility by the Disabled (PO Box 356, Malverne, NY 11565; phone: 516-887-5798). A travelers' referral service that acts as an intermediary with tour operators and agents worldwide, and provides information on accessibility at various locations. A membership program, *Access* charges a onetime $35 registration fee.
Accessible Journeys (35 W. Sellers Ave., Ridley Park, PA 19078; phone: 215-747-0171). Arranges for medical professionals to be traveling companions — registered or licensed practical nurses, therapists, or doctors (all are experienced

travelers). Several prospective companions' profiles and photos are sent to the client for perusal and, if one is acceptable, the "match" is made. The client usually pays all travel expenses for the companion, plus a set fee to compensate for wages the companion would be making at his or her usual job.

Accessible Tours/Directions Unlimited (720 N. Bedford Rd., Bedford Hills, NY 10507; phone: 914-241-1700 in New York State; 800-533-5343 elsewhere in the continental US). Arranges group or individual tours for disabled persons traveling in the company of able-bodied friends or family members. Accepts the unaccompanied traveler if completely self-sufficient.

Evergreen Travel Service (4114 198th St. SW, Suite 13, Lynnwood, WA 98036-6742; phone: 206-776-1184 or 800-435-2288 throughout the US and Canada). It offers worldwide tours for people who are disabled (Wings on Wheels Tours), sight-impaired/blind (White Cane Tours), hearing-impaired/deaf (Flying Fingers Tours), or mentally disabled (Happiness Tours). It also offers a program for people who are not disabled but who want a slower pace (Lazybones Tours), and arranges special programs for people who need dialysis.

Flying Wheels Travel (143 W. Bridge St., Box 382, Owatonna, MN 55060; phone: 507-451-5005 or 800-535-6790 throughout the US and Canada). Handles both tours and individual arrangements.

Sprout (893 Amsterdam Ave., New York, NY 10025; phone: 212-222-9575). Arranges travel programs for mildly and moderately disabled teens and adults.

USTS Travel Horizons (11 E. 44th St., New York, NY 10017; phone: 212-687-5121 in New York State or 800-487-8787 elsewhere in the US). Travel agent and registered nurse Mary Ann Hamm designs trips for individual travelers requiring all types of kidney dialysis and handles arrangements for the dialysis.

Whole Person Tours (PO Box 1084, Bayonne, NJ 07002-1084; phone: 201-858-3400). Owner Bob Zywicki travels the world with his wheelchair and offers a lineup of escorted tours (many conducted by him) for the disabled. Call for current itinerary at the time you plan to travel. *Whole Person Tours* also publishes *The Itinerary,* a quarterly newsletter for disabled travelers (see the publication source list above).

Travelers who would benefit from being accompanied by a nurse or physical therapist also can hire a companion through *Traveling Nurses' Network,* a service provided by Twin Peaks Press (PO Box 129, Vancouver, WA 98666; phone: 800-637-CALM or 206-694-2462). For a $10 fee, clients receive the names of three nurses, whom they can then contact directly; for a $125 fee, the agency will make all the hiring arrangements for the client. Travel arrangements also may be made in some cases — the fee for this further service is determined on an individual basis.

A similar service is offered by *MedEscort International* (ABE International Airport, PO Box 8766, Allentown, PA 18105; phone: 800-255-7182 in the continental US; elsewhere, call 215-791-3111). Clients can arrange to be accompanied by a nurse, paramedic, respiratory therapist, or physician through *MedEscort*. The fees are based on the disabled traveler's needs. This service also can assist in making travel arrangements.

Hints for Single Travelers

Just about the last trip in human history on which the participants were neatly paired was the voyage of Noah's Ark. Ever since, passenger lists and tour groups have reflected the same kind of asymmetry that occurs in real life, as countless individuals set forth to see the world unaccompanied (or unencumbered, depending on your outlook) by spouse, lover, companion, or relative. Unfortunately, traveling alone can turn a traveler into a second class citizen.

The truth is that the travel industry is not very fair to people who vacation by themselves. People traveling alone almost invariably end up paying more than individuals traveling in pairs. Most travel bargains, including package tours, accommodations, resort packages, and cruises, are based on *double occupancy* rates. This means that the per-person price is offered on the basis of two people traveling together and sharing a double room (which means they each will spend a good deal more on meals and extras). The single traveler will have to pay a surcharge, called a single supplement, for exactly the same package. In extreme cases, this can add as much as 35% — and sometimes more — to the basic per-person rate.

Don't despair, however. In Toronto, there are scores of smaller hotels and other hostelries where, in addition to a cozier atmosphere, prices still are quite reasonable for the single traveler.

The obvious, most effective alternative is to find a traveling companion. Even special "singles' tours" that promise no supplements usually are based on people sharing double rooms. Perhaps the most recent innovation along these lines is the creation of organizations that "introduce" the single traveler to other single travelers. Some charge fees, while others are free, but the basic service offered is the same: to match an unattached person with a compatible travel mate. Among such organizations are the following:

Odyssey Network (118 Cedar St., Wellesley, MA 02181; phone: 617-237-2400). Originally founded to match single women travelers, this company now includes men in its enrollment. *Odyssey* offers a quarterly newsletter for members who are seeking a travel companion, and occasionally organizes small group tours. Membership (which includes newsletter subscription) is $50.

Partners-in-Travel (PO Box 491145, Los Angeles, CA 90049; phone: 213-476-4869). Members receive a list of singles seeking traveling companions; prospective companions make contact through the agency. The membership fee is $40 per year and includes a chatty newsletter (6 issues per year).

Travel Companion Exchange (PO Box 833, Amityville, NY 11701; phone: 516-454-0880). This group publishes a newsletter for singles and a directory of individuals looking for travel companions. On joining, members fill out a lengthy questionnaire and write a small listing (much like an ad in a personal column). Based on these listings, members can request copies of profiles and contact prospective traveling companions. It is wise to join well in advance of your planned vacation so that there's enough time to determine compatibility and plan a joint trip. Membership fees, including the newsletter, are $30 for 6 months or $60 a year for a single-sex listing.

Travel in Two's (239 N. Broadway., Suite 3, N. Tarrytown, NY 10591; phone: 914-631-8409). For city programs, this company matches up solo travelers and then customizes programs for them. The firm also puts out a quarterly *Singles Vacation Newsletter,* which costs $7.50 per issue or $20 per year.

In addition, a number of tour packagers cater to single travelers. These companies offer packages designed for individuals interested in vacationing with a group of single travelers or in being matched with a traveling companion. Among the better established of these agencies are the following:

Cosmos: This tour operator offers a number of package tours with a guaranteed-share plan whereby singles who wish to share rooms (and avoid paying the single supplement) are matched by the tour escort with individuals of the same sex and charged the basic double-occupancy tour price. Contact the firm at one of its three North American branches: 95-25 Queens Blvd., Rego Park, NY 11374 (phone: 800-221-0090 or 718-268-7000); 5301 S. Federal Circle, Littleton, CO

80123 (phone 800-221-0090); 1061 Eglinton Ave. W., Toronto, Ontario M6C 2C9, Canada (phone: 416-787-1281). *Cosmos* offers a 12-day Eastern US and Canada Grand Tour, with stops in Boston, Montreal, New York City, and Toronto.

Grand Circle Travel (347 Congress St., Boston, MA 02210; phone: 617-350-7500 or 800-221-2610). Arranges extended vacations, escorted tours, and cruises for the over-50 traveler. Membership, which is automatic when you book a trip through *Grand Circle,* includes travel discounts and other extras, such as a Pen Pals service for singles seeking travel companions. Offers a 15-day Grand Canadian Capitals tour, with stops in Toronto, the Algonquin Provincial Park, Montreal, Niagara Falls, Ottawa, and Quebec City.

Marion Smith Singles (611 Prescott Pl., N. Woodmere, NY 11581; phone: 516-791-4852, 516-791-4865, or 212-944-2112). Specializes in tours for singles ages 20 to 50, who can choose to share accommodations to avoid paying single-supplement charges.

Saga International Holidays (222 Berkeley St., Boston MA 02116; phone: 617-451-6808 or 800-343-0273). A subsidiary of a British company specializing in older travelers, many of them single, *Saga* offers a broad selection of packages for people age 60 and over or those 50 to 59 traveling with someone 60 or older. Although anyone can book a *Saga* trip, a club membership (no fee) includes a subscription to their newsletter, as well as other publications and travel services — such as a matching service for single travelers. Offers a 13-day Ontario and Quebec Historic Provinces tour, which includes stops in Toronto, Montreal, Niagara Falls, Ottawa, and Quebec City.

Singles in Motion (545 W. 236th St., Suite 1D, Riverdale, NY 10463; phone: 718-884-4464). Offers a number of packages for single travelers, including tours, cruises, and excursions focusing on outdoor activities such as hiking and biking.

A good book for single travelers is *Traveling On Your Own,* by Eleanor Berman, which offers tips on traveling solo and includes information on trips for singles. Available in bookstores, it also can be ordered by sending $12.95, plus postage and handling, to Random House, Order Dept., 400 Hahn Rd., Westminster, MD 21157 (phone: 800-733-3000).

Single travelers also may want to subscribe to *Going Solo,* a newsletter that offers helpful information on going on your own. Issued eight times a year, a subscription costs $29. Contact Doerfer Communications, PO Box 1035, Cambridge, MA 02239 (phone: 617-876-2764).

Hints for Older Travelers

 Special discounts and more free time are just two factors that have given Americans over age 65 a chance to see the world at affordable prices. Senior citizens make up an ever-growing segment of the travel population, and the trend among them is to travel more frequently and for longer periods of time.

PLANNING: When planning a vacation, prepare your itinerary with one eye on your own physical condition and the other on your interests. One important factor to keep in mind is not to overdo anything and to be aware of the effects that the weather may have on your capabilities.

Older travelers may find the following publications of interest:

Going Abroad: 101 Tips for the Mature Traveler offers tips on preparing for your trip, commonsense precautions en route, and some basic travel terminology.

This concise free booklet is available from *Grand Circle Travel,* 347 Congress St., Boston, MA 02210 (phone: 800-221-2610 or 617-350-7500).

The International Health Guide for Senior Citizen Travelers, by Dr. W. Robert Lange, covers such topics as trip preparations, food and water precautions, adjusting to weather and climate conditions, finding a doctor, motion sickness, jet lag, and so on. Also includes a list of resource organizations that provide medical assistance for travelers. It is available for $4.95, plus $1 in postage, from Pilot Books, 103 Cooper St., Babylon, NY 11702 (phone: 516-422-2225).

Mature Traveler is a monthly newsletter that provides information on travel discounts, places of interest, useful tips, and other topics of interest for travelers 49 and up. To subscribe, send $24.95 to GEM Publishing Group, PO Box 50820, Reno, NV 89513 (phone: 702-786-7419).

Senior Citizen's Guide To Budget Travel In The US And Canada, by Paige Palmer, provides specific information on economical travel options for senior citizens. To order, send $4.95, plus postage and handling, to Pilot Books (address above).

Take a Camel to Lunch and Other Adventures for Mature Travelers, by Nancy O'Connell, offers offbeat and unusual adventures for travelers over 50. Available at bookstores or directly from Bristol Publishing Enterprises (PO Box 1737, San Leandro, CA 94577; phone: 800-346-4889 or 510-895-4461) for $8.95, plus shipping and handling.

Travel Tips for Older Americans is a useful booklet that provides good, basic advice. This US State Department publication (stock number: 044-000-02270-2) can be ordered by sending a check or money order for $1 to the Superintendent of Documents (US Government Printing Office, Washington, DC 20420) or by calling 202-783-3238 and charging the order to a credit card.

Unbelievably Good Deals & Great Adventures That You Absolutely Can't Get Unless You're Over 50, by Joan Rattner Heilman, offers travel tips for older travelers, including discounts on accommodations and transportation, as well as a list of organizations for seniors. It is available for $7.95 (plus shipping and handling) from Contemporary Books, 180 N. Michigan Ave., Chicago, IL 60601 (phone: 312-782-9181).

HEALTH: Health facilities generally are maintained by individual Canadian provinces, but Blue Cross usually is honored throughout Canada. Pre-trip medical and dental checkups are strongly recommended. In addition, be sure to take along any prescription medication you need, enough to last *without a new prescription* for the duration of your trip; pack all medications with a note from your doctor for the benefit of airport authorities. If you have specific medical problems, bring prescriptions and a "medical file" composed of the following:

1. A summary of your medical history and current diagnosis.
2. A list of drugs to which you are allergic.
3. Your most recent electrocardiogram, if you have heart problems.
4. Your doctor's name, address, and telephone number.

DISCOUNTS AND PACKAGES: Since guidelines change from place to place, it is a good idea to inquire in advance about discounts on accommodations, transportation, tickets to theater and concert performances and movies, entrance fees to museums, national monuments, and other attractions. Senior citizens with identification are eligible for a large variety of discounts across Canada. Some discounts are only available to Canadians, but many others are available to anyone over 65. For instance, depending on the local management, discounts of 10% to 25% often are available at a variety of hotel chains, including *Holiday Inn, Howard Johnson, Marriott, Rodeway Inns,* and *Sheraton.* In addition, both *Air Canada* and *Canadian Airlines International* offer discounts on fares to those 62 and over (and often one traveling companion per senior). Given the continuing changes in the airline industry, however, these discounted fares may not be available when you purchase your tickets. For more information on current prices and applicable restrictions, contact the individual carriers.

Some discounts, however, are extended only to bona fide members of certain senior citizens organizations. Because the same organizations frequently offer package tours to both domestic and international destinations, the benefits of membership are twofold: Those who join can take advantage of discounts as individual travelers and also reap the savings that group travel affords. In addition, because the age requirements for some of these organizations are quite low (or nonexistent), the benefits can begin to accrue early.

In order to take advantage of these discounts, you should carry proof of your age (or eligibility): for Canadians, a special card issued by the province; for older visitors from the US and other countries, a driver's license, passport, birth certificate, membership card in a recognized senior citizens organization, or a Medicare card should be sufficient.

Among the organizations dedicated to helping older travelers see the world are the following:

American Association of Retired Persons (*AARP;* 601 E St. NW, Washington, DC 20049; phone: 202-434-2277). The largest and best-known of these organizations. Membership is open to anyone 50 or over, whether retired or not; dues are $8 a year, $20 for 3 years, or $45 for 10 years, and include spouse. The *AARP* Travel Experience Wordwide program, available through *American Express Travel Related Services,* offers members travel programs designed exclusively for older travelers. Members can book these services by calling *American Express* at 800-927-0111 for land and air travel.

Mature Outlook (Customer Service Center, 6001 N. Clark St., Chicago, IL 60660; phone: 800-336-6330). Through its *Travel Alert,* tours, cruises, and other vacation packages are available to members at special savings. Hotel and car rental discounts and travel accident insurance also are available. Membership is open to anyone 50 years of age or older, costs $9.95 a year, and includes a bimonthly newsletter and magazine, as well as information on package tours.

National Council of Senior Citizens (1331 F St. NW, Washington, DC 20004; phone: 202-347-8800). Here, too, the emphasis is on keeping costs low. This nonprofit organization offers members a different roster of package tours each year, as well as individual arrangements. Although most members are over 50, membership is open to anyone (regardless of age) for an annual fee of $12 per person or couple, or $30 for 3 years. Lifetime membership costs $150. For information, contact its affiliated travel agency *Vantage Travel Service* (phone: 800-322-6677).

Certain travel agencies and tour operators offer special trips geared to older travelers. Among them are the following:

Evergreen Travel Service (4114 198th Ave. SW, Suite 13, Lynnwood, WA 98036-6742; phone: 206-776-1184 or 800-435-2288 throughout the US and Canada). This specialist in trips for persons with disabilities recently introduced Lazybones Tours, a program offering leisurely trips for older travelers. Most programs are first class or deluxe, and include an escort.

Gadabout Tours (700 E. Tahquitz Way, Palm Springs, CA 92262; phone: 619-325-5556 or 800-521-7309 in California; 800-952-5068 elsewhere in the US). Offers escorted tours and cruises throughout Canada. Offers an 18-day Fall Foliage Spectacular, with stops in Toronto, Montreal, Ottawa, Quebec City, and Washington, DC.

Grand Circle Travel (347 Congress St., Boston, MA 02210; phone: 800-221-2610 or 617-350-7500). Caters exclusively to the over-50 traveler and packages a large variety of escorted tours, cruises, and extended vacations. Membership, which is automatic when you book a trip through *Grand Circle,* includes discount certificates on future trips and other travel services, such as a matching service for single travelers and a helpful free booklet, *Going Abroad: 101 Tips for Mature Travelers* (see the source list above).

OmniTours (104 Wilmot Rd., Deerfield, IL 60015; phone: 800-962-0060 or 708-374-0088). Offers combination air and rail group tours designed for travelers 50 years and older. Their itineraries include a 9-day rail tour that visits Montreal, Ottawa, Quebec City, and Toronto.

Saga International Holidays (222 Berkeley St., Boston MA 02116; phone: 617-451-6808 or 800-343-0273). A subsidiary of a British company catering to older travelers, *Saga* offers a broad selection of packages for people age 60 and over or those 50 to 59 traveling with someone 60 or older. Although anyone can book a *Saga* trip, a club membership (no fee) includes a subscription to their newsletter, as well as other publications and travel services.

Many travel agencies, particularly the larger ones, are delighted to make presentations to help a group of senior citizens select destinations. A local chamber of commerce should be able to provide the names of such agencies. Once a time and place are determined, an organization member or travel agent can obtain group quotations for transportation, accommodations, meal plans, and sightseeing. Larger groups usually get the best breaks.

Another choice open to older travelers is a trip that includes an educational element. *Elderhostel,* a nonprofit organization, offers educational programs at schools worldwide. Most Canadian programs run for 1 week, and include double occupancy accommodations in hotels or student residence halls and all meals. Elderhostelers must be at least 60 years old (younger if a spouse or companion qualifies), in good health, and not in need of special diets. For a free catalogue describing the program and current offerings, contact *Elderhostel* (75 Federal St., Boston, MA 02110; phone: 617-426-7788) or *Elderhostel Canada* (308 Wellington St., Kingston, Ontario K7K 7A7, Canada; phone: 613-530-2222). Those interested in the program also can purchase an informational videotape for $5.

Hints for Traveling with Children

What better way to encounter the world's variety than in the company of the young, wide-eyed members of your family? Their presence does not have to be a burden or an excessive expense. The current generation of discounts for children and family package deals can make a trip together quite reasonable.

A family trip to Toronto will be an investment in your children's future, making geography and history come alive to them, and leaving a sure memory that will be among the fondest you will share with them someday. Their insights will be refreshing to you; their impulses may take you to unexpected places with unexpected dividends.

PLANNING: Here are several hints for making a trip with children easy and fun.

1. Children, like everyone else, will derive more pleasure from a trip if they know something about their destination before they arrive. Begin their education about a month before you leave. Using maps, travel magazines, and books, give children a clear idea of where you are going and how far away it is.

2. Children should help to plan the itinerary, and where you go and what you do should reflect some of their ideas. If they already know something about the sites they'll visit, they will have the excitement of recognition when they arrive.
3. Familiarize your children with Canadian dollars. Give them an allowance for the trip and be sure they understand just how far it will or won't go.
4. Give children specific responsibilities: The job of carrying their own flight bags and looking after their personal things, along with some other light chores, will give them a stake in the journey.
5. Give each child a travel diary or scrapbook to take along.

Children's books about Canada provide an excellent introduction to the country and culture and can be found at many general bookstores and in libraries.

And for parents, *Travel With Your Children* (*TWYCH;* 45 W. 18th St., 7th Floor, New York, NY 10011; phone: 212-206-0688) publishes a newsletter, *Family Travel Times,* that focuses on families with young travelers and offers helpful hints. An annual subscription (10 issues) is $35 and includes a copy of the "Airline Guide" issue (updated every other year), which focuses on the subject of flying with children. This special issue is also available separately for $10.

Another newsletter devoted to family travel is *Getaways.* This quarterly publication provides reviews of family-oriented literature, activities, and useful travel tips. To subscribe, send $25 to *Getaways,* Att. Ms. Brooke Kane, PO Box 8282, McLean, VA 22107 (phone: 703-534-8747).

Also of interest to parents traveling with their children is *How to Take Great Trips With Your Kids,* by psychologist Sanford Portnoy and his wife, Joan Flynn Portnoy. The book includes helpful tips from fellow family travelers, tips on economical accommodations and touring by car, recreational vehicle, and train, as well as over 50 games to play with your children en route. It is available for $8.95, plus shipping and handling, from Harvard Common Press, 535 Albany St., Boston, MA 02118 (phone: 617-423-5803).

Another book on family travel, *Travel with Children,* by Maureen Wheeler, offers a wide range of practical tips on traveling with children, and includes accounts of the author's family travel experiences. It is available for $10.95, plus shipping and handling, from Lonely Planet Publications, 155 Filbert St., Oakland, CA 94607 (phone: 510-893-8555).

Adventure Travel North America, by Pat Dickerman (Adventure Guides, 36 E. 57th St., New York, NY 10022; phone: 800-252-7899 or 212-355-6334; $18, plus shipping and handling), is a good source of companies featuring family travel adventures. Also see *Great Vacations with Your Kids,* by Dorothy Jordan (Dutton; $12.95), *What to Do with the Kids This Year: One Hundred Family Vacation Places with Time Off for You!,* by Jane Wilford and Janet Tice (Globe Pequot Press; $8.95), and *Super Family Vacations,* by Martha Shirk (HarperCollins; $14).

Finally, parents arranging a trip with their children may want to contact *Let's Take the Kids* (1268 Devon Ave., Los Angeles, CA 90024; phone: 800-726-4349 or 213-274-7088), an information service specializing in family travel. Although they do not arrange or book trips, this organization provides parents with information and advice on questions they may have about accommodations, itineraries, transportation, and other aspects of a planned vacation. They also offer a parent travel network, whereby parents who have been to a particular destination can evaluate it for others.

PLANE: Begin early to investigate all available discounts and charter flights, as well as any package deals and special rates offered by the major airlines. Booking is sometimes required up to 2 months in advance. You may well find that charter companies offer no reductions for children, or not enough to offset the risk of last-minute delays or other inconveniences to which charters are subject. The major scheduled airlines, on the other hand, almost invariably provide hefty discounts for children.

When you make your reservations, tell the airline that you are traveling with a child.

Children ages 2 through 11 generally travel at about a 20% to 30% discount off regular full-fare adult ticket prices on international flights. This children's fare, however, usually is much higher than the excursion fare, which is applicable to any traveler regardless of age. An infant under 2 years of age usually can travel free if it sits on an adult's lap. A second infant without a second adult would pay the fare applicable to children ages 2 through 11.

Although some airlines will, on request, supply bassinets for infants, most carriers encourage parents to bring their own safety seat on board, which then is strapped into the airline seat with a regular seat belt. This is much safer — and certainly more comfortable — than holding the child in your lap. If you do not purchase a seat for your baby, you have the option of bringing the infant restraint along on the off-chance that there might be an empty seat next to yours — in which case some airlines will let you use that seat at no charge for your baby and infant seat. However, if there is no empty seat available, the infant seat no doubt will have to be checked as baggage (and you may have to pay an additional charge), since it generally does not fit under the seat or in the overhead racks. The safest bet is to pay for a seat.

Be forewarned: Some safety seats designed primarily for use in cars do not fit into plane seats properly. Although nearly all seats manufactured since 1985 carry labels indicating whether they meet federal standards for use aboard planes, actual seat sizes may vary from carrier to carrier. At the time of this writing, the FAA was in the process of reviewing and revising the federal regulations regarding infant travel and safety devices — it was still to be determined if children should be *required* to sit in safety seats and whether the airlines will have to provide them.

If using one of these infant restraints, you should try to get bulkhead seats, which will provide extra room to care for your child during the flight. You also should request a bulkhead seat when using a bassinet — again, this is not as safe as strapping the child in. On some planes bassinets hook into a bulkhead wall; on others they are placed on the floor in front of you. (Note that bulkhead seats often are reserved for families traveling with children.) As a general rule, babies should be held during takeoff and landing.

Request seats on the aisle if you have a toddler or if you think you will need to use the bathroom frequently. Carry onto the plane all you will need to care for and occupy your children during the flight — formula, diapers, a sweater, books, favorite stuffed animals, and so on. Dress your baby simply, with a minimum of buttons and snaps, because the only place you may have to change a diaper is at your seat or in a small lavatory.

On some airlines, you also can ask for a hot dog, hamburger, or even a fruit plate instead of the airline's regular lunch or dinner if you give at least 24 hours' notice. Some, but not all, airlines have baby food aboard and the flight attendant can warm a bottle for you. While you should bring along toys from home, also ask about children's diversions. Some carriers have terrific free packages of games, coloring books, and puzzles.

When the plane takes off and lands, make sure your baby is nursing or has a bottle, pacifier, or thumb in its mouth. This sucking will make the child swallow and help to clear stopped ears. A piece of hard candy will do the same for an older child.

Parents traveling by plane with toddlers, children, or young teenagers may want to consult *When Kids Fly,* a free booklet published by Massport (Public Affairs Department, 10 Park Plaza, Boston, MA 02116-3971; phone: 617-973-5600), which includes helpful information on airfares for children, infant seats, what to do in the event of overbooked or cancelled flights, and so on.

■ **Note:** Newborn babies, whose lungs may not be able to adjust to the altitude, should not be taken aboard an airplane. And some airlines may refuse to allow a pregnant woman in her 8th or 9th month to fly. Check with the airline ahead of time, and carry a letter from your doctor stating that you are fit to travel — and indicating the estimated date of birth.

Things to Remember

1. If you are visiting many sites, pace the days with children in mind. Break the trip into half-day segments, with running around or "doing" time built in.

2. Don't forget that a child's attention span is far shorter than an adult's. Children don't have to see every sight or all of any sight to learn something from their trip; watching, playing with, and talking to other children can be equally enlightening.

3. Let your children lead the way sometimes; their perspective is different from yours, and they may lead you to things you would never have noticed on your own.

4. Remember the places that children love to visit: aquariums, zoos, amusement parks, nature trails, and so on. Among the activities that may pique their interest are bicycling, boat trips, visiting planetariums and children's museums, and viewing natural habitat exhibits. Children's favorites in Toronto include *Centreville,* a magical theme park made just for children. *Funstation* is just that, with its mini-golf courses, remote-control boats and cars, and bumper cars. Just outside of Toronto, there's *Wild Water Kingdom* and its inviting 20,000-square-foot tidal-wave pool. Nature lovers will enjoy *African Lion Safari* in nearby Cambridge, where lions, rhinos, and other creatures of the wild roam free for all to view.

On the Road

Credit and Currency

 It may seem hard to believe, but one of the greatest (and least understood) costs of travel is money itself. Your one single objective in relation to the care and retention of your travel funds is to make them stretch as far as possible. When you do spend money, it should be on things that expand and enhance your travel experience, with no buying power lost due to carelessness or lack of knowledge. This requires more than merely ferreting out the best airfare or the most charming budget hotel. It means being canny about the management of money itself. Herewith, a primer on making money go as far as possible when traveling.

CURRENCY: Travelers from the US should have little difficulty with matters of exchange in Canada. Both countries have money systems based on 100 cents to the dollar, although the US dollar and the Canadian dollar are not equal in value. The value of Canadian currency in relation to the US dollar fluctuates daily, affected by a wide variety of phenomena.

Although US dollars usually are accepted in Canada, you certainly will lose a percentage of your dollar's buying power if you do not take the time to convert it into the local legal tender. By paying for goods and services in local currency, you save money by not negotiating invariably unfavorable exchange rates for every small purchase, and avoid difficulty where US currency is not readily — or happily — accepted. *Throughout this book, unless specifically stated otherwise, prices are given in US dollars.*

There is no limit to the amount of US currency that can be brought into Canada. To avoid problems anywhere along the line, it's advisable to fill out any customs forms provided when leaving the US on which you can declare all money you are taking with you — cash, traveler's checks, and so on. US law requires that anyone taking more than $10,000 into or out of the US must report this fact on customs form No. 4790, which is available at all international airports or from any office of US Customs. If taking over $10,000 out of the US, you must report this *before* leaving the US; if returning with such an amount, you should include this information on your customs declaration. Although travelers usually are not questioned by customs officials about currency when entering or leaving, the sensible course is to observe all regulations just to be on the safe side.

In Toronto, as in the rest of Canada, you will find the official rate of exchange posted in banks, airports, money exchange houses, hotels, and some shops. As a general rule, expect to get more local currency for your US dollar at banks than at any other commercial establishment. Exchange rates do change from day to day, and most banks offer the same (or very similar) exchange rates. (In a pinch, the convenience of cashing money in your hotel — sometimes on a 24-hour basis — *may* make up for the difference in the exchange rate.) Don't try to bargain in banks or hotels — no one will alter the rates for you.

Money exchange houses are financial institutions that charge a fee for the service of exchanging dollars for local currency. When considering alternatives, be aware that although the rate varies among these establishments, the rates of exchange offered are bound to be less favorable than the terms offered at nearby banks — again, don't be surprised if you get fewer Canadian dollars for your US dollar than the rate published in the papers.

That said, however, the following rules of thumb are worth remembering:

Rule number one: Never (repeat: *never*) exchange more than $10 for foreign currency at hotels, restaurants, or retail shops. If you do, you are sure to lose a significant amount of your US dollar's buying power. If you do come across a storefront exchange counter offering what appears to be an incredible bargain, there's too much counterfeit specie in circulation to take the chance.

Rule number two: Estimate your needs carefully; if you overbuy, you lose twice — buying and selling back. Every time you exchange money, someone is making a profit, and rest assured it isn't you. Use up foreign notes before leaving, saving just enough for last-minute incidentals, and tips.

Rule number three: Learn the local currency quickly and keep abreast of daily fluctuations in the exchange rate. These are listed in the *International Herald Tribune* daily for the preceding day, as well as in every major newspaper in Canada. Rates change to some degree every day. For rough calculations, it is quick and safe to use round figures, but for purchases and actual currency exchanges, carry a small pocket calculator to help you compute the exact rate. Inexpensive calculators specifically designed to convert currency amounts for travelers are widely available.

When changing money, don't be afraid to ask how much commission you're being charged, and the exact amount of the prevailing exchange rate. In fact, in any exchange of money for goods or services, you should work out the rate before making any payment.

TRAVELER'S CHECKS: It's wise to carry traveler's checks instead of (or in addition to) cash, since it's possible to replace them if they are stolen or lost. Issued in various denominations and available in both US and Canadian dollars, with adequate proof of identification (credit cards, driver's license, passport), traveler's checks are as good as cash in most hotels, restaurants, stores, and banks.

You will be able to cash traveler's checks fairly easily throughout Canada. However, even in metropolitan areas, such as Toronto, don't assume that restaurants, small shops, and other establishments are going to be able to change checks of large denominations.

Although traveler's checks are available in some foreign currencies, such as Canadian dollars, the exchange rates offered by the issuing companies in the US generally are far less favorable than those available from banks both in the US and abroad. Therefore, it usually is better to carry the bulk of your travel funds abroad in US dollar–denomination traveler's checks.

Every type of traveler's check is legal tender in banks around the world, and each company guarantees full replacement if checks are lost or stolen. After that the similarity ends. Some charge a fee for purchase, others are free; you can buy traveler's checks at almost any bank, and some are available by mail. Most important, each traveler's check issuer differs slightly in its refund policy — the amount refunded immediately, the accessibility of refund locations, the availability of a 24-hour refund service, and the time it will take for you to receive replacement checks. For instance, *American Express* guarantees replacement of lost or stolen traveler's checks in under 3 hours at any *American Express* office — other companies may not be as prompt. (Travelers should keep in mind that *American Express*'s 3-hour policy is based on a traveler's being able to provide the serial numbers of the lost checks. Without these numbers, refunds can take much longer.)

We cannot overemphasize the importance of knowing how to replace lost or stolen checks. All of the traveler's check companies have agents around the world, both in their own name and at associated agencies (usually, but not necessarily, banks), where refunds can be obtained during business hours. Most of them also have 24-hour toll-free telephone lines, and some even will provide emergency funds to tide you over on a Sunday.

Be sure to make a photocopy of the refund instructions that will be given to you by the issuing institution at the time of purchase. To avoid complications should you need to redeem lost checks (and to speed up the replacement process), keep the purchase receipt and an accurate list, by serial number, of the checks that have been spent or cashed. You may want to incorporate this information in an "emergency packet," also including the numbers of the credit cards you are carrying, and any other bits of information you shouldn't be without. Always keep these records separate from the checks and the original records themselves (you may want to give them to a traveling companion to hold).

Several of the major traveler's check companies charge 1% for the acquisition of their checks; others don't. To receive fee-free traveler's checks you may have to meet certain qualifications — for instance, *Thomas Cook* checks issued in US currency are free if you make your travel arrangements through its travel agency; *American Express* traveler's checks are available without charge to members of the *American Automobile Association (AAA)*. Holders of some credit cards (such as the *American Express Platinum* card) also may be entitled to free traveler's checks. The issuing institution (e.g., the particular bank at which you purchase them) may itself charge a fee. If you purchase traveler's checks at a bank in which you or your company maintains significant accounts (especially commercial accounts of some size), the bank may absorb the 1% fee as a courtesy.

American Express, Bank of America, Citicorp, MasterCard, Thomas Cook, and *Visa* all offer traveler's checks. Here is a list of the major companies issuing traveler's checks and the numbers to call in the event that loss or theft makes replacement necessary:

American Express: To report lost or stolen checks in the US and Canada, call 800-221-7282.

Bank of America: To report lost or stolen checks in the US, call 800-227-3460. In Canada, call 415-624-5400, collect, 24 hours.

Citicorp: To report lost or stolen checks in the US, call 800-645-6556. In Canada, call 813-623-1709, collect.

MasterCard: Note that *Thomas Cook MasterCard* (below) is now handling all *MasterCard* traveler's checks, inquiries, and refunds.

Thomas Cook MasterCard: To report lost or stolen checks in the US, call 800-223-7373; in Canada, call 609-987-7300, collect.

Visa: To report lost or stolen checks throughout the US and Canada, call 800-227-6811.

CREDIT CARDS: Some establishments you may encounter during the course of your travels may not honor any credit cards and some may not honor all cards, so there is a practical reason to carry more than one. Most US credit cards, including the principal bank cards, are honored in Canada. The following is a list of credit cards that enjoy wide domestic and international acceptance:

American Express: Cardholders can cash personal checks for traveler's checks and cash at *American Express* or its representatives' offices in the US and Canada up to the following limits (within any 21-day period): $1,000 for *Green* and *Optima* cardholders; $5,000 for *Gold* cardholders; and $10,000 for *Platinum* cardholders. Check cashing also is available to cardholders who are guests at participating hotels in the US and Canada (up to $250) and, for holders of airline tickets, at participating airlines (up to $50). Free travel accident, baggage, and car rental insurance is provided if the ticket or rental is charged to the card; additional insurance also is available for additional cost. For further information or to report a lost or stolen *American Express* card, call 800-528-4800 throughout the continental US and Canada.

Carte Blanche: Free travel accident, baggage, and car rental insurance if ticket or rental is charged to card; additional insurance also is available at additional cost. For medical, legal, and travel assistance worldwide, call 800-356-3448 throughout the US and Canada. For further information or to report a lost or stolen *Carte Blanche* card, call 800-525-9135 throughout the US and Canada.

Diners Club: Emergency personal check cashing for cardholders staying at participating hotels and motels in the US (up to $250 per stay). Free travel accident, baggage, and car rental insurance if ticket or rental is charged to card; additional insurance also is available for an additional fee. For medical, legal, and travel assistance worldwide, call 800-356-3448 throughout the US and Canada. For further information or to report a lost or stolen *Diners Club* card, call 800-525-9135 throughout the US and Canada.

Discover Card: Offered by a subsidiary of *Sears, Roebuck & Co.,* it provides cardholders with cash advances at numerous automatic teller machines and *Sears* stores throughout the US. For further information and to report a lost or stolen *Discover* card, call 800-DISCOVER throughout the US; in Canada, call 302-323-7834, collect.

MasterCard: Cash advances are available at participating banks worldwide. Check with your issuing bank for information. *MasterCard* also offers a 24-hour emergency lost card service; call 800-826-2181 throughout the US and Canada; in Canada you can also call 314-275-6690, collect.

Visa: Cash advances are available at participating banks worldwide. Check with your issuing bank for information. *Visa* also offers a 24-hour emergency lost card service; call 800-336-8472 throughout the US. Once in Canada, call 415-570-3200, collect.

SENDING MONEY ABROAD: If you have used up your traveler's checks, cashed as many emergency personal checks as your credit card allows, drawn on your cash advance line to the fullest extent, and still need money, have it sent to you via one of the following services:

American Express (phone: 800-926-9400 for an operator). Offers a service called "MoneyGram," completing money transfers generally within 15 minutes. The sender can go to any *American Express Travel Office* or MoneyGram agent location in the US and transfer money by presenting cash or credit card — *Discover, MasterCard, Visa,* or *American Express Optima* card (no other *American Express* or other credit cards are accepted). *American Express Optima* cardholders also can arrange for this transfer over the phone. To collect at the other end, the receiver must show identification (passport, driver's license, or other picture ID) or answer a test question at an *American Express Travel Office* (there are over 3,000) or at a branch of an affiliated bank in Canada. For further information on this service, call 800-543-4080.

Western Union Telegraph Company (phone: 800-325-4176 throughout the US). A friend or relative can go, cash in hand, to any *Western Union* office in the US, where, for a charge of $50 or less (it varies with the amount of the transaction), the funds will be transferred to one of *Western Union*'s branch offices. When the money arrives, you will not be notified — you must go to the *Western Union* branch office to inquire. Transfers generally take only about 15 minutes. The funds will be turned over in Canadian currency, based on the rate of exchange in effect on the day of receipt. For a higher fee, the US party to this transaction may call *Western Union* with a *MasterCard* or *Visa* number to send up to $2,000.

If you are literally down to your last cent, and you have no other way to obtain cash, the nearest US consulate (see *Legal Aid and Consular Services,* in this section) will let you call home to set these matters in motion.

CASH MACHINES: Automatic teller machines (ATMs) are increasingly common worldwide. If your bank participates in one of the international ATM networks (most do), the bank will issue you a "cash card" along with a personal identification code or number (also called a PIC or PIN). You can use this card at any ATM in the same electronic network to check your account balances, transfer monies between checking and savings accounts, and — most important for a traveler — withdraw cash instantly. Network ATMs generally are located in banks, commercial and transportation centers, and near major tourist attractions.

Some financial institutions offer exclusive automatic teller machines for their own customers only at bank branches. At the time of this writing, ATMs that *are* connected generally belong to one of the following two international networks:

> *CIRRUS:* Has over 75,000 ATMs worldwide, including 117 in Toronto. *Master-Card* and *Visa* cardholders also may use their cards to draw cash against their credit lines. For more information on the *CIRRUS* network and the location of the nearest ATM call 800-4-CIRRUS; for all other information contact your financial institution.

> *PLUS:* Has over 60,000 automatic teller machines worldwide, including 513 in Toronto. *MasterCard* and *Visa* cardholders also may use their cards to draw cash against their credit lines. For a free directory listing the locations of these machines and further information on the *PLUS* network, call 800-THE-PLUS.

Information about these networks is available at member bank branches, where you can obtain free booklets listing the locations worldwide. Note that a recent change in banking regulations permits financial institutions to subscribe to both the *CIRRUS* and *PLUS* systems, allowing users of either network to withdraw funds from ATMs at participating banks.

Time Zones, Business Hours, and Public Holidays

 TIME ZONES: Canada is divided into six time zones, but because the two most northeasterly zones — Newfoundland standard time and Atlantic standard time — are only a half hour apart, there is no more than a 5½-hour difference between its east and west coasts. Traveling west from Atlantic standard time, the zones get earlier by hour intervals.

Greenwich Mean Time — the time in Greenwich, England, at longitude 0°0′ — is the base from which all other time zones are measured. Areas in zones west of Greenwich have earlier times and are called Greenwich Minus; those to the east have later times and are called Greenwich Plus. For example, New York City — which falls into the Greenwich Minus 5 time zone — is 5 hours earlier than Greenwich, England.

Toronto is in the eastern standard time zone, which means that the time is 5 hours earlier than it is in Greenwich, England.

Daylight savings time in Canada, as in the US, begins on the first Sunday in April and continues until the last Sunday in October.

Canadian timetables use a 24-hour clock to denote arrival and departure times, which means that hours are expressed sequentially from 1 AM. By this method, 9 AM is recorded as 0900, noon as 1200, 1 PM as 1300, 6 PM as 1800, midnight as 2400, and so on. For example, the departure of a train at 7 AM will be announced as "0700"; one leaving at 7 PM will be announced as "1900."

BUSINESS HOURS: In Toronto, as throughout Canada, business hours are fairly standard and similar to those in the US: 9 AM to 5 PM, Mondays through Fridays. While an hour lunch break is customary, employees often take it in shifts so that service is not interrupted, especially at banks and other public service operations.

Banks traditionally are open from 10 AM to 3 PM, Mondays through Thursdays, and until 6 PM on Fridays, but, as in the US, the trend is toward longer hours. Banks generally are closed on Saturdays and Sundays, although in major cities some banks offer services on Saturday mornings.

Retail stores usually are open from 10 AM to 6 PM, Mondays through Saturdays. They often are open until 9 PM on Thursday and Friday nights. Most major stores are closed on Sundays.

PUBLIC HOLIDAYS: In Toronto the public holidays (and their dates this year) are as follows:

New Year's Day (January 1)
Good Friday (April 9)
Easter Monday (April 12)
Victoria Day (May 24)
Canada Day (July 1)
Civic Holiday (August 2)
Labour Day (September 6)
Thanksgiving (October 11)
Remembrance Day (November 11)
Christmas Day (December 25)
Boxing Day (December 26)

Mail, Telephone, and Electricity

MAIL: The main post office in Toronto (25 The Esplanade; phone: 416-973-2433) is open from 8 AM to 2 PM, Mondays through Fridays. Stamps also are available at most hotel desks. Vending machines for stamps are outside post offices and in stores in shopping centers.

Letters between Canada and the US have been known to arrive in as short a time as 5 days, but it is a good idea to allow at least 10 days for delivery in either direction. If your correspondence is important, you may want to send it via a special courier service: *Federal Express* (Aetna Centre, 145 King St. W.; phone: 416-369-9485) or *DHL* (115 City View Dr.; phone: 416-240-9999). The cost is considerably higher than sending something via the postal service — but the assurance of its timely arrival may be worth it.

There are several places that will receive and hold mail for travelers in Toronto. Mail sent to you at a hotel and clearly marked "Guest Mail, Hold for Arrival" is one safe approach. Canadian post offices, including the main city offices, also will extend this service to you if the mail is sent to you in care of General Delivery. To inquire about this service, in Toronto call the post office at 416-973-2433. Also, don't forget to bring identification (driver's license, credit cards, birth certificate, or passport) with you when you go to collect it. Mail must be collected in person.

If you are an *American Express* customer (a cardholder, a carrier of *American Express* traveler's checks, or traveling on an *American Express Travel Related Services* tour) you can have mail sent to its office in Toronto. Letters are held free of charge — registered mail and packages are not accepted. You must be able to show an *American Express* card, traveler's checks, or a voucher proving you are on one of the company's tours to qualify. Those who aren't clients cannot use the service. Mail should be addressed to you, care of *American Express,* and should be marked "Client Mail Service."

While the US Embassy and consulates in Canada will not under ordinary circumstances accept mail for tourists, they *may* hold mail for US citizens in an emergency situation or if the papers sent are particularly important. It is best to inform them either by separate letter or cable, or by phone (particularly if you are in the country already), that you will be using their address for this purpose.

 TELEPHONE: The procedure for calling any number in Canada is the same as when calling within the US: Dial the area code + the local number. The reverse procedure — dialing a number in the US from Canada — is the same.

The area code for Toronto is 416.

Public telephones are available just about everywhere if you are in a city or town — including transportation terminals, hotel lobbies, restaurants, drugstores, libraries, post offices, and other municipal buildings. They also may be found at rest stops along major highways, at major tourist centers, and in resort areas. Roadside booths can be found just about anywhere. The average price of a local call is CN 25¢.

Although you can use a telephone-company credit card number on any phone, pay phones that take major credit cards (*American Express, MasterCard, Visa,* and so on) are increasingly common, particularly in transportation and tourism centers. Also now available is the "affinity card," a combined telephone calling card/bank credit card that can be used for domestic and international calls. Cards of this type include the following:

> *AT&T/Universal* (phone: 800-662-7759).
> *Executive Telecard International* (phone: 800-950-3800).
> *Sprint Visa* (phone: 800-877-4646).

Similarly, *MCI VisaPhone* (phone: 800-866-0099) can add phone card privileges to the services available through your existing *Visa* card. This service allows you to use your *Visa* account number, plus an additional code, to charge calls on any touch-tone phone in the US and Canada.

The nationwide number for information is the same as in the US, 555-1212. If you need a number in another area code, dial the area code + 555-1212. (If you don't know the area code, simply dial 0 for an operator who can tell you.) In Toronto, you also have the option of dialing 411 for local information.

Long-distance rates are charged according to when the call is placed: weekday daytime; weekday evenings; and nights, weekends, and holidays. Least expensive are the calls you dial yourself from a private phone at night, and on weekends and major holidays. It generally is more expensive to call from a pay phone than it is to call from a private phone, and you must pay for a minimum 3-minute call. If the operator assists you, calls are more expensive. This includes credit card, bill-to-a-third-number, collect, and time-and-charge calls, as well as person-to-person calls, which are the most expensive. Rates are fully explained in the front of the white pages of every telephone directory.

Hotel Surcharges – Avoiding operator-assisted calls can cut costs considerably and bring rates into a somewhat more reasonable range — except for calls made through hotel switchboards. One of the most unpleasant surprises travelers encounter in many foreign countries is the amount they find tacked onto their hotel bill for telephone calls, because foreign hotels routinely add on astronomical surcharges. Before calling from your hotel room, inquire about any surcharges the hotel may impose. These can be excessive, but are avoidable by calling collect, using a telephone credit card (see above), or calling from a public pay phone. (Note that when calling from your hotel room, even if the call is made collect or charged to a credit card number, some establishments still may add on a nominal line usage charge — so ask before you call.)

Emergency Number – As in the US, dial 911 in Toronto in the event of an emergency. Operators at this number will get you the help you need from the police, fire department, or ambulance service.

■**Note:** An excellent resource for planning your trip is *AT&T's Toll-Free 800 Directory,* which lists thousands of companies with 800 numbers, both alphabetically (white pages) and by category (yellow pages), including a wide range of travel services — from travel agents to transportation and accommodations. Issued in a consumer edition for $9.95 and a business edition for $14.95, both are available from *AT&T Phone Centers* or by calling 800-426-8686. Another useful directory for use before you leave and on the road is the *Toll-Free Travel & Vacation Information Directory* ($4.95 postpaid from Pilot Books, 103 Cooper St., Babylon, NY 11702; phone: 516-422-2225).

ELECTRICITY: Canada has the same electrical current system as that in the US: 110 volts, 60 cycles, alternating current (AC). US appliances running on standard current can be used throughout Canada without adapters or convertors.

Staying Healthy

The surest way to return home in good health is to be prepared for medical problems that might occur while on vacation. Below we've outlined some things about which you need to think before you go.

BEFORE YOU GO: Older travelers or anyone suffering from a chronic medical condition, such as diabetes, high blood pressure, cardiopulmonary disease, asthma, or ear, eye, or sinus trouble, should consult a physician before leaving home. Those with conditions requiring special consideration when traveling should think about seeing, in addition to their regular physician, a specialist in travel medicine. For a referral in a particular community, contact the nearest medical school or ask a local doctor to recommend such a specialist. Dr. Leonard Marcus, a member of the *American Committee on Clinical Tropical Medicine and Travelers' Health,* provides a directory of more than 100 travel doctors around the world. For a copy, send a 9- by 12-inch self-addressed, stamped envelope to Dr. Marcus at 148 Highland Ave., Newton, MA 02165 (phone: 617-527-4003).

Also be sure to check with your insurance company ahead of time about the applicability of your hospitalization and major medical policies away from home; many policies do not apply. Older travelers should know that Medicare does not make payments outside the US and its territories. If your medical policy does not protect you while you're traveling, there are comprehensive combination policies specifically designed to fill the gap. (For a discussion of medical insurance and a list of inclusive combination policies, see *Insurance,* in this section.)

First Aid – Put together a compact, personal medical kit including Band-Aids, first-aid cream, antiseptic, nose drops, insect repellent, aspirin, an extra pair of prescription glasses or contact lenses (and a copy of your prescription for glasses or contact lenses), sunglasses, over-the-counter remedies for diarrhea, indigestion, and motion sickness, a thermometer, and a supply of those prescription medicines you take regularly.

In a corner of your kit, keep a list of all the drugs you have brought and their purpose, as well as duplicate copies of your doctor's prescriptions (or a note from your doctor). As brand names may vary in different countries, it's a good idea to ask your doctor for the generic name of any drugs you use so that you can ask for their equivalent should you need a refill. It also is a good idea to ask your doctor to prepare a medical identification card that includes such information as your blood type, your social security number, any allergies or chronic health problems you have, and your medical insurance information. Considering the essential contents of your medical kit, keep it with you, rather than in your checked luggage.

MINIMIZING THE RISKS: Travelers to Canada do not face the same health risks as might be encountered in visiting some other destinations in this hemisphere (such as Mexico and South America). Certainly travel always entails *some* possibility of injury or illness, but neither is inevitable and, with some basic precautions, your trip should proceed untroubled by ill health.

Sunburn – Even in Canada the burning power of the sun can quickly cause severe sunburn or sunstroke. To protect yourself against these ills, wear sunglasses, take along a broad-brimmed hat and cover-up, and, most important, use a sunscreen lotion.

Food and Water – Tap water in Toronto, as throughout Canada, generally is quite pure, so feel free to drink it. However, in rural areas, the local water supply may not be thoroughly purified, and local residents either have developed immunities to the natural bacteria or boil the water for drinking. You also should avoid swimming in or drinking water from freshwater streams, rivers, or pools, as they may be contaminated with leptospira, which cause a bacterial disease called leptospirosis (the symptoms resemble influenza). Milk is pasteurized throughout Canada, and dairy products are safe to eat, as are fruit, vegetables, meat, poultry, and fish.

MEDICAL AID IN TORONTO: Nothing ruins a vacation or business trip more effectively than sudden injury or illness. Fortunately, should you need medical attention, competent health professionals perfectly equipped to handle any medical problem can be found throughout the country. All hospitals are prepared for emergency cases, and many hospitals also have walk-in clinics to serve people who do not really need emergency service, but who have no place to go for immediate medical attention. Medical institutes in Canada, especially in the larger cities, generally provide the same basic specialties and services that are available in the US.

Emergency Treatment – You will find, in the event of an emergency, that most tourist facilities — transportation companies and hotels — are equipped to handle the situation quickly and efficiently. If a bona fide emergency occurs, the fastest way to get attention may be to take a taxi to the emergency room of the nearest hospital. In Toronto go to *Mt. Sinai Hospital* (600 University Ave.; phone: 416-596-4200) and *Toronto General Hospital* (200 Elizabeth St.; phone: 416-395-3111). Both are major facilities with advanced life-support equipment and technology to deal with acute medical situations. An alternative is to dial the free national "emergency" number — 911 in Canada — used to summon the police, fire department, or an ambulance.

Non-Emergency Care – If a doctor is needed for something less than an emergency, there are several ways to find one. If you are staying in a hotel or at a resort, ask for help in reaching a doctor or other emergency services, or for the house physician, who may visit you in your room or ask you to visit an office.

It also usually is possible to obtain a referral through a US consulate (see addresses and phone numbers below) or directly through a hospital, especially if it is an emergency.

Pharmacies and Prescription Drugs – If you have a minor medical problem, a pharmacist might offer some help. In Toronto, one 24-hour drugstore is the *Shopper Drug Mart,* with locations at 2428 Eglinton (phone: 416-757-1154); Dufferin and Lawrence (phone: 416-787-0238); Lucliffe Building (phone: 416-979-2424); and 2500 Hurontario St. (phone: 416-896-2500).

Bring along a copy of any prescription you may have from your doctor in case you should need a refill. In the case of minor complaints, Canadian pharmacists *may* fill a foreign prescription; however, do not count on this. In most cases, you will need a local doctor to rewrite the prescription. Even in an emergency, a traveler will more than likely be given only enough of a drug to last until a local prescription can be obtained.

ADDITIONAL RESOURCES: Emergency assistance also is available from the various medical programs designed for travelers who have chronic ailments or whose illness requires them to return home:

International Association for Medical Assistance to Travelers (IAMAT; 417 Center St., Lewiston, NY 14092; phone: 716-754-4883). Entitles members to the services of participating doctors around the world, as well as clinics and hospitals in various locations. Participating physicians agree to adhere to a basic charge of around $50 to see a patient referred by *IAMAT.* To join, simply write to *IAMAT;* in about 3 weeks you will receive a membership card, the booklet of members, and an inoculation chart. A nonprofit organization, *IAMAT* appreciates donations; with a donation of $25 or more, you will receive a set of worldwide climate charts detailing weather and sanitary conditions. (Delivery can take up to 5 weeks, so plan ahead.)

International Health Care Service (New York Hospital–Cornell Medical Center, 525 E. 68th St., Box 210, New York, NY 10021; phone: 212-746-1601). This service provides a variety of travel-related health services, including a complete range of immunizations at moderate per-shot rates. A pre-travel counseling and immunization package costs $255 for the first family member and $195 for each additional member; a post-travel consultation is $175 to $275, plus lab work. Consultations are by appointment only, from 4 to 8 PM Mondays through Thursdays, although 24-hour coverage is available for urgent travel-related problems. In addition, sending $4.50 (with a self-addressed envelope) to the address above will procure the service's publication, *International Health Care Travelers Guide,* a compendium of facts and advice on health care and diseases around the world.

International SOS Assistance (PO Box 11568, Philadelphia, PA 19116; phone: 800-523-8930 or 215-244-1500). Subscribers are provided with telephone access — 24 hours a day, 365 days a year — to a worldwide, monitored, multilingual network of medical centers. A phone call brings assistance ranging from a telephone consultation to transportation home by ambulance or aircraft, or, in some cases, transportation of a family member to wherever you are hospitalized. Individual rates are $35 for 2 weeks of coverage ($3.50 for each additional day), $70 for 1 month, or $240 for 1 year; couple and family rates also are available.

Medic Alert Foundation (2323 N. Colorado, Turlock, CA 95380; phone: 800-ID-ALERT or 209-668-3333). If you have a health condition that may not be readily perceptible to the casual observer — one that might result in a tragic error in an emergency situation — this organization offers identification emblems specifying such conditions. The foundation also maintains a computerized central file from which your complete medical history is available 24 hours a day by phone (the telephone number is clearly inscribed on the emblem). The onetime membership fee (between $35 and $50) is based on the type of metal from which the emblem is made — the choices range from stainless steel to 10K gold-filled.

TravMed (PO Box 10623, Baltimore, MD 21204; phone: 800-732-5309 or 410-296-5225). For $3 per day, subscribers receive comprehensive medical assistance while abroad. Major medical expenses are covered up to $100,000, and special transportation home or of a family member to wherever you are hospitalized is provided at no additional cost.

Helpful Publications – Practically every phase of health care — before, during, and after a trip — is covered in *The New Traveler's Health Guide,* by Drs. Patrick J. Doyle and James E. Banta. It is available for $4.95, plus postage and handling, from Acropolis Books Ltd., 13950 Park Center Rd., Herndon, VA 22071 (phone: 800-451-7771 or 703-709-0006).

The *Traveling Healthy Newsletter,* which is published six times a year, also is brimming with health-related travel tips. For a year's subscription, which costs $24, contact Dr. Karl Neumann (108-48 70th Rd., Forest Hills, NY 11375; phone: 718-268-7290). A sample issue is available for $4. Dr. Neumann also is the editor of the useful free booklet *Traveling Healthy,* which is available by writing to the *Travel Healthy Program* (Clark O'Neill Inc., 1 Broad Ave., Fairview, NJ 07022; phone: 201-947-3400).

For more information regarding preventive health care for travelers, contact the *International Association for Medical Assistance to Travelers* (*IAMAT;* 417 Center St., Lewiston, NY 14092; phone: 716-754-4883). The Centers for Disease Control also publishes an interesting booklet, *Health Information for International Travel.* To order send a check or money order for $5 to the Superintendent of Documents (US Government Printing Office, Washington, DC 20402), or charge it to your credit card by calling 202-783-3238. For information on vaccination requirements, disease outbreaks, and other health information pertaining to traveling abroad, you also can call the Centers for Disease Control's 24-hour International Health Requirements and Recommendations Information Hotline: 404-332-4559.

■**Note:** Those who are unable to take a reserved flight due to personal illness or who must fly home unexpectedly due to a family emergency should be aware that airlines may offer a discounted airfare (or arrange a partial refund) if the traveler can demonstrate that his or her situation is indeed a legitimate emergency. Your inability to fly or the illness or death of an immediate family member usually must be substantiated by a doctor's note or the name, relationship, and funeral home from which the deceased will be buried. In such cases, airlines often will waive certain advance purchase restrictions or you may receive a refund check or voucher for future travel at a later date. Be aware, however, that this bereavement fare may not necessarily be the least expensive fare available and, if possible, it is best to have a travel agent check all possible flights through a computer reservations system (CRS).

Legal Aid and Consular Services

There are crucial places to keep in mind when outside the US, namely, the US Embassy (100 Wellington St., Ottawa, Ontario K1P 5T1, Canada; phone: 613-238-4470) and the US consulates (in Toronto, the consulate is at 360 University Ave.; phone: 416-595-1700).

If you are injured or become seriously ill, or if you encounter legal difficulties, the consulate is the first place to turn, although its powers and capabilities are limited. It will direct you to medical assistance and notify your relatives if you are ill; it can advise you of your rights and provide a list of English-speaking lawyers if you are arrested, but it cannot interfere with the local legal process.

For questions about US citizens arrested abroad, how to get money to them, and other useful information, call the *Citizen's Emergency Center* of the Office of Special Consular Services in Washington, DC, at 202-647-5225. (For further information about this invaluable hotline, see below.)

A consulate exists to aid citizens in serious matters, such as illness, destitution, and the above legal difficulties. It is not there to aid in trivial situations, such as canceled reservations or lost baggage, no matter how important these matters may seem to the victimized tourist. If you should get sick, the US consul can provide names of English-speaking doctors and dentists, as well as the names of local hospitals and clinics; the consul also will contact family members in the US and help arrange special ambulance service for a flight home. In a situation involving "legitimate and proven poverty" of an US citizen stranded abroad without funds, the consul will contact sources of money (such as family or friends in the US), apply for aid to agencies in foreign countries, and in a last resort — which is *rarely* — arrange for repatriation at government expense, although this is a loan that must be repaid. And in case of natural disasters or civil unrest, consulates around the world handle the evacuation of US citizens if it becomes necessary.

As mentioned above, the US State Department operates a *Citizens' Emergency Center,* which offers a number of services to US citizens traveling abroad and their families at home. In addition to giving callers up-to-date information on trouble spots, the center will contact authorities abroad in an attempt to locate a traveler or deliver an urgent message. In case of illness, death, arrest, destitution, or repatriation of a US citizen on foreign soil, it will relay information to relatives at home if the consulate is unable to do so. Travel advisory information is available 24 hours a day to people with touch-tone phones (phone: 202-647-5225). Callers with rotary phones can get information at this number from 8:15 AM to 10 PM (eastern standard time) on weekdays; 9 AM to 3 PM on Saturdays. In the event of an emergency, this number also may be called during these hours. For emergency calls only, at all other times, call 202-634-3600 and ask for the duty officer.

Drinking and Drugs

DRINKING: The legal drinking age is 19 in Toronto. All beer, wine, and liquor are available only at government liquor stores.

Licensed restaurants, hotels, lounges, and bars are found throughout Toronto, though some may sell only wine or beer. The hours during which bars and restaurants may serve liquor vary, though traditionally bar closing time is between midnight and 3 AM. Liquor stores are required to close on Sundays and holidays, but some alcoholic beverages may be purchased on Sundays, usually only with meals, at authorized dining rooms, restaurants, and private clubs.

Visitors to Canada may bring in 40 ounces (about 1 gallon) of liquor or wine, or 288 ounces of beer or ale (24 12-ounce cans, 18 16-ounce cans) as personal baggage, duty-free. Anything in excess of this amount is subject to duties and taxes and requires a provincial permit. If excess liquor is declared, it will be held by Canada Customs at the point of entry for 30 days. A receipt will be issued, and the owner can claim it upon return. People leaving Canada from a point other than their point of entry can make arrangements to have their property returned at the point of departure.

DRUGS: Illegal narcotics are as prevalent in Canada as in the US, but the moderate legal penalties and vague social acceptance that marijuana has gained in the US has no equivalent in Canada. Due to the international war on drugs, enforcement of drug laws is becoming increasingly strict throughout the world. Local Canadian narcotics officers and customs officials are renowned for their absence of understanding and lack of a sense of humor — especially where foreigners are involved.

Opiates and barbiturates, and other increasingly popular drugs — "white powder" substances like heroin and cocaine, and "crack" (the cocaine derivative) — continue to be of major concern to narcotics officials. It is important to bear in mind that the type or quantity of drugs involved is of minor importance. According to a spokesperson for the Royal Canadian Mounted Police, stiff penalties have been imposed on drug offenders convicted of possessing mere *traces* of illegal drugs. Persons arrested are subject to the laws of the country they are visiting, and there isn't much the US consulate can do for drug offenders beyond providing a list of lawyers. The best advice we can offer is this: Don't carry, use, buy, or sell illegal drugs.

Those who carry medicines that contain a controlled drug should be sure to have a current doctor's prescription with them. Ironically, travelers can get into almost as much trouble coming through US Customs with over-the-counter drugs picked up abroad that contain substances that are controlled in the US. Cold medicines, pain relievers, and the like often have codeine or codeine derivatives that are illegal, except by prescription, in the US. Throw them out before leaving for home.

■ **Be forewarned:** US narcotics agents warn travelers of the increasingly common ploy of drug dealers asking travelers to transport a "gift" or other package back to the US. Don't be fooled into thinking that the protection of US law applies abroad — accused of illegal drug trafficking, you will be considered guilty until you prove your innocence. In other words, do not, under any circumstances, agree to take anything across the border for a stranger.

Tipping

While tipping is at the discretion of the person receiving the service, CN 50¢ is the rock-bottom tip for anything, and CN$1 is the current customary minimum for small services. *(Please note that the gratuities suggested below are given in Canadian dollars.)*

In restaurants, tip between 10% and 20% of the bill's total before tax is added. For average service in an average restaurant, a 15% tip to the waiter is reasonable, although one should never hesitate to penalize poor service or reward excellent and efficient attention by leaving less or more.

Although it's not necessary to tip the maître d' of most restaurants — unless he or she has been especially helpful in arranging a special party or providing a table (slipping the maître d' something in a crowded restaurant *may,* however, get you seated sooner or procure a preferred table) — when tipping is appropriate, the least amount should be CN$5. In the finest restaurants, where a multiplicity of servers are present, plan to tip 5% to the captain. The sommelier (wine waiter) is entitled to a gratuity of approximately 10% of the price of the bottle of wine.

In allocating gratuities at a restaurant, pay particular attention to what has become the standard credit card charge form, which now includes separate places for gratuities for waiters and/or captains. If these separate boxes are not on the charge slip, simply ask the waiter or captain how these separate tips should be indicated. In some establishments, tips indicated on credit card receipts may not be given to the help, so you may want to leave tips in cash.

In a large hotel, where it's difficult to determine just who out of a horde of attendants actually performed particular services, it is perfectly proper for guests to ask to have an extra 10% to 15% added to their bill. For those who prefer to distribute tips themselves, a chambermaid generally is tipped at the rate of around CN$1 a day. Tip the concierge and hall porter for specific services only, with the amount of such gratuities dependent on the level of service provided. For any special service you receive in a hotel, a tip is expected — CN$1 being the minimum for a small service.

Bellhops, doormen, and porters at hotels and transportation centers generally are tipped at the rate of CN$1 per piece of luggage, along with a small additional amount if a doorman helps with a cab or car. Taxi drivers should get about 15% of the total fare. And if you arrive without Canadian currency, tip in US dollars.

Miscellaneous tips: Sightseeing tour guides should be tipped. If you are traveling in a group, decide together what you want to give the guide and present it from the group at the end of the tour ($1 per person is a reasonable tip). If you have been individually escorted, the amount paid should depend on the degree of your satisfaction, but it should not be less than 10% of the tour price. Museum and monument guides usually are tipped, and it is a nice touch to tip a caretaker who unlocks a small church or turns on the light in a chapel. In barbershops and beauty parlors, tips also are expected, but the percentages vary according to the type of establishment — 10% in the most expensive salons; 15% to 20% in less expensive establishments. (As a general rule, the person who washes your hair should get a small additional tip.) Washroom attendents should get a small tip — they usually set out a little plate with a coin already on it indicating the suggested denomination.

Tipping always is a matter of personal preference. In the situations covered above, as well as in any others that arise where you feel a tip is expected or due, feel free to express your pleasure or displeasure. Again, never hesitate to reward excellent and efficient attention and to penalize poor service. Give an extra gratuity and a word of thanks when someone has gone out of his or her way for you. Either way, the more personal the act of tipping, the more appropriate it seems. And if you didn't like the service — or the attitude — don't tip.

Duty-Free Shopping and Goods and Services Tax

DUTY-FREE SHOPS: If common sense says that it always is less expensive to buy goods in an airport duty-free shop than to buy them at home or in the streets of a foreign city, travelers should be aware of some basic facts. Duty-free, first of all, does not mean that the goods travelers buy will be free of duty when they return to the US. Rather, it means that the shop has paid no import tax in acquiring goods of foreign make, because the goods are not to be used in the country where the shop is located. This is why duty-free goods are available only in the restricted, passengers-only area of international airports or are delivered to departing passengers on the plane. In a duty-free store, travelers save money only on goods of foreign make because they are the only items on which an import tax would be charged in any other store. There usually is no saving on locally made items, but in provinces such as Ontario that impose provincial sales and good and services taxes (see below) that are refundable to foreigners, the prices in airport duty-free shops also subtract this tax, sparing travelers the often cumbersome procedures they otherwise have to follow to obtain a PST or GST refund.

Beyond this, there is little reason to delay buying locally made merchandise and/or souvenirs until reaching the airport. In fact, because airport duty-free shops usually pay high rents, the locally made goods they sell may well be more expensive than they would be in downtown stores. The real bargains are foreign goods, but — let the buyer beware — not all foreign goods are automatically less expensive in an airport duty-free shop. You can get a good deal on even small amounts of perfume, costing less than the usually required minimum purchase, tax-free. Other fairly standard bargains include spirits, smoking materials, cameras, clothing, watches, chocolates, and other food and luxury items — but first be sure to know what these items cost elsewhere. Terrific savings do exist (they are the reason for such shops, after all), but so do overpriced items that an unwary shopper might find equally tempting. In addition, if you wait to do your shopping at airport duty-free shops, you will be taking the chance that the desired item is out of stock or unavailable.

Duty-free shops are located at Lester B. Pearson International Airport and Toronto Island Airport.

GOODS AND SERVICES TAX: Commonly abbreviated as GST, this 7% tax is levied by Canada on a wide range of purchases and payments for services, including package tours, car rentals, accommodations, and meals.

The tax is intended for residents (and already is included in the price tag), but visitors are also required to pay it unless they have purchases shipped by the store directly to an address abroad. If visitors pay the tax and take purchases with them, however, they generally are entitled to a refund.

The amount of the tax rebate claimed must be for a minimum of CN$7 — which means your expenditures in Canada for accommodations and other applicable purchases (there's no GST refund for food) must be at least CN$100 (CN$107, including the tax). Visitors are entitled to make up to four rebate claims per year, or purchases can be accumulated on any number of visits and one claim made for the calendar year. Visitors can mail the rebate forms after returning home (again, forms are available where goods are purchased), or at instant-rebate centers at points of departure from Canada such as duty-free shops and border crossings. (Any rebate claim for tax on a day's expenditure of CN$500 or more must be processed by mail.) Note that rebates through the mail are issued in US dollars; instant rebates are in Canadian dollars. If you have any questions about the tax while you're in Canada, call the information hotline that has been set up by Revenue Quebec, Visitor Rebate Program, Ottawa, Ontario K1A 1J5, Canada (phone: 800-66-VISIT or 613-991-3346).

In addition, most provinces impose a provincial sales tax (PST) on most items, including food and lodging. These taxes vary from province to province; in Ontario it is 8% on goods and services and a tax refund is provided to foreign visitors. Forms to use when applying for the PST refund are available by contacting the Retail Sales Tax District Office, 2300 Yonge St., 10th Floor, Toronto, Ontario M4P 1H6, Canada (phone: 800-ONTARIO or 416-965-4008).

■ **Buyer Beware:** You may come across shops *not* at airports that call themselves duty-free shops. These require shoppers to show a foreign passport but are subject to the same rules as other stores, including paying import duty on foreign items. What "tax-free" means in the case of these establishments is something of an advertising strategy: They are announcing loud and clear that they do, indeed, offer the PST/GST refund service — sometimes on the spot (minus a fee for higher overhead). Prices may be no better at these stores, and could be even higher due to this service.

Customs and Returning to the US

When you return to the United States, you must declare to the US Customs official at the point of entry everything you have bought or acquired while in Canada. To speed up the process, keep all your receipts handy and try to pack your purchases together in an accessible part of your suitcase.

DUTY-FREE ARTICLES: In general, the duty-free allowance for US visitors return-ing from abroad is $400. This duty-free limit covers purchases that accompany you and are for personal use. This limit includes items used or worn while in Canada, souvenirs for friends, and gifts received during the trip. A flat 10% duty based on the "fair retail value in country of acquisition" is assessed on the next $1,000 worth of merchandise brought in for personal use or gifts. Amounts above these two levels are dutiable at a variety of rates. The average rate for typical tourist purchases is about 12%, but you can find out rates on specific items by consulting *Tariff Schedules of the United States* in a library or at any US Customs Service office.

Families traveling together may make a joint declaration to customs, which permits one member to exceed his or her duty-free exemption to the extent that another falls short. Families also may pool purchases dutiable under the flat rate. A family of three, for example, would be eligible for up to a total of $3,000 at the 10% flat duty rate (after each member had used up his or her $400 duty-free exemption) rather than three separate $1,000 allowances. This grouping of purchases is extremely useful when considering the duty on a duty-tariff item, such as jewelry or a fur coat.

Personal exemptions can be used once every 30 days; in order to be eligible, an individual must have been out of the country for more than 48 continuous hours. If any portion of the exemption has been used once within any 30-day period or if your trip is less than 48 hours long, the duty-free allowance is cut to $25. (Keep in mind, however, that the $25 exemption may not be grouped with family members.)

There are certain articles, however, that are duty-free only up to certain limits. The $25 limit includes the following: 10 cigars (not Cuban), 50 cigarettes, and 4 ounces of perfume. Individuals eligible for the full $400 duty-free limit are allowed 1 carton of cigarettes (200), 100 cigars, and 1 liter of alcoholic beverages if the traveler is over 21. Under federal law, alcohol above this allowance is liable for both duty and an Internal Revenue tax. Note, however, that states are allowed to impose additional restrictions and penalties of their own, including (in Arizona and Utah, for example) confiscation of any quantities of liquor over the statutory limit. Antiques, if they are 100 or more years old and you have proof from the seller of that fact, are duty-free, as are paintings and drawings if done entirely by hand.

To avoid paying duty twice, register the serial number of computers, watches, and electronic equipment with the nearest US Customs bureau before departure; receipts of insurance policies also should be carried for other foreign-made items.

Gold, gold medals, bullion, and up to $10,000 in currency or negotiable instruments may be brought into the US without being declared. Sums over $10,000 must be declared in writing.

The allotment for individual "unsolicited" gifts mailed from abroad (no more than one per day per recipient) is $50 retail value per gift. These gifts do not have to be declared and are not included in your duty-free exemption (see below). Although you should include a receipt for the purchases with each package, the examiner is empow-ered to impose a duty based on his or her assessment of the value of the goods. The duty owed is collected by the US Postal Service when the package is delivered. More information on mailing packages home from abroad is contained in the US Customs Service pamphlet *Buyer Beware, International Mail Imports* (see below for where to write for this and other useful brochures).

CLEARING CUSTOMS: This is a simple procedure. If your purchases total no more than the $400 duty-free limit, you need only make an oral declaration to the customs inspector. If entering with more than $400 worth of goods, you must submit a written declaration.

It is illegal not to declare dutiable items; not to do so, in fact, constitutes smuggling, and the penalty can be anything from stiff fines and seizure of the goods to prison sentences. There is a basic rule to buying goods abroad, and it should never be broken:

If you can't afford the duty on something, don't buy it. Your list or verbal declaration should include all items purchased in Canada, as well as gifts received there, purchases made at the behest of others, the value of repairs, and anything brought in for resale in the US.

Do not include in the list items that do not accompany you, i.e., purchases that you have mailed or had shipped home. These are dutiable in any case, even if for your own use and even if the items that accompany your return from the same trip do not exhaust your duty-free exemption. It is a good idea, if you have accumulated too much while abroad, to mail home any personal effects (made and bought in the US) that you no longer need rather than your foreign purchases. These personal effects pass through US Customs as "American goods returned" and are not subject to duty.

FORBIDDEN IMPORTS: US residents are prohibited from bringing certain goods into the US from Canada, including any Cuban-made goods and items from North Korea, Vietnam, or Cambodia.

Narcotics, plants (unless specifically exempt and free of soil), and many types of food are not allowed into the US. Drugs are totally illegal, with the exception of medication prescribed by a physician. It's a good idea not to travel with too large a quantity of any given prescription drug (however, in the event that a pharmacy is not open when you need it, bring along several extra doses) and to have the prescription on hand in case any question arises either abroad or when re-entering the US.

Tourists have long been forbidden to bring into the US foreign-made, US-trade-marked articles purchased abroad (if the trademark is recorded with US Customs) without written permission. It's now permissible to enter with one such item in your possession as long as it's for personal use.

Tourists who want to bring Canadian plants into the US should know that house-plants usually are permitted; however, those transporting outdoor plants and fruit trees must have a plant certificate from an office of Agriculture Canada. For more information, contact Plant Protection Division, Export Division, Food Production and Inspection Branch, Agriculture Canada, Ottawa, Ontario K1A 0C6, Canada (phone: 613-995-7900).

The US Customs Service implements the rigorous Department of Agriculture regulations concerning the importation of vegetable matter, seeds, bulbs, and the like. Living vegetable matter may not be imported without a permit, and everything must be inspected, permit or not. Approved items (which do not require a permit) include dried bamboo and woven items made of straw; beads made of most seeds (but not jequirity beans — the poisonous scarlet and black seed of the rosary pea) and some viable seeds; cones of pine and other trees; roasted coffee beans; most flower bulbs; flowers (without roots); dried or canned fruits, jellies, or jams; polished rice, dried beans, and teas; herb plants (not witchweed); nuts (but not acorns, chestnuts, or any nuts with outer husks); dried lichens, mushrooms (including truffles), shamrocks, and seaweed; and most dried spices.

Other processed foods and baked goods usually are okay. Regulations on meat products generally depend on the country of origin and manner of processing. As a rule, commercially canned meat, hermetically sealed and cooked in the can so that it can be stored without refrigeration, is permitted, but not all canned meat fulfills this requirement.

The US Customs Service also enforces federal laws that prohibit the entry of articles made from the furs or hides of animals on the endangered species list. Beware of shoes, bags, and belts made of crocodile and certain kinds of lizard, and anything made of tortoiseshell; this also applies to preserved crocodiles, lizards, and turtles sometimes sold in gift shops. Most coral — particularly black coral — also is restricted (although small quanitites of coral incorporated into jewelry or other craft items usually are permitted). And if you're shopping for big-ticket items, beware of fur coats made from the skins of spotted cats. They are sold abroad, but they will be confiscated upon your return to the US, and there will be no refund. For information about other animals on the endangered species list, contact the Department of the Interior, US Fish and Wildlife Service (Publications Unit, 4401 N. Fairfax Dr., Room 130, Arlington, VA 22203; phone: 703-358-1711), and ask for the free publication *Facts About Federal Wildlife Laws.*

Also note that some foreign governments prohibit the export of items made from certain species of wildlife, and the US honors any such restrictions. Before you go shopping in any foreign country, check with the US Department of Agriculture (G110 Federal Bldg., Hyattsville, MD 20782; phone: 301-436-8010) and find out what items are prohibited from the country you will be visiting.

The US Customs Service publishes a series of free pamphlets with customs information. It includes *Know Before You Go,* a basic discussion of customs requirements pertaining to all travelers; *Buyer Beware, International Mail Imports; Travelers' Tips on Bringing Food, Plant, and Animal Products into the United States; Importing a Car; GSP and the Traveler; Pocket Hints; Currency Reporting; Pets, Wildlife, US Customs; Customs Hints for Visitors (Nonresidents);* and *Trademark Information for Travelers.* For the entire series or individual pamphlets, write to the US Customs Service (PO Box 7474, Washington, DC 20044) or contact any of the seven regional offices — in Boston, Chicago, Houston, Long Beach (California), Miami, New Orleans, and New York.

Note that the US Customs Service has a tape-recorded message whereby callers using touch-tone phones can obtain free pamphlets on various travel-related topics; the number is 202-566-8195. These pamphlets provide great briefing material, but if you still have questions when you're in Canada, contact the nearest US consulate or the US Embassy.

Religion on the Road

 The surest source of information on religious services in an unfamiliar country is the desk clerk of the hotel or guesthouse in which you are staying; the local tourist information office, a US consul, or a church of another religious affiliation also may be able to provide this information. For a full range of options, joint religious councils often print circulars with the addresses and times of services of houses of worship in the area. These often are printed as part of general tourist guides provided by the local tourist and convention center, or as part of a "what's going on" guide to the city. Many newspapers also print a listing of religious services in their area in weekend editions. You also can check the yellow pages of the phone book under "Churches" and call for more information.

You may want to use your vacation to broaden your religious experience by joining an unfamiliar faith in its service. This can be a moving experience, especially if the service is held in a church, synagogue, or temple that is historically significant or architecturally notable. You almost always will find yourself made welcome and comfortable.

■ **Note:** For those interested in a spiritual stay while in Canada, *Catholic America: Self-Renewal Centers and Retreats,* by Patricia Christian-Meyer, lists approximately 20 self-renewal centers throughout Canada. To order, send $13.95 to John Muir Publications, PO Box 613, Sante Fe, NM 87504 (phone: 800-888-7504 or 505-982-4078).

Sources and Resources

Tourist Information Offices

The Canadian tourist offices and consulates in the US generally are the best sources of local travel information, and most of their many, varied publications are free for the asking. For the best results, request general information on specific provinces or cities, as well as publications relating to your particular areas of interest: accommodations, special events, sports, guided tours, and facilities for specific sports. There is no need to send a self-addressed, stamped envelope with your request, unless specified. For information on Toronto, contact the *Metropolitan Toronto Convention and Visitors Association (MTCVA;* 207 Queen's Quay W., Suite 590, Toronto, Ontario M5J 1A7, Canada; phone: 800-363-1990 or 416-368-9821). The *MTCVA* also maintains convenient outdoor kiosks around town that provide quick information; its city map is especially helpful and includes an insert on the subway system.

Canadian Embassy and Consulates in the US

The Canadian government maintains an embassy and several consulates in the US. These are empowered to sign official documents and to notarize copies of US documents, which may be necessary for those papers to be considered legal abroad. Below is a list of the Canadian Embassy and consulates in the US.

Atlanta: Canadian Consulate (1 CNN Center, Suite 400, South Tower, Atlanta, GA 30303; phone: 404-577-6810).
Dallas: Canadian Consulate (750 N. St. Paul St., Suite 1700, Dallas, TX 75201; phone: 214-922-9806).
Los Angeles: Canadian Consulate (300 S. Grand Ave., Los Angeles, CA 90071; phone: 213-687-7432).
New York City: Canadian Consulate (1251 Ave. of the Americas, New York, NY 10020; phone: 212-768-2442).
San Francisco: Canadian Consulate (50 Fremont St., Suite 2100, San Francisco, CA 94105; phone: 415-495-6021).
Washington, DC: Canadian Embassy (501 Pennsylvania Ave. NW, Washington, DC 20001; phone: 202-682-1740).

Theater and Special Event Tickets

As you read this book, you will learn about events that may spark your interest — everything from music festivals and special theater seasons to sporting championships — along with telephone numbers and addresses to which to write for descriptive brochures, reservations, or tickets. The Canadian government tourist offices can supply information on these and other special events and festivals that take place in Toronto, though they cannot in all cases provide the actual program or detailed information on ticket prices.

Since many of these occasions often are fully booked well in advance, think about having your reservation in hand before you go. In some cases, tickets may be reserved over the phone and charged to a credit card, or you can send an international money order or foreign draft. If you do write, remember that any request from the US should be accompanied by an International Reply Coupon to ensure a response (send two of them for an airmail response). These international coupons, money orders, and drafts are available at US post offices.

Books, Magazines, and Newsletters

BOOKS: Throughout GETTING READY TO GO, numerous books and brochures have been recommended as good sources of further information on a variety of topics. In many cases, these are publications of the various tourism authorities and are available in any of their offices both here and abroad.

Suggested Reading – The list below comprises books we have come across and think worthwhile; it is by no means complete, but meant merely to start you on your way. Unless indicated, all the books listed here are in print, but you also may want to do some additional research at your local library. These titles include some informative guides to special interests, solid historical accounts, and books that call attention to things you might not notice otherwise.

General Travel

The Adventure Guide to Canada, by Pam Hobbs (Hunter Publishing; $15.95).

The Best Bicycle Tours of Eastern Canada: Twelve Breathtaking Tours Through Quebec, Ontario, Newfoundland, Nova Scotia, New Brunswick, & Prince Edward Island, by Jerry Dennis (Henry Holt; $14.95).

Birnbaum's Canada 1993, edited by Alexandra Mayes Birnbaum (HarperCollins; $17).

Budget Traveler's Guide to Great Off-Beat Vacations in the US and Canada, by Paige Palmer (Pilot Books; $4.95).

Canada: A Travel Survival Kit, by Mark Lightbody and Tom Smallman (Lonely Planet; $19.95).

Canadian Bed and Breakfast Guide, by Gerda Pantel (Chicago Review Press; $12.95).

The Canadian Canoeing Companion: An Illustrated Guide to Paddling Canada's Wilderness, by Alex Narvey (Thunder Enlightening Press; $16.95).

Country Inns, Lodges, and Historic Hotels, Canada, by Anthony Hitchcock (Burt Franklin Press; $10.95).

O Canada: Travels in an Unknown Country, by Jan Morris (HarperCollins; $20).

Toronto's Best-Kept Secrets: And New Views of Old Favorites, by Mike Michaelson (Passport Books; $9.95).

Toronto: The Ultimate Guide, by Margaret and R. Mackenzie (Chronicle Books; $11.95).

History and Culture

Canadian Folklore, by Edith Fowke (Oxford University Press; $9.95).

Contours of Canadian Thought, by A. B. McKillop (University of Toronto Press; $13.95).

The Penguin History of Canada, by Kenneth McNaught (Penguin Books; $8.95).

A Reader's Guide to Canadian History, in 2 volumes, edited by D. A. Muise (University of Toronto Press; $14.95 per volume).

Sweet Promises: A Reader in Indian-White Relations in Canada, edited by J. R. Miller (University of Toronto Press; $24.95).

Literature

Anne Hébert: Selected Poems (Bookslinger; $10).

Black Robe, by Brian Moore (Fawcett Books; $4.99).

The Enthusiasms of Robertson Davies, by Robertson Davies; edited by Judith Skelton Grant (Penguin; $9.95).

Friend of My Youth, by Alice Munro (Penguin; $8.95).

Home Sweet Home: My Canadian Album, by Mordecai Richler (Random House; $16.95).

The Oxford Book of Canadian Ghost Stories, edited by Alberto Manguel (Oxford University Press; $15.95).

The Oxford Book of Canadian Short Stories in English, edited by Margaret Atwood (Oxford University Press; $27.95).

The Oxford Illustrated Literary Guide to Canada, by Albert and Theresa Moritz (Oxford University Press; $39.95).

Surfacing, by Margaret Atwood (Fawcett Books; $4.95).

In addition, *Culturgrams* is a handy series of pamphlets that provides a good sampling of information on the people, cultures, sights, and bargains to be found in over 90 countries around the world. Each four-page, newsletter-size leaflet covers one country, and Canada is included in the series. The topics included range from customs and courtesies to lifestyles and demographics. These fact-filled pamphlets are published by the David M. Kennedy Center for International Studies at Brigham Young University; for an order form contact the group c/o Publication Services (280 HRCB, Provo, UT 84602; phone: 800-528-6279 or 801-378-6528). When ordering from 1 to 5 *Culturgrams,* the price is $1 each; 6 to 49 pamphlets cost 50¢ each; and for larger quantities, the price per copy goes down proportionately.

MAGAZINES: As sampling the regional fare is likely to be one of the highlights of any visit, you will find reading about local edibles worthwhile either before you go or after you return. *Gourmet,* a magazine specializing in food, frequently carries mouth-watering articles on food and restaurants in Canada, although its scope is much broader. It is available at newsstands nationwide for $2.50 an issue, or as a subscription for $18 a year from *Gourmet,* PO Box 53789, Boulder, CO 80322 (phone: 800-365-2454).

There are numerous additional magazines for every special interest available; check at your library information desk for a directory of such publications, or look over the selection offered at a well-stocked newsstand.

NEWSLETTERS: Throughout GETTING READY TO GO we have mentioned specific newsletters which our readers may be interested in consulting for further information.

One of the very best sources of detailed travel information is *Consumer Reports Travel Letter*. Published monthly by Consumers Union (PO Box 53629, Boulder, CO 80322-3629; phone: 800-234-1970), it offers comprehensive coverage of the travel scene on a wide variety of fronts. A year's subscription costs $37; 2 years, $57.

In addition, the following travel newsletters provide useful up-to-date information on travel services and bargains:

> *Entree* (PO Box 5148, Santa Barbara, CA 93150; phone: 805-969-5848). This newsletter caters to a sophisticated, discriminating traveler with the means to explore the places mentioned. Subscribers have access to a 24-hour hotline providing information on restaurants and accommodations around the world. Monthly; a year's subscription costs $59.
>
> *The Hideaway Report* (Harper Assocs., PO Box 50, Sun Valley, ID 83353; phone: 208-622-3193). This monthly source highlights retreats — including Canadian idylls — for sophisticated travelers. A year's subscription costs $90.
>
> *Romantic Hideaways* (217 E. 86th St., Suite 258, New York, NY 10028; phone: 212-969-8682). This newsletter leans toward those special places made for those traveling in twos. A year's subscription for this monthly publication costs $65.
>
> *Travel Smart* (Communications House, 40 Beechdale Rd., Dobbs Ferry, NY 10522; phone: 914-693-8300 in New York; 800-327-3633 elsewhere in the US). This monthly covers a wide variety of trips and travel discounts. A year's subscription costs $44.

■ **Computer Services:** Anyone who owns a personal computer and a modem can subscribe to a database service providing everything from airline schedules and fares to restaurant listings. Two such services of particular use to travelers are *CompuServe* (5000 Arlington Center Blvd., Columbus, OH 43220; phone: 800-848-8199 or 614-457-8600; $39.95 to join, plus a $2 monthly fee and usage fees of $6 to $22 per hour) and *Prodigy Services* (445 Hamilton Ave., White Plains, NY 10601; phone: 800-822-6922, 800-PRODIGY, or 914-993-8000; $12.95 per month's subscription, plus variable usage fees). Before using any computer bulletin-board services, be sure to take precautions to prevent downloading of a computer "virus." First install one of the programs designed to screen out such nuisances.

Weights and Measures

When traveling in Toronto, you'll find that just about every quantity, whether it is distance, length, weight, or capacity, will be expressed in unfamiliar terms. In fact, this is true for travel almost everywhere in the world, since the US is one of the last countries to make its way to the metric system. Your trip to Toronto may serve to familiarize you with what may one day be the weights and measures at your grocery store.

There are some specific things to keep in mind during your trip. Fruits and vegetables at a market generally are recorded in kilos (kilograms), as are your luggage at the airport and your body weight. (This latter is particularly pleasing to people of significant size, who, instead of weighing 220 pounds, hit the scales at a mere 100 kilos.) A kilo equals 2.2 pounds and 1 pound is .45 of a kilo. Body temperature usually is measured in degrees centigrade or Celsius rather than on the Fahrenheit scale, so that a normal body temperature is 37C, not 98.6F, and freezing is 0 degrees C rather than 32F.

Gasoline is sold by the liter (approximately 3.8 liters to a gallon). Tire pressure gauges and other equipment measure in kilograms per square centimeter rather than pounds per square inch. Highway signs are written in kilometers rather than miles (1 mile equals 1.6 km; 1 km equals .62 mile). And speed limits are in kilometers per hour, so think twice before hitting the gas when you see a speed limit of 100. That means 62 miles per hour.

The tables and conversion factors listed below should give you all the information you will need to understand any transaction, road sign, or map you encounter during your travels.

CONVERSION TABLES **METRIC TO US MEASUREMENTS**		
Multiply:	**by:**	**to convert to:**
LENGTH		
millimeters	.04	inches
meters	3.3	feet
meters	1.1	yards
kilometers	.6	miles
CAPACITY		
liters	2.11	pints (liquid)
liters	1.06	quarts (liquid)
liters	.26	gallons (liquid)
WEIGHT		
grams	.04	ounces (avoir.)
kilograms	2.2	pounds (avoir.)
US TO METRIC MEASUREMENTS		
LENGTH		
inches	25.0	millimeters
feet	.3	meters
yards	.9	meters
miles	1.6	kilometers
CAPACITY		
pints	.47	liters
quarts	.95	liters
gallons	3.8	liters
WEIGHT		
ounces	28.0	grams
pounds	.45	kilograms
TEMPERATURE $°F = (°C \times 9/5) + 32$ $°C = (°F - 32) \times 5/9$		

APPROXIMATE EQUIVALENTS		
Metric Unit	**Abbreviation**	**US Equivalent**
LENGTH		
meter	m	39.37 inches
kilometer	km	.62 mile
millimeter	mm	.04 inch
CAPACITY		
liter	l	1.057 quarts
WEIGHT		
gram	g	.035 ounce
kilogram	kg	2.2 pounds
metric ton	MT	1.1 tons
ENERGY		
kilowatt	kw	1.34 horsepower

Cameras and Equipment

Vacations are everybody's favorite time for taking pictures and home movies. After all, most of us want to remember the places we visit — and show them off to others. Here are a few suggestions to help you get the best results from your travel photography or videography. For more information see *A Shutterbug's Toronto* in DIVERSIONS.

BEFORE THE TRIP

If you're taking your camera or camcorder out after a long period in mothballs, or have just bought a new one, check it thoroughly before you leave to prevent unexpected breakdowns or disappointing pictures.

1. Still cameras should be cleaned carefully and thoroughly, inside and out. If using a camcorder, run a head cleaner through it. You also may want to have your camcorder professionally serviced (opening the casing yourself will violate the manufacturer's warranty). Always use filters to protect your lens while traveling.
2. Check the batteries for your camera's light meter and flash, and take along extras just in case yours wear out during the trip. For camcorders, bring along extra Nickel-Cadmium (Ni-Cad) batteries; if you use rechargeable batteries, a recharger will cut down on the extras.
3. Using all the settings and features, shoot at least one test roll of film or one videocassette, using the type you plan to take along with you.

EQUIPMENT TO TAKE ALONG

Keep your gear light and compact. Items that are too heavy or bulky to be carried comfortably on a full-day excursion will likely remain in your hotel room.

1. Invest in a broad camera or camcorder strap if you now have a thin one. It will make carrying the camera much more comfortable.
2. A sturdy canvas, vinyl, or leather camera or camcorder bag, preferably with padded pockets (not an airline bag), will keep your equipment organized and easy to find. If you will be doing much shooting around the water, a waterproof case is best.
3. For cleaning, bring along a camel's hair brush that retracts into a rubber squeeze bulb. Also take plenty of lens tissue, soft cloths, and plastic bags to protect equipment from dust and moisture.

FILM AND TAPES: If you are concerned about airport security X-rays damaging rolls of undeveloped still film (X-rays do not affect processed film) or tapes, store them in one of the lead-lined bags sold in camera shops. This possibility is not as much of a threat as it used to be, however. In both the US and Canada, incidents of X-ray damage to unprocessed film (exposed or unexposed) are few because low-dosage X-ray equipment is used virtually everywhere. If you're traveling without a protective bag, you may want to ask to have your photo equipment inspected by hand. One type of film that should never be subjected to X-rays is the very high speed ASA 1000 film; there are lead-lined bags made especially for it — and, in the event that you are refused a hand inspection, this is the only way to save your film. The walk-through metal detector devices at airports do not affect film, though the film cartridges may set them off.

You should have no problem finding film or tapes in Toronto. When buying film, tapes, or photo accessories the best rule of thumb is to stick to name brands with which you are familiar. The availability of film processing labs and equipment repair shops will vary.

THE CITY

TORONTO

There was a time when Toronto was content with its position as Canada's second city, and willingly deferred to Montreal as the spicier, more intriguing Canadian travel destination. But anyone who visits the city today knows that the so-called Queen City's former lethargic attitude has changed dramatically. A vibrant rhythm has replaced the old puritanical chord, and a new spirit flows through the city's bustling streets. After-dark entertainment has a vital, exciting beat; restaurants have grown in number and variety; and modern structures are being built as rapidly as old neighborhoods are being restored. Toronto has truly developed a strong cosmopolitan personality.

The dreams of farm kids and immigrants and a surprising combination of economic and sociological factors have transformed Toronto from a minor North American city into the financial, commercial, and communications center of Canada. This change is reflected in the ethnic composition of the population, the character of the city, and even in its physical profile. Dominating the skyline are two buildings, the CN Tower — a 1,815-foot communications tower that is the tallest freestanding structure in the world — and Royal Bank Plaza, whose two triangular towers appear to be made of solid gold (actually, there are 2,500 ounces of gold in the windows). The construction and eminence of both structures symbolize the city's ascendancy, a rise that occurred during the past 2 decades.

One of the fastest-growing cities in North America, Toronto has long surpassed Montreal as the Canadian city with the largest metropolitan population (Toronto's is about 3.5 million, with over 2.1 million in the city itself). Toronto claims to have the greatest ethnic diversity of any major city in the world. Some 80 nationalities speaking 16 different languages are represented here. The city has the largest Italian population outside of Italy, as well as large numbers of East Indians, Portuguese, Ukrainians, Germans, Asians, West Indians, and substantial other minority communities, all with their own newspapers and traditions.

Mass-scale immigration was responsible for Toronto's evolution as an international city. Growth was spurred initially by a large influx of refugees from the war-ravaged countries of Western and Central Europe, who came in a great wave during the early 1950s in search of jobs. These immigrants, as well as the natives, have transformed Toronto from a minor city into the metropolis it is today. Jobs brought people, and people brought more jobs. Thousands of industrial plants in and around the city account for about one-fifth of all manufacturing in Canada. A third of the country's purchasing power is located within a 100-mile radius of Toronto; most of the nation's companies are headquartered here, and many international companies maintain offices in Toronto as well.

Rising on the north bank of Lake Ontario, Toronto covers 244 square miles, embracing six municipalities that stretch from the flat, central downtown section to numerous hills in the sprawling suburbs. The city is laid out on a rectangular grid, but the neat order of the plan is interrupted by a green belt of wooded ravines created by two small rivers — the Humber and the Don — that cut through the city. The miles of wooded parkland along the rivers are among Toronto's prime recreational areas; summer and winter, residents use the space to hike, jog, and cross-country ski.

Lake Ontario has a wide, deep harbor that can accommodate oceangoing vessels, making Toronto a major port on the St. Lawrence Seaway. The waterfront area close to downtown has been renovated and is now the site of Harbourfront, a government-funded complex that includes recreational, cultural, and crafts centers, restaurants, and residential and commercial complexes. Also bordering the lake are Harbour Square, exclusive, modern highrise apartments, and the *Westin Harbour Castle,* a spectacular double-towered luxury hotel. Beaches, walkways, and marinas stretch along the lakefront.

Downtown rises to the north. Innovative architecture characterizes the city — the banking towers; City Hall, with its two curved towers surrounding a lower rotunda; *Eaton Centre,* the spacious shopping gallery that looks more like a huge greenhouse (inside are some of the best shops in Canada); the public library, designed by Raymond Moriyama (a Japanese-Canadian architect living in Toronto, he also built the *Ontario Science Centre*); and numerous other avant-garde buildings.

The construction of these buildings and complexes has contributed to the transformation of a city that only 30 years ago was an almost provincial town. The history of the city began over 400 years ago, when the Huron Indians set up camp at the end of their portage connecting Lake Huron to Lake Ontario. They called the site Toronto, the Huron word for "meeting place." French fur traders discovered it in the early 18th century and built a fort here in 1720. In 1759, they burned it to the ground during the Seven Years War to prevent its falling into British hands and from that time, French influence waned and Toronto's history and character were predominantly British. Indeed, as late as 1951, almost three-quarters of its population was of British descent.

In 1793, Lieutenant Governor John Graves Simcoe of Upper Canada took the first step in securing the tiny colony from US invaders by founding a town on this site. The land where metropolitan Toronto now sits had been purchased by the Missisauga Indians 6 years earlier, and Simcoe believed it would be a safer site than Niagara-on-the-Lake near the US border, which was then the capital. His British overseers agreed and Great Britain soon proclaimed the town the capital of Upper Canada; Loyalist refugees from the US were welcomed with open arms. They named the settlement York, after the Duke of York, the son of George III — the major opponent of the American Revolution. But despite the building of Yonge Street (the so-called longest street in the world) begun in 1794 at what is now Eglinton Avenue, the village grew slowly and earned the dubious sobriquet "Muddy York" because the land was swampy, causing its streets to be almost impassable.

During the War of 1812 between Britain and the US, the town was attacked by US troops, who destroyed the Parliament buildings and archives and stole the mace, the symbol of British sovereignty and authority. The invaders withdrew 4 days later, on May 1, 1813, and then reoccupied it for 2 more days that summer before withdrawing for good. The British retaliated by marching on Washington and burning all of its public buildings. (Before setting fire to the presidential mansion, a regiment of Scottish soldiers finished off a fine dinner prepared for the president, then proceeded to burn as much of the house as possible, leaving only a scorched outer shell. It was rebuilt quickly and painted white, thus bringing it in line with its sobriquet "the White House.") In 1934, President Franklin D. Roosevelt returned the mace to the government of Ontario as a gesture of international goodwill.

The city was incorporated in 1834, and its name reverted from York to the original Toronto. Since then, the most remarkable aspect about Toronto has been its growth. By 1901 its population had reached 200,000, and its business extended throughout Canada. The Toronto of that era was an anglicized town, its character heavily influenced by and indebted to classic English traits. Its business world was run like a very select British club, with the reins of financial and corporate power held tightly in a few hands. The view of what made a good and satisfying life was vividly perceived and rigidly maintained. Until World War II, Toronto was a WASP town — white, Anglo-Saxon, and Protestant — and so immersed in the work ethic that anything that even looked like fun was assumed to be harmful, sinful, prideful, or all three. Life in the city was governed by a stringent series of blue laws. In the words of the late Gordon Sinclair, Toronto's outspoken radio and TV broadcaster, "Everyday life was dreary enough, but Sundays were murder. Everything but the churches shut down tight. *Eaton's* (the major department store) even drew its curtains to prevent the small enjoyment of window shopping on the Sabbath."

What turned Toronto the Good into Toronto the Human was the infusion of cultures from several continents during the last 50 years. These groups have brought their customs, cultures, and cuisines with them, and they have utterly changed the city's character. Toronto has become a city of neighborhoods. Thousands of Greeks live in the East End around Danforth Avenue at the end of Bloor Street, and elsewhere there are large communities of Italians, Ukrainians, and Hungarians. Bordering Chinatown is a Portuguese neighborhood distinguished by its lovely pastel-painted houses. Toronto is home to a sizable German population as well, although its members tend not to live in any easily defined ethnic enclave. In nearby *Kensington Market,* most of these cultures meet to buy from and sell to one another. Strongly Portuguese and Caribbean, with some Italians and Jews, this market is where everyone can get just about everything. And as inexpensive as the goods always are, they become even less expensive if the buyer speaks the native tongue of the seller.

Toronto celebrates its ethnicity every year at the end of June in a 10-day blowout known as *Caravan.* Various groups set up pavilions in churches and community centers, offering the public food, drink, handicrafts, art, songs and dances, all from the Old Country. Visitors buy a "passport" and go from pavilion to pavilion on an around-the-world tour, stopping here for some Greek baklava, there for a demonstration of Ukrainian folk dancing, around the corner for an earful of Caribbean steel-band music. In the course of a day's ramble, you can have Italian pasta washed down by Irish coffee or a potent Polish liqueur.

A more lasting gift from Toronto's newer residents has been the proliferation of theaters, clubs, and ethnic restaurants and, even more important, the effect such social and cultural offerings have had on living habits in the city. With so much to choose from, Toronto has opened up at night. Residents are determined that the city center should not be a daytime-only experience, and a good deal of the most recent construction — the last wave of which added so many of the buildings that now make the city's skyline unique — fosters and encourages this feeling. Mixed development downtown — commercial and residential complexes — keeps people in the heart of the city. Instead of becoming a ghost town after working hours, downtown Toronto remains vibrant, drawing people to its nightlife.

A concomitant movement has awakened in the city's neighborhoods. Thirty-five years ago, Toronto appeared to be following the American model: a city center for business in the day, with rings of ever more affluent suburbs around it. When the great numbers of immigrants arrived, they moved into the older neighborhoods, where they established communities with strong bonds and natural cohesion. This movement has been extended to downtown commercial neighborhoods in recent years by the young middle class, who years ago might have moved to the suburbs.

The phenomenon that sparked the revival of the decaying neighborhoods was the election in 1972 of a reform city council, which reversed developers' plans for massive demolition to make way for inner-city high-rises and instead promoted city-run nonprofit housing, rent control, and tenants' rights. (Today it seems inconceivable that old City Hall was almost torn down to make way for an earlier version of ultra-posh *Eaton Centre,* but it's true.) The mood of the residents changed and, with the support of the city, the restoration of the old neighborhoods began in earnest. One small group of 200 people managed to save their historic church — the Church of the Holy Trinity — from destruction during the construction of *Eaton Centre.* Not only did developers revise their plans to protect the sanctity of the lovely little church, one of the oldest houses of worship in the city, but they changed the plans to ensure that sun would still shine on the building.

Toronto residents created and still maintain a lively and livable city. It boasts showplaces, like the spectacular *Ontario Science Centre;* the Metro Toronto Zoo, one of the largest and best in the world; and the *SkyDome* stadium. But the city is worth a visit for even more fundamental reasons. Its number one tourist attraction is its healthy urban environment. As Canada's leading metropolis, it has achieved a balance between progress and preservation. Wherever Toronto's heading, much of the rest of urban Canada is likely soon to follow. And much of the rest of urban North America might do well to take note.

TORONTO AT-A-GLANCE

SEEING THE CITY: The best way to grasp the lay of the land is from the CN Tower, Toronto's most visible and famous landmark. The property of *Canadian National,* the publicly owned railway, this communications tower is the world's tallest freestanding structure. From the base of the reflecting pool, the tower stretches 1,815 feet and 5 inches. (There are taller TV antennas, but they're supported by guy wires and thus are not freestanding.) Four exterior glass elevators whisk visitors 1,122 feet up to the Sky Pod, which has an outdoor observation deck, an indoor deck with zoom lens peritelescopes, the world's highest revolving restaurant, *Top of Toronto,* and a nightclub called *Sparkles.* On a clear day, Buffalo, Niagara Falls, and everything in between is visible. The Sky Pod level also contains a broadcasting studio and communications equipment. Another elevator leads to the 1,500-foot level, where you can look up at the transmission mast and down on everything else, except the jets approaching Pearson International Airport, northwest of the city. Open daily. Admission charge. 301 Front St. W. (phone: 360-8500).

Toronto is designed on a grid, which makes it easy to walk around downtown; however, nearly all streets have names rather than numbers, so finding a specific address can be difficult for a newcomer. The north end of the city is bounded by Highway 401, and Lake Ontario borders the south. Yonge Street is the main north-south arterial, and other north-south streets are designated by blue street signs. Bloor Street (which becomes Danforth Avenue east of the viaduct) is the main east-west thoroughfare, and other east-west streets have yellow signs. Downtown extends from Bloor south to Lake Ontario, between Spadina (Spa-*dye*-na) Avenue and Jarvis Street. Midtown covers the area north of Bloor to Eglinton Avenue.

SPECIAL PLACES: Unless you have a special need to take your car into the central city, don't. Toronto streets can get very congested, and on-street parking is severely restricted during peak hours. Parking lots exist, but they are expensive. Overtime parking at meters can end in a CN$52 ticket, and parking in a restricted zone can result in towing and payment of CN$150 to retrieve your car. Your best bet is to use Toronto's modern, efficient, clean, and safe public transit system (see *Getting Around*). The *Toronto Transit Commission* has extensive routes and will get you anywhere you want to go in metropolitan Toronto for a single fare.

DOWNTOWN

SkyDome – Set on 8 acres, this 31-story amphitheater is one of the world's largest, with a capacity for 60,000 spectators. Home of the *Blue Jays* baseball team and the Canadian Football League's Toronto *Argonauts,* it also hosts other major-league sporting events, plus concerts, exhibitions, and more. The amphitheater has a retractable dome roof that covers the stadium during inclement weather and opens up when the weather is good. It also boasts the world's largest scoreboard/replay machine, SkyVision (35 by 115 feet), along with an 800-seat restaurant overlooking one of the football end-zones, several bars, a health club, a 364-suite hotel with 70 rooms overlooking the stadium, a *Hard Rock Café,* and a *McDonald's* with seating for 500 people. Parking is limited, and most fans will have to reach the stadium via public transportation (for information, call 393-4636). 277 Front St. W. (phone: 341-3663).

Royal Ontario Museum – Affectionately referred to as *ROM,* it's Canada's largest public museum — made even larger after an $83-million renovation and expansion project — which features collections drawn from 20 science, art, and archaeology departments. *ROM* is well known for its Chinese collections, and the Bat Cave and Dinosaur Gallery are popular with kids of all ages. The European Gallery, Gallery of Birds, and the Ethnology Gallery of Native Peoples of North America are the most recent additions. Mummies are on exhibit in the Egypt-Nubia Gallery. The adjacent *McLaughlin Planetarium* presents Laserium shows Wednesdays through Sundays (call 586-5750 for show times and admission prices; children under 6 not admitted). Original star shows also are presented every few months; for more information, call 586-5736. The museum's Sigmund Samuel Building features Canadian decorative arts and crafts (14 Queen's Park Crescent W.; phone: 586-5549), and *ROM*'s *George R. Gardiner*

Museum of Ceramic Art (111 Queen's Park; phone: 586-8080) is the only specialized ceramics museum in North America. The *ROM Shop* is a cornucopia of gifts from around the world. The main museum and the Samuel Building are closed Mondays between *Labour Day* and *Victoria Day;* the *Gardiner Museum* and planetarium are closed Mondays; the entire complex is closed on *Christmas* and *New Year's Day.* Admission charge. 100 Queen's Park (phone: 586-5549). Subway exit: Museum.

Provincial Parliament Buildings – Located in Queen's Park, now synonymous with the provincial legislature, that pile of pink Romanesque rock is the back of the provincial Parliament buildings; from the front they are striking brownstones. Enthroned beside the buildings is a statue of a regally resplendent Queen Victoria. Her equally regal son, Edward VII, astride his sturdy steed, has become a shrine for local pigeons. Sir John A. Macdonald, Canada's first prime minister and the chief architect of Canadian Confederation, and George Brown, his political as well as personal adversary, who first proposed a federal system of government, also are represented here. Here's a bit of Canadiana to put these two characters in proper perspective: Once, during a legislative debate, Brown accused Macdonald of being drunk — a fairly safe accusation. Macdonald's reply was immortalized in the annals of Canadian history: "Better Sir John A. drunk," he said, "than George Brown sober." Queen's Park, with its sweeping lawns and old trees, is a favorite picnic ground, with outdoor musical events held regularly during the summer. Guided tours are offered on weekdays during the winter (no admission charge; call for times); in the summer, tours are conducted daily, every hour. The legislature convenes on Mondays through Wednesdays from 1:30 to 6 PM and on Thursdays from 10 AM to 12 PM. Queen's Park Crescent at University Ave. (phone ahead to book a tour: 965-4028). Subway exit: Museum or Queen's Park.

Ontario Hydro – Up and to the right of Queen's Park is the mirrored, concave building that is the headquarters of Canada's largest power producing and distributing organization. It employs a radical heating system, eliminating the traditional boiler: Heat provided by interior lighting and old-fashioned body warmth is recirculated throughout the building. Technical tours (not for the general public) are by appointment only. 700 University Ave. (phone: 592-3345). Subway exit: Queen's Park.

University of Toronto – Before continuing south on University Avenue, detour 1 block west to one of North America's better universities, dating from 1827. The campus sprawls over several city blocks; the best route for a short tour is around King's College Circle. Take a look inside Hart House, the Gothic student center built with Massey money (the family of the late Hollywood actor Raymond and his brother, Vincent, former Governor-General of Canada). Among the other buildings are the Old Observatory, University College, Knox College, and the Medical Sciences Building. Many scientific firsts have occurred in this last building: Dr. Frederick Banting and Dr. Charles Best isolated insulin in 1922; the first electric heart pacemaker was developed; and Pablum, the first precooked vitamin-enriched cereal, was formulated. Student guides lead free walking tours at 10:30 AM, 1 PM, and 2:30 PM Mondays through Fridays during June, July, and August. Groups should book ahead. Hart House (Alumni and Community Relations, University of Toronto, 21 King's College Cir.; phone: 978-5000). Subway exit: Museum or St. George.

Tour of the Universe – For those who've always wondered what it's like to be an astronaut, this futuristic attraction is a must-see. The year is 2019. "Astronauts" are checked in by security, insert their 3-D pass into a computer terminal, and pass through customs. Then it's blast-off time for a simulated ride to Jupiter. Open daily year-round. Admission charge. At the base of the CN Tower (phone: 364-3134). Subway exit: Union Station.

Mary Pickford's Birthplace – Along stately University Avenue, with its wide, flowered median, are the city's most famous hospitals — Toronto General, Mt. Sinai, and Hospital for Sick Children. In the gardens of "Sick Kids" on the east side of

University Avenue is a plaque and bronze bust commemorating the birthplace of Gladys Marie Smith, better known as Mary Pickford, America's Sweetheart. (Incidentally, Miss Pickford requested her Canadian citizenship back; it was granted in October 1978.) 55 University Ave. Subway exit: St. Andrew.

Chinatown – Several blocks downtown (north of City Hall; west of *Eaton Centre*) is the focal point of Toronto's Chinese, Korean, and Japanese communities: Here you'll find many interesting grocery stores and restaurants. The best places to eat are *Macay Court* (405 Dundas St. W.; phone: 596-1172) and *Young Lok* (122 St. Patrick St.; phone: 593-9819; also see *Eating Out*). The original Chinatown at Gerrard Street and Broadview Avenue has become "Vietnam Town." Another Chinatown is in the suburb of Scarborough. Subway exit: St. Patrick.

City Hall and Nathan Phillips Square – This distinctive modern complex was designed by Finnish architect Viljo Revell. Two curved towers of unequal height focus on the low-domed Council Chamber, which, from an aerial view, resembles a giant eye. Surrounding the buildings is a square named for Toronto's longtime mayor Nathan Phillips, who initiated plans for a new City Hall back in 1957. The square is a popular gathering place and the site of special events during the summer. The reflecting pool and fountains circulate 12,000 gallons of water a minute. In summer, office workers dip their toes in the pool; in winter they skate on its frozen surface. *The Archer*, a bronze Henry Moore sculpture, was purchased with public donations to adorn the square after the city council refused to buy it. Free tours are conducted daily (call for times). Bay and Queen Sts. (phone: 392-7341). Subway exit: Queen or Osgoode.

Eaton Centre – A modern 4-level shopping gallery, the center has a high glass roof, lots of space and light, marble floors, trees, plants, flowers, and benches. *Eaton's*, an institution in Canadian merchandising (whose founder, Timothy Eaton, first set up shop in Toronto in 1869), has its plush flagship store here. In addition, the center houses another 300 shops, boutiques, and restaurants. One entire level is underground. For a bite or a beer, drop into *Elephant and Castle* (phone: 598-4455), or call a friend from the red, English-style phone kiosk out front. You'll find the best ice cream in the city at *Swensen's* (phone: 979-1249). The gallery was constructed in accordance with Toronto's policy for architectural preservation and was built around two of the city's oldest buildings, Trinity Church and Scadding House, the former home of an early Toronto historian. Shops and some restaurants are open daily. 220 Yonge St. (phone: 598-2322). Subway exit: Dundas.

Bank Towers – Canada's five major banks have offices in these high-rise office-commercial complexes that dominate the Toronto skyline. All four complexes are linked underground by concourses that house shops, cinemas, and restaurants. The tallest of the buildings is the white marble, 72-story Bank of Montreal building, known as First Canadian Place because it was Canada's first chartered bank. Most striking is the Royal Bank Plaza, two triangular towers of 41 and 26 stories respectively, with serrated walls and windows covered with 2,500 ounces of gold. Inside there's a cascading fountain and an international art collection featuring Venezuelan Jesús Soto's sculpture composed of 8,600 20-inch-long aluminum tubes. You can't miss it — the work is 100 feet high and 60 feet wide and occupies more than half the space in the hall. Commerce Court is a stainless-steel skyscraper with 7,400 windows of double-glazed reflective glass. The three jet-black buildings are the Toronto Dominion Centre; the lobby often has art exhibits. The fifth major bank tower is the Bank of Nova Scotia, or "Scotia Bank" tower. King and Bay Sts. Subway exit: King.

Art Gallery of Ontario – The highlight here is the *Henry Moore Sculpture Centre*, the largest public collection of his work, displayed with related drawings, prints, studio material, and photography donated by Moore. Of the gallery's permanent collection, over half is the work of Canadian artists, including a wide variety of paintings and sculpture from the early 19th century through the present. Old Masters, Impressionists, and early 20th-century artists are also represented. The museum recently completed an extensive expansion and renovation, refurbishing its 20 galleries and adding another 30; the additional space will house contemporary works of Canadian and international painters, sculpture, drawings, and Inuit artwork. Connected to the gallery by an underground walkway is the *Grange,* a charming museum located in Toronto's oldest remaining brick house (ca. 1817). Some say it's haunted, but the atmosphere is cheery and the furnishings delightful. Vera, the upstairs "maid," often greets visitors, and goods baked fresh from the hearth are sold Tuesdays, Thursdays, and Saturdays. Facing the front lawn of Grange Park. Closed Mondays. Admission charge covers entrance to the gallery and the *Grange.* Gallery at 317 Dundas St. W., between McCaul and Beverley Sts. (phone: 977-0414). Subway exit: St. Patrick.

Yorkville – Once a hangout for Toronto hippies before they headed west, this area is now the chicest in the city. Renovated townhouses, boutiques with designer fashions and expensive jewelry, quiet courtyards, wrought-iron lampposts, and art galleries flank the narrow streets. There are several cafés where patrons can sit by a window box sipping an aperitif and watching the world go by. Yorkville Village was incorporated in 1853, and eagle-eyed explorers will find the original coat of arms — brewer, smith, brickmaker, carpenter, and farmer — outside many of the specialty stores. *Hazelton Lanes* (55 Avenue Rd.) is a classy commercial-residential complex with some 70 boutiques and an outdoor courtyard that is transformed into an ice skating rink in winter. Some of the most expensive chocolate around is sold at *Teuscher of Switzerland* (55 Avenue Rd.; phone: 961-1303), which imports its goodies from Zurich; try the champagne truffles — a tasty way to bankruptcy. Bounded by Bloor St., Avenue Rd., Bay St., and Scollard St. Subway exit: Bay.

Queen Street West – The up-and-coming cousin to Yorkville, this once-moribund stretch just west of City Hall now hums with colorful street life, sidewalk jewelry vendors, and an assortment of shops selling everything from new and used furniture and books to state-of-the-art computers. Nearby is the Ontario College of Art, whose proximity played a big role in the development of this area: When graduates from the acclaimed art school needed places to show their work, they began opening shops along this street. High-fashion highlights include *Twinkle Toes* (No. 320; phone: 340-7349) for men's and women's footwear; *Next* (No. 348; phone: 599-9497) for boots; *Club Monaco* (No. 403; phone: 979-5633) for sportswear, plus an inexpensive lunch counter offering sandwiches, salads, and cappuccino. From John St. to Spadina Ave. Subway exit: Osgoode.

Kensington Market – A colorful, artsy area jammed with cafés, street musicians, and shops where everything from salted fish and fresh produce to clothing and stereos is sold. This outdoor market has character — lots of it — and a heavy ethnic flavor. Jewish, Portuguese, Caribbean, and Italian influences are apparent. The market is at its best on Saturday mornings. Closed Sundays. College and Dundas Sts., west of Spadina. Subway exit: St. Patrick.

St. Lawrence Market – This is another great marketplace. Erected in 1844 to serve as Toronto's first City Hall, it's now a clearinghouse for farmers, butchers, and fishmongers. Saturday's the big day here, when the area farmers truck their produce to the *Farmers' Market* across the street. Open Tuesdays through Saturdays. 95 Front St. E. Subway exit: Union.

Casa Loma – This magnificent, rambling, eccentric, turreted mansion was built between 1911 and 1914 by Sir Henry Pellatt — a pioneer of the use of hydroelectric power in Canada — to house the collection of antique furniture and grandiose art he had collected from the greatest galleries of Europe during his career as one of Toronto's most successful financiers. He imported European craftsmen to build this 98-room mock-medieval castle, which features a secret staircase; a conservatory, with elegant bronze doors; vast, carpeted horse stables, lined in mahogany and marble, connected to the house by an 800-foot tunnel; "Peacock Alley," a corridor running the length of the house, copied and named after the Peacock Alley in the royal residence of Windsor Castle; the Great Hall, with suits of armor and a 60-foot ceiling; the Oak Room, where three artisans worked for 3 years to chisel the French oak paneling; and 15 bathrooms, 25 fireplaces, and a wine cellar with space for 1,700 bottles. In the 1920s, Toronto's electric utilities went public and the city took over his company. Sir Henry found the cost of upkeep beyond even his ample means; Casa Loma was taken by the city for back taxes, and Sir Henry had to auction most of his Chippendales and Reynoldses to keep body and soul together. For a while the place fell victim to mice and disrepair. In 1937, the *Kiwanis Club* of West Toronto restored the castle and still runs it today as a tourist attraction, with proceeds going to community projects. The *Garden Club of Toronto* renovated Casa Loma's 10 acres of gardens. Be sure to climb the two towers; the Norman Tower is open and the Scottish Tower is enclosed. In summer, you can come back Saturday nights for ballroom dancing under the stars that shine through the dome of the old Conservatory. Open daily from 10 AM to 4 PM. Handicap access. Admission charge includes self-guided audio tours or guided tours can be arranged in advance. 1 Austin Terr. (phone: 923-1171). Subway exit: Spadina; then walk 2 blocks north.

Spadina – This house, whose Indian name means "hill," is located just east of Casa Loma. Built in 1866 as a home for James Austin, major shareholder in Consumer Gas and founder of the Dominion Bank (now the Toronto Dominion), it has 50 rooms and halls, which were completely restored by the Toronto Historic Board. Most of the Victorian and Edwardian furnishings belonged to the family, and many pieces were made by the Jakes & Haye Company in Toronto. The Palm Room, with its space filled with flowers, and the gentlemen's billiard parlor have been maintained in the genteel style of one of Toronto's first families. Four generations of Austins lived here until the historic board obtained it and opened the doors to the public, and the *Garden Club of Toronto* took on the landscaping, planting more than 300 varieties of flowers and plants. Open daily. Admission charge. Wheelchair access. 285 Spadina Rd. (phone: 392-6910). Subway exit: Spadina. Walk two blocks north of the station. Parking is available at Casa Loma.

Fort York – This site marks the founding of Toronto in 1793, when a small garrison was constructed to protect the entrance to Toronto Bay. A force of British soldiers marched on Washington, DC, in 1813 to avenge the successful invasion of this fort and the burning of the government buildings during a battle in the War of 1812. In the attack on the US capital, the public buildings were burned, including the presidential mansion, which was rebuilt quickly and painted white. Today the defensive walls of old Fort York surround gunpowder magazines, soldiers' barracks, and officers' quarters. There are other restored structures on site and guards in period costume conduct tours. Open daily. Admission charge. On Garrison Rd. off Fleet St., between Bathurst St. and Strachan Ave., near Exhibition Pl. Take the No. 511 Bathurst Streetcar to the stop after Front St. (phone: 392-6907).

Mackenzie House – This row house honors one of the most colorful and spirited early political leaders in English Canada. A populist whose reform views in his own newspaper, the *Colonial Advocate,* earned him a dedicated following among laborers and farmers, William Lyon Mackenzie became the first Mayor of Toronto for 9 months from 1834 to 1835. But his views veered to the extreme, and in December 1837 he fomented an uprising of 750 rural supporters that took the form of two skirmishes in and near Toronto. The Upper Canada Rebellion of 1837 (as it became known), the only one of its kind in Ontario, was quickly put down, and Mackenzie fled to the US. Still a popular man with Canadian elitists, he returned under amnesty 12 years later, but many of his supporters were hanged or sent to prison camps in Australia. Mackenzie served as a member of the legislative assembly for 8 years upon his return. The row house that a committee of his friends bought for him has not changed much since he lived here: Costumed guides will show you pieces from 1857, from clothing and kitchen utensils to heavy period furniture and linen tablecloths. There is also a reconstructed print shop which tells the story of this political visionary. Open daily. Admission charge. Near *Eaton Centre* at 82 Bond St. (phone: 392-6915). Subway exit: Dundas.

High Park – Covering 400 acres at the west end of town, this is the largest recreation area in the city. Open and wooded spaces and ravines are the restful setting for two playgrounds, sports facilities (swimming, tennis, baseball, soccer, and lawn bowling), and a small zoo and bird sanctuary. Grenadier Pond is a great spot to fish, row, and feed the ducks; and Hillside Gardens, three beautiful and elaborate gardens on the west side, are popular locations for wedding photographs. In the evenings during July and August, members of the *Canadian Stage Company* perform *The Dream in High Park,* a free outdoor staging of *A Midsummer Night's Dream.* Colborne Lodge Dr. Subway exit: High Park.

Colborne Lodge – This 1837 Regency country cottage was once the home of John G. Howard, city engineer and architect. He gave much of the present High Park to the city, which acquired the lodge in 1876 in return for a lifetime annuity for Howard and his wife. A living museum with costumed staff re-creating Victorian times, it is furnished with period pieces and fine examples of early Canadian art. The Howards had both summer and winter kitchens, a wine cellar, and one of the first examples of indoor plumbing in North America. Verandahs on three sides of the house take advantage of views of Lake Ontario to the south and Grenadier Pond to the west. Open daily. Admission charge. Colborne Lodge Dr. in High Park (phone: 392-6916). Subway exit: High Park.

Cabbagetown – In the eastern part of town, bordered by Sherbourne, Don Valley Parkway, and Bloor Street East, this is Toronto's best-preserved Victorian neighborhood. Once called "the largest Anglo-Saxon slum in North America," it is now among the city's trendiest places to live. For a bit of country in the city, visit *Riverdale Farm* (201 Winchester St.; phone: 392-6794), a tiny working farm with a Victorian-style farmhouse, an 1858 barn, and a menagerie of cows, sheep, pigs, ducks, geese, turkeys, chickens, goats, and horses. The farm is open daily from 9 AM to 4 PM; no admission charge. Subway exit: College; then take the Carlton Streetcar east to Parliament St.

OUTDOORS

Ontario Place – A 96-acre theme park on the edge of Lake Ontario, it is part playground, part exposition and cultural center, and mostly lush green park. The cinesphere, a giant structure shaped like a dimpled basketball and spiked with luminous eyeballs, houses a curved 6-story movie screen, where films are shown in the winter. At the *Forum* (capacity 10,000), music lovers can listen to the *Toronto Symphony,* to jazz, or to popular performers. Children's Village is an imaginative area for kids under 12 years old (there's even a height restriction of 58 inches). The Pavilion, a series of interconnected pods built right in Lake Ontario, houses good restaurants and exhibits. The west island features a wilderness flume ride and water stage facility showcasing Ontario talent. Open daily from mid-May to *Labour Day.* Admission charge. 955 Lakeshore Blvd. W. (phone: 965-7711). Subway exit: Union; then take the *Harbourfront Rapid Transit Line* west to the last stop and walk a quarter of a mile along the lakeshore.

Harbourfront – The federal government restored this 92-acre waterfront area and built a recreation/culture complex. The Metropolitan Toronto Convention and Visitors Association has its offices (with a designer foyer and contemporary art exhibit) in the Queen's Quay Terminal. From May to October, at the refurbished terminal and surrounding park, visitors can shop, dine, listen to jazz, make crafts, participate in sports, examine old steam engines, feed the ducks, or just watch the ships go by. The area is divided into several sections: York Quay, with an art gallery, theater, and café featuring jazz and poetry readings; Spadina Quay, with a marina and picnic facilities; and

Bathurst Quay, with a park and cooperative housing projects. There's also a year-round antiques and flea market, and in the summer there's a sailing school. Open daily. No admission charge, although sometimes there's a charge for specific events. 235 Queen's Quay W. (phone: 973-3000). Subway exit: Union; then take *Harbourfront Rapid Transit Line* west to York St.

Toronto Islands – This archipelago off the Toronto shore of Lake Ontario known locally as "The Island" encompasses Hanlan's Point, Ward's Island, Centre Island, Algonquin Island, and four small islands. The 15-minute ferry ride is the least expensive and quickest escape from the intensity of city life. (The islands are populated by 650 people, at least one sly red fox, and thousands of Canada geese and mallards.) Cars aren't allowed on the ferry; bicycles (you may bring your own on weekdays only) and foot power are the standard modes of transportation. Centre Island, the most popular, has 612 acres of park, picnic grounds, restaurants, boating, a barnyard zoo, and Centreville, a child-size replica of a 19th-century Ontario village with lots of rides (open May 24 to *Labour Day*). Ward's Island and Hanlan's Point have fewer facilities and attract fewer people, but swimming is good at Ward's Island, and public tennis courts are available at Hanlan's Point. There also are boat rentals. Subway exit: Union.

SUBURBS

Ontario Science Centre – A spectacular facility that was built in 1967 at a cost of $30 million to mark Canada's centennial. Since then, it has attracted millions of visitors from all over the world to its scientific and technological exhibits, which stress interaction and participation and demonstrate that science can be fun. Designed by Raymond Moriyama, the structure is extremely well integrated with its environment. It is built into a ravine; visitors enter at the top of a cliff and work their way down on glass-enclosed escalators that overlook a lush, wooded valley. Inside, there are many different exhibits — Food/Earth Hall, Hall of Communication, Hall of Life, Hall of Transportation, Science Arcade, Hall of the Atom — as well as demonstrations, films, and theaters with multimedia shows. One of the most popular new exhibits is the interactive Space Hall, which features the Challenger Learning Centre, a hands-on space shuttle mission. There are far too many things to see and do to cover everything, even in several visits. There are no guided tours, so visitors may set their own pace, plotting a course with the help of the *Science Centre*'s map. Wherever they decide to head, visitors will find plenty of opportunities to participate: pitting their wits against a computer in a game of Hangman; making a machine talk; receiving a charge of static electricty that makes their hair stand on end; or testing their fitness, their reflexes, or their perception. Hosts knowledgeable about science are around to assist those who want guidance. Open daily. Admission charge. 770 Don Mills Rd. (phone: 429-4100).

Metro Toronto Zoo – This impressive zoo is one of the largest in the world. Stretched between two arms of the Rouge River, these 710 acres of river valley and eight pavilions have been shaped to simulate the natural habitats of the zoo's nearly 4,000 animal residents. The geographic regions represented include Africa, Australia, Eurasia, Indo-Malaysia, North America, and South America. The largest area, the African Pavilion, is equipped with ponds and a jungle atmosphere to keep the gorillas, hippos, and monkeys feeling right at home. Orangutans and gibbons swing through trees in the rain forest environment of Indo-Malaysia. Other settings accommodate polar bears, alligators, zebras, Japanese macaques, and South African fur seals. A slow, rubber-wheeled train negotiates the 3½-mile path though the Canadian Domain, where deer, Arctic wolves, caribou, moose, and antelope play. Seeing the zoo easily can take up a full day. There are several ways to approach a visit: In addition to the train, there are a variety of walking tours. Open daily. Admission charge. Just north of Hwy. 401 on Meadowvale Rd., 10 miles (16 km) east of the Don Valley Pkwy. (phone: 392-5900, or 392-5901 for recorded information).

Black Creek Pioneer Village – This restored 19th-century town depicts life in a rural Ontario village over a hundred years ago. The buildings include a homestead and farm, a general store, a blacksmith's shop, a town hall, and a flour mill. Costumed folk in last century's fashions perform tasks such as shoeing horses, making butter, and weaving rugs. Open daily in summer; the buildings are closed in January and February, but there's a sports program with skating, and horse-drawn sleigh rides. Admission charge. There is no easy way to get here, but if you have the time, the scenic route is west along the Gardiner Expressway to Jane Street and north 12 miles (18 km) to Steeles Avenue. Jane St. at Steeles Ave. W. (phone: 736-1733; for recorded information, 661-6610).

McMichael Canadian Art Collection – These attractive galleries, built of hand-hewn logs and fieldstone and set amidst 100 acres of breathtaking conserved land overlooking the Humber River Valley, shelter many works of the Group of Seven, an informal school of artists who broke away from traditional British painting early in the 20th century and immortalized the Canadian landscape. There are also exhibits of Northwest Coast, Inuit, and contemporary Indian art. Lively weekend programs include tours, talks, films, and Sunday afternoon jazz concerts. There's a full-service restaurant and book and gift shop with exclusive hand-crafted Canadian goods. Open daily during the summer; closed Mondays from November through April. Admission charge. In Kleinburg, about 25 miles (40 km) north of Toronto. Take Highway 401 West and exit at Highway 400 North, then take Major Mackenzie Drive west to Kleinburg and follow the signs (phone: 893-1121).

Canada's Wonderland – Canada's major theme park is just 20 miles (32 km) northwest of downtown Toronto. The park features five live stage shows and some 30 thrilling rides, including the only stand-up looping roller coaster in Canada. Shops and restaurants line International Street, which leads to six theme areas. Top entertainers perform in the *Kingswood Music Theatre* (capacity 15,000). The children's and adult's pay-one-price passports allow unlimited use of the park for the day (*Kingswood* not included). Open daily June to September, weekends from May through mid-October. On Hwy. 400 between Rutherford Rd. and Major Mackenzie Dr. (phone: 832-7000 or 832-2205).

Trillium Terminal 3 – This could be the only airport terminal worth a visit even if you're not traveling by plane. The $520-million international terminal — the first in Canada to be privately developed, owned, and operated — at Lester B. Pearson International Airport has been called a "transportation theme park." Designed to recall a 19th-century European railway station, with high-vaulted glass and steel ceilings, it features the recently built *Swissôtel* (see *Checking In*), a food court with 80 restaurants and concessions, and a posh shopping mall that includes North America's first *Harrods* — of London fame.

■**EXTRA SPECIAL:** Just 82 miles (131 km) southwest of Toronto is Niagara Falls, one of the most powerful waterfalls in the world, as well as one of the Western Hemisphere's major tourist attractions. The falls are formed as the waters of Lake Erie race downhill to join Lake Ontario, becoming the Niagara River en route. The river gathers strength and power in the narrows and then plunges more than 150 feet to form the famous falls. A small island in the river splits this whitewater juggernaut at the point of its mighty dive, dividing it into two falls instead of one. While 9 feet shorter than the American Falls, the Canadian (or Horseshoe) Falls, 158 feet high, channel nearly 90% of the total flow of over 120 million gallons per minute. Many Canadian waterfalls are higher but none approaches it in volume. The city of Niagara Falls, Ontario, calls itself "The Honeymoon Capital of the World" and "The World's Most Famous Address." There are several ways to see the falls — from a tower or helicopter ride, on one of the four *Maid of the Mist* sightseeing boats that carry visitors to the base of the Horseshoe Falls, or from one of the restaurants that overlook them. Take Queen Elizabeth Way (QEW) West 82 miles (130 kms) to Niagara Falls.

SOURCES AND RESOURCES

TOURIST INFORMATION: For general information, brochures, maps, and a copy of an annually updated guide to Toronto's hotels, restaurants, and attractions, contact the Metropolitan Toronto Convention and Visitors Association in the Queen's Quay Terminal, along the waterfront (207 Queen's Quay W., Suite 509; phone: 368-9821 or 800-363-1990 in the US; fax: 867-3995). The association maintains several outdoor kiosks that provide quick information and a permanent Visitor Information Centre outside *Eaton Centre* (Yonge and Dundas Sts.; phone: 979-3133). Its city map has plenty of helpful information and an insert on the subway routes.

The Ontario Ministry of Tourism is a good information source for activities taking place not only in Toronto but also in its environs. Write or call in advance to obtain an information packet (Queen's Park, Toronto, Ontario M7A 2E5; phone: 965-4008 or 800-268-3735 in the US). They also have a year-round Visitor Information Centre in *Eaton Centre* and summer kiosks in various spots around town.

The best street maps of Toronto are in the *Perly's* city street guide, used by all the city's taxi drivers. The *Toronto Guidebook,* edited by Alexander Ross (Grey de Pencier Publications; CN$4.95), is the best local guide. The *Toronto Book,* edited by William Kilbourn (Gage Publishing Co.; CN$35), is a good anthology of Toronto literature past and present. And if you're browsing in a city bookstore, look for other works by Kilbourn or anything written by Mike Filey — both local historians who have chronicled at length various features of the city, from the history of its streetcars to the interesting aspects of strolling through its cemeteries.

Local Coverage – The *Toronto Globe and Mail* appears every morning except Sundays; the tabloid-size *Sun* comes out daily; the *Toronto Star* is the country's largest daily newspaper; and the *Financial Post,* owned by the *Sun,* is a morning daily.

Toronto Life is a monthly magazine that features the latest restaurants, theater, music, and fashion, as well as the movers and shakers who shape the life and direction of the city. *About Town,* a quarterly booklet with lists of what's going on in town, is available from the Metropolitan Toronto Convention and Visitors Association. *Where Toronto* is a monthly magazine distributed free to hotel guests by the *Hotel Association of Metropolitan Toronto;* it's also available from the Metropolitan Toronto Convention and Visitors Association. *NOW* and *EYE* magazines are two weekly tabloids available free at most newsstands, bars, and cafés. Both cover the city's entertainment scene and print information about music, film, theater, and shopping.

CFTO-TV is the local affiliate of the CTV national network; CBLT-TV is the local affiliate of the Canadian Broadcasting Corporation (CBC); CBLFT-TV is the CBC's French-language station; TVO is Ontario's educational station; CFMT-TV is the city's multicultural channel; CITY-TV is the Toronto-based creator of MuchMusic, Canada's version of MTV; and the Global network is another Toronto-based station. In addition, all the US networks — ranging from ABC to Fox — are available through cable and disk hookup (in fact, the original role of the CN Tower was as a huge television and radio antenna).

CBL-AM (740) is the national radio network; it features talk shows, music, and news. CBL-FM (94.1) is its FM counterpart, and CJBC-AM (860) is its French-language version. CFRB-AM (1010) is a major news, talk, and music station; CMIX-FM (99.9) plays a mixture of contemporary music and oldies; CHUM-AM (1050) and CJCL-AM (1430) are oldies stations. CHUM-FM (104.5), CHFI-FM (98.1), CJEZ-FM (97.3), CMFK-FM (96.3), and CKFM-FM (99.9) play adult contemporary music; CILQ-FM (107) and CFTR-AM (680) have a younger rock-music audience. CJRT-FM (91.1) features classical music and jazz; CKYC-AM (590) plays country music; and CHIN-AM (1540) and CHIN-FM (100.7) broadcast ethnic (mostly Italian) music and news.

Food – *Toronto Life* and *Metropolitan Toronto Events Guide* list most of the established restaurants and many newcomers. In addition, all of the daily newspapers feature restaurant reviews, as do *NOW* and *EYE* magazines and *Where Toronto*.

TELEPHONE: The area code for Toronto is 416.

CURRENCY: All prices are quoted in US dollars unless otherwise indicated.

Sales Tax – Ontario has a provincial sales tax of 8%. In addition, a 7% federal tax, called the Goods and Services Tax (GST), is levied on all purchases, including hotel and restaurant bills. In many cases, however, visitors can receive refunds of both the provincial and federal taxes. Most stores that deal with tourists carry Ontario tax rebate information; tax rebate forms can be obtained at every airport and border crossing. Make sure to retain all receipts so that when you return home, you can calculate your entitled tax rebate. For more GST rebate information, see *Duty-Free Shopping and Goods and Services Tax* in GETTING READY TO GO.

GETTING AROUND: Car Rental – All major North American firms are represented: *Avis* (Hudson Bay Centre, 80 Bloor St. E.; phone: 964-2051); *Budget* (141 Bay St.; phone: 364-7104); *Hertz* (39 Richmond St. W.; phone: 363-9022); and *Tilden* (at Union Station, 65 Front St. W; phone: 364-4191). All of these companies have offices throughout downtown and in the outlying areas of the city. The *Canadian Automobile Association* (2 Carlton St.; phone: 966-3000) has a reciprocal agreement with the *American Automobile Association,* should you have problems with your car.

Public Transit – The *Toronto Transit Commission* (*TTC*) operates an efficient, modern system covering over 700 miles of routes. The *TTC* publishes a handy pocket-size *Ride Guide* available free from station collectors, from the *TTC* Center at Bloor-Yonge subway station, by calling 393-INFO (393-4636), or by writing to the *TCC* (1900 Yonge St., Toronto, Ontario M4S 1Z2). Some 2,300 vehicles — buses, trolleys, streetcars, and subways — make up this interconnecting system. The exact change or a token is required for the first fare, but transfers along the same route are free (including subway-bus-trolley transfers). The cash fare is CN$2, but you can save money by using tokens: a package of two tokens costs CN$3; five tokens cost CN$6.50, and ten cost CN$13. Special family passes are available for use on Sundays and holidays. The subways are clean and safe. For information on routes and fares, call the *TTC* information line between 7 AM and 11:30 PM (phone: 393-4636).

Sightseeing Tours – *Gray Coach* (610 Bay St.; phone: 979-3511) has excellent bus tours of the city during summer months with passenger pickups at all major hotels and the main bus terminal. The *TTC* also offers a tour of the city on one of its restored antique trolleys; call the *TTC* for information (phone: 393-4636) or check with any hotel.

Taxi – Cabs are easy to hail on any downtown street, and there are taxi stands at every hotel. Major cab companies are *Beck's Taxi* (phone: 449-6911), *Co-op Taxi* (phone: 364-8161), *Diamond Cab* (phone: 366-6868), *Metro* (phone: 363-5611), and *Yellow Cab* (phone: 363-4141),.

 SPECIAL EVENTS: For 10 days in January, the *Toronto International Boat Show* brings yachting enthusiasts to *Exhibition Place,* at the *Canadian National Exhibition (CNE)* grounds; later that month, motorcycle buffs converge for the 3-day *Toronto Motorcycle Show* (phone: 695-0311). In February, the 10-day *International Auto Show* fills the downtown Metro Toronto Convention Centre with state-of-the-art and possible future automobile designs (phone: 585-8000).

The *Toronto Sportsmen's Show,* held in March, draws hundreds of thousands of visitors during its annual 10-day run at the *CNE* grounds. The show features displays of the most up-to-date sporting equipment and technology and provides information about hunting and fishing lodges throughout North America (phone: 393-6076).

In May, the *International Children's Festival* features over 100 performances by international companies. Free activities include jugglers, mimes, and more. Harbourfront (235 Queen's Quay W.; phone: 973-3000).

Two music festivals held in June bring huge crowds to Toronto from as far away as Chicago. The *du Maurier Ltd. Downtown Jazz Festival* features concerts — many of them free — in city squares, concert halls, theaters, clubs, and street corners (phone: 363-8717). And the *Harbourfront Jazz Festival* offers free music in the outdoor concert spaces, indoor cafés, and grassy parks that make up the 3-mile-long waterfront area (phone: 973-3000).

At the end of June, the *Caravan* festival is held, and most of Toronto's 80 ethnic communities set up national pavilions in church basements, school gyms, public halls, and tents to show off their cuisines, music, dance, costumes, and traditions. Patrons purchase a ticket in the form of a passport, which gets "stamped" at each pavilion visited during their international tour. For information, contact the *Metro Caravan* (263 Adelaide St. W.; phone: 977-0466).

The *Benson & Hedges International Fireworks Festival,* which lasts for 2 weeks in June and July, brings together the most talented pyrotechnicians from around the world, who compete for the most spectacular presentation. The best place from which to view these celestial sights is the *Ontario Place* grounds. For more information, call 965-6332.

The *Canada Day* holiday weekend in July always brings the *International Picnic,* a free bash sponsored by the multilingual radio station CHIN. It features everything from pie-eating contests and games to music and a parade. For information, contact CHIN (637 College St.; phone: 531-9991).

In mid-July, Toronto plays host to the *Molson Indy* auto race, during which cars roar through the streets near the lakeshore and barrel past bleachers that are specially built along the harborfront. For information, contact *Molson Indy* (phone: 595-5445). Held about the same time is the annual *Outdoor Art Exhibition,* in which dozens of artists display their work in and around Nathan Phillips Square.

Caribana is a 10-day West Indies carnival that takes place during the August 1 weekend. Its highlight is a colorful parade that winds through town, complete with floats and Caribbean displays, reggae music, and street-corner stands selling grilled jerk pork. For information, call 925-5435 or refer to *About Town* or *Where Toronto.*

The *Canadian National Exhibition* is the city's big fair, running for 3 weeks from mid-August to *Labour Day.* The *CNE* grounds are filled from dawn to dusk with crowds testing out the midway rides, playing games of chance, visiting the food and auto pavilions, viewing the agricultural exhibits, and attending nightly concerts on the bandstand. For information, contact *Canadian National Exhibition,* Lakeshore Blvd. (phone: 393-6000).

The first 2 weeks of September are a cineast's dream, as the annual *Festival of Festivals* introduces more than 300 films from around the world. International film-makers, movie stars, and journalists crowd into the city for this prestigious public festival. For information, contact the *Festival of Festivals,* 69 Yorkville Ave. (phone: 967-7371).

Also taking place in the beginning of September is the 4-day-long *Canadian Open Golf Championship,* held at the *Glen Abbey Golf Course.* For information, contact the course at 1333 Dorval Rd., Oakville (phone: 844-1811).

The 13th edition of the *International Festival of Authors* at *Harbourfront* features some of the finest writers from around the world for 9 days in September. Events include readings, lectures, on-stage interviews, and the popular Lives & Times presenta-tions (featuring prominent biographers and critics speaking on their subjects), plus the *Book-Keepers Café,* with free appraisals of up to ten of your favorite old books (phone: 973-4000). *Artsweek,* for 9 days in September and October, offers free special events in all arts disciplines: behind-the-scenes tours, rehearsals, workshops, and perform-ances. It's held throughout the city (phone: 597-8223).

The *Royal Agricultural Winter Fair* at *Exhibition Place* on Lakeshore Boulevard is billed as the largest agricultural fair under one roof (27½ acres). The fair runs for 10 days in mid-October and traditionally marks the beginning of winter. Its *Royal Horse Show* attracts international competition in every field (phone: 393-6400).

 MUSEUMS: The *Art Gallery of Ontario* distributes an excellent guidebook with information about more than 30 galleries around the city. In addition to those described in detail in *Special Places,* other interesting museums to visit include the following:

Gibson House – A restored 19th-century home. Closed Mondays (except Monday holidays). Admission charge. 5172 Yonge St. (phone: 225-0146). Subway exit: North York Centre.

Hockey Hall of Fame and Museum – A must-see for the hockey enthusiast. The *Stanley Cup,* North America's oldest professional sports trophy, is here (the NHL team that wins the cup each year gets to hold it for 1 month), as well as most of the sport's other famous trophies — *Challenge Cup, Canada Cup,* and all of the National Hockey League's major prizes. Officially endorsed by the NHL, the Canadian Amateur Hockey Association, and the International Ice Hockey Federation, the museum has exhibits devoted to famous goalies, hockey skates and sticks used by the sport's great players, and other celebrated paraphernalia; there are also audiovisual presentations and other regular programs. The museum is temporarily closed while it moves to a new down-town location at the corner of Front and Yonge Streets; it is scheduled to reopen early this summer. Lakeshore Blvd., Exhibition Pl. (phone: 595-1345). Subway exit: Union.

Marine Museum of Upper Canada – The last surviving structure of seven buildings built in 1841 to replace the original Fort York, it now features exhibits on the history of shipping and waterways. There is a fine display of model ships and marine artwork, as well as an audiovisual presentation for marine buffs on the economic history of the Great Lakes. Open daily year-round except *Christmas, Boxing Day* (December 26), and *New Year's Day.* Admission charge. Lakeshore Blvd., Stanley Barracks, Exhibition Pl. (phone: 392-6827). Subway exit: Union.

Market Gallery – On the second level of the *St. Lawrence Market,* this display chronicles the history of Toronto through old photographs. Until 1899, this was the site of Toronto's second City Hall, and the city's extensive archival and artistic collec-tions are housed here. Closed Mondays and Tuesdays. No admission charge. 95 Front St. E. (phone: 392-7604). Subway exit: Union.

Museum of History of Medicine – Known for its Egyptian mummy, on which an autopsy has been performed, and for the Drake Collection of pediatric artifacts, this museum features exhibits that span 5,000 years of health care, from the ancient world to the 20th century. Open weekdays year-round. No admission charge but donations requested. Academy of Medicine, 288 Bloor St. W. (phone: 922-0564). Subway exit: St. George.

Museum of Textiles – Tucked away in a condominium building, just a few blocks east of the *Ontario Gallery of Art,* is the only museum in Canada devoted to handmade textiles and carpets. Exhibits range from complex loom-woven tapestries to pounded and painted barkcloth. A special gallery is devoted to contemporary artists. Wheelchair accessible. Closed Mondays. Admission charge. 55 Centre Ave. (phone: 599-5515). Subway exit: St. Patrick.

R. C. Harris Water Filtration Plant – In spite of its less than intriguing name, this building — which is still in operation — offers some fine examples of Art Deco design and marble work. Weekend tours only. No admission charge. At the extreme eastern end of the Beach area. Queen St. E. at Victoria Park (phone: 392-8209). Subway exit: Queen St.; then take the Neville Park Streetcar east to the end of the line.

 SHOPPING: Toronto is a good shopping city with stores carrying imported goods and native crafts — everything from Swiss chocolate to Eskimo soapstone sculpture. There's a broad selection of shopping areas as well, ranging from the exclusive *Hazelton Lanes,* which houses the biggest names in fashion and design, to *Kensington Market* (see *Special Places*). There's more to shopping here than initially meets the eye — some 1,400 shops are underground, many of them in *Eaton Centre* (see *Special Places*). Here you'll find many goods not readily found elsewhere in town, such as Scottish woolen knits, Eskimo carvings and prints, as well as the ubiquitous *Blue Jays* merchandise.

Most native Torontonians know what bargains can be found in which areas. Those looking for clothing head to the Spadina Avenue area, the established garment district, where they can find merchandise for a third of the prices charged at shops in the Bloor-Yonge area or at the chic Yorkville boutiques. Specialty items — like an authentic Chinese wok — can be tracked down along the Dundas West strip of Chinatown; funky fashions can be found in the quirky little shops that line Queen Street West; and more expensive items — from a designer suit to a new yacht — can be purchased in the smart shops of Queen's Quay Terminal.

Antiques – The ideal spot for browsing in myriad antiques-cum-kitsch shops is on Queen Street West, between University Avenue and Bathurst Street, or at the ever-popular *Harbourfront Antique Market* (390 Queen's Quay W.; phone: 340-8377), which houses hundreds of dealers purveying everything from furniture to tiny toy soldiers, under one huge roof. Scattered throughout the city are more specialized shops, such as *Hickl-Szabo Antiques and Fine Art* (66 Avenue Rd.; phone: 962-4140), which has a good selection of artwork; the *Old Lamp Shop* (1582 Queen St. E.; phone: 466-7275), with unusual old lamps and fixtures; *Lorenz Antiques* (701 Mt. Pleasant Ave.; phone: 487-2066), which has silver and china; the *Map Room* (18 Birch Ave.; phone: 922-5153) carries historical maps and globes; and *Pao & Moltke Ltd.* (21 Avenue Rd.; phone: 925-6197), which has an unusual assortment of Chinese antiques.

Art – Toronto's numerous art galleries feature everything from historic Canadian art (The Group of Seven) to popular contemporary pieces (Robert Bateman) to photojournalism (Ottmar Bierwagen). Many galleries occupy the Yorkville section; one could easily spend an entire day browsing in a dozen galleries in only a few short blocks. For some genuine Canadian pieces, visit the *Evelyn Amis Gallery* (14 Hazelton Ave.; phone: 961-0878) or *Libby's of Toronto* (463 King St. E.; phone: 364-3730), which specializes in contemporary Canadian art. *Marci Lipman Graphics* (231 Avenue Rd.; phone: 922-7061) has an extensive collection of prints and posters. Both the *Marianne Friedland Gallery* (122 Scollard St.; phone: 961-4900) and the *Mira Godard Gallery* (22

Hazelton Ave.; phone: 964-8179) are preeminent in the city. Also noteworthy are *Moos* (136 Yorkville Ave.; phone: 922-0627) and *Nancy Poole's Studio* (16 Hazelton Ave.; phone: 964-9050). And there are a number of good galleries under one roof at 80 Spadina Avenue. Those interested in photography should visit the *Jane Corkin Gallery* (179 John St.; phone: 979-1980), which features both historical and modern works.

Books, Magazines, and Newspapers – *Abelard Books* (89 Harbord St.; phone: 960-9076) carries first editions; *Britnell's* (765 Yonge St.; phone: 924-3321) stocks hard-to-find titles; and *Old Favourites* (250 Adelaide St. W.; phone: 977-2944) has the city's largest collection of old and rare tomes. Science fiction buffs should visit *Bakku Science Fiction Book Shoppe* (282 Queen St. W.; phone: 596-8161); those looking for how-to books should go to the nearby *Can-Do Bookstore* (311 Queen St. W.; phone: 977-2351). *Coles, The World's Biggest Bookstore* (20 Edward St.; phone: 977-7009) lives up to its name: You can find just about any book on its rows and rows of shelves. For art books, try *David Mirvish Books on Art* (596 Markham St.; phone: 531-9975) or *Edwards Books and Art* (356 Queen St. W.; phone: 596-0126). *Gulliver's Travel Bookshop* (609 Bloor St. W.; phone: 537-7700) should satisfy those touched by wanderlust; the *Longhouse Bookstore* (497 Bloor St. W.; phone: 921-9995) specializes in Canadian subjects and authors; and *Theatrebooks* (25 Bloor St. W.; phone: 922-7175) carries a vast range of books dealing with the world of drama.

The *Book Cellar* (142 Yorkville Ave.; phone: 925-9955) and the nearby *Maison de la Presse Internationale* (124 Yorkville Ave.; phone: 928-0418) are both good spots for international newspapers and magazines. The best-known shop of this kind is the *Lichtman's News and Books* chain, whose main store is at Yonge and Richmond Sts. (phone: 368-7390).

China, Crystal, and Silver – *Ashley China* (50 Bloor St. W.; phone: 964-2900) carries the finest and most distinctive English bone china dinnerware, as well as a huge selection of the best silver, crystal, and china tableware, all greatly discounted. *Georg Jensen* (90A Bloor St. W.; phone: 924-7707) features fine and costly silver and stainless-steel table settings, jewelry, and some furniture. The *Irish Import House* (444 Yonge St. W.; phone: 595-0500) offers a 15% discount on Waterford and Belleek and also sells tweeds, linens, and other Irish goods at lower-than-usual prices.

Chocolate – Swiss chocolates are air-expressed weekly from Zurich to *Teuscher Switzerland* in *Hazelton Lanes* at 55 Avenue Rd. (phone: 961-1303).

Cigars – *Winston & Holmes* is Toronto's foremost tobacconist. Cuban cigars are on hand at several locations (including 138 Cumberland St.; phone: 968-1290). Another recommended smokeshop is *Havana House* (in *Hazelton Lanes* at 55 Avenue Rd.; phone: 927-9070; and across the street, at 30 Avenue Rd.; phone: 927-7703). *Tobacco Haven* (595 Bay St.; phone: 593-6655) has a wide selection of pipes and a walk-in humidor.

Clothing – Bloor Street is the Toronto equivalent of New York's Fifth Avenue; several of its shops offer sophisticated fashions, including *Holt Renfrew & Co.* (50 Bloor St. W.; phone: 922-2333). Also on Bloor are *Harry Rosen* (80 Bloor St. W.; phone: 972-0556), one of a chain of men's stores with good taste and high — but not outrageous — prices; and *David's* (Bloor St. at Bay St.; phone: 920-1000) for pricey purses and costly women's shoes. *Hazelton Lanes* features many shops with distinctive apparel, including *Chez Catherine* (20A *Hazelton Lanes;* phone: 967-5666). For gritty chic, check out the stores on Queen Street West; for suburban trendiness head for Yonge Street North. Some stores to explore: *Ms. Emma Designs* (274 Queen St. W.; phone: 598-2472), which features stylish, comfortable clothes made from fine silk, cotton, wool, and linen; *Mr. Mann, Tailor and Shirtmaker* (41 Avenue Rd.; phone: 968-2022), for expensive men's attire; *Madelaine Children's Fashions* (106 Yorkville Ave.; phone: 968-2022) for practical children's clothes; and *Tilley Endurables* (207

Queen's Quay W.; phone: 865-9910) for original clothing designed with sportsfolk and travelers in mind.

Crafts – The *Guild Shop* (140 Cumberland St.; phone: 921-1721) is a nonprofit retail outlet for Canadian craftspeople. Returning US residents do not have to pay duty on original works of Inuit art. The *Pottery Shop* (140 Yorkville Ave.; phone: 923-1803) specializes in hand-crafted clay and glass pieces. *Natara's Collection* (1396 Yonge St.; phone: 928-0846) has hand-finished lace. *Yonge at Art* (Scadding House, 6 Trinity Sq., next to *Eaton Centre;* phone: 598-0245) offers reasonably priced goods, including jewelry and toys, hand-crafted by Canadians; the shop is run by the *Inner City Angels,* and proceeds support their charity programs.

Eskimo Art – The *Eskimo Art Gallery* (458 Queen's Quay W.; phone: 591-9004) displays hundreds of native sculptures from the northern reaches of Canada. The *Inuit Gallery of Eskimo Art* (9 Prince Arthur Ave.; phone: 921-9985) features primitive Eskimo carvings, sculptures, prints, and wall hangings, and *Kiva Arts* (52 McCaul St.; phone: 971-5176) has native works from all over North America.

Furs – The Spadina Avenue garment district — where most of the city's retail furriers are located — is the best place for comparison shopping. In the Balfour Building alone (119 Spadina Ave.), there are dozens of showrooms and specialty shops, such as *Aristotelis Creation* (phone: 598-4511), which specializes in fur hats. Also in the area are *Alaska Furs* (116 Spadina Ave.; phone: 967-1115), *Class Furs Company 89* (383 Adelaide St. W.; phone: 360-6568), *Green Brothers Fur Manufacturing* (332 Richmond St. W.; phone: 593-8860), and *Paul Magder Furs* (202 Spadina Ave.; phone: 363-6077), one of the most prominent furriers in town. There are other worthwhile emporia throughout the city — try *Eaton's Fur Salon* (in *Eaton Centre;* phone: 343-2111) or the upscale *Alan Cherry* (33 Avenue Rd.; phone: 967-1115) — but the garment district has far and away the best prices.

Jewelry – Both casual shoppers and connoisseurs call at the *Gold Shoppe* (25 Bloor St. W.; phone: 923-5565) for antique jewelry and silver. *European Jewellery* (390 Bay St.; phone: 369-0009; and 111 Bloor St. W.; phone: 967-7201) features elegant and distinctive pieces. *Fraleigh Jewellery & Gemologists* in the *Four Seasons Toronto* hotel (21 Avenue Rd.; phone: 924-2296) and at other locations has estate and antique jewelry; *Wendy Portman Fine Jewellery* (at the *Inter-Continental Hotel,* 220 Bloor St. W.; phone: 920-7676) sells contemporary and estate jewelry. For handmade jewelry, *Skin and Bones* (180 Queen St. W.; phone: 599-0216) has a good selection of native items, while master craftsman Richard Booth, whose creations are on display at 138 Cumberland St. (phone: 960-3207), custom-designs pieces for his clients.

Leather Goods – A good range of quality and styles can be found in any *Danier Leather and Suede* store, in several locations throughout the city including *Eaton Centre* (phone: 979-3131) and their factory outlet (365 Weston Rd.; phone: 762-6631). Another good place is the aptly named *Half Price Leather* (116 Spadina Ave.; phone: 360-4276). *Lanzi of Italy* (123 Yorkville Ave.; phone: 964-2582) and *Hermès* (in *Hazelton Lanes* at 55 Avenue Rd.; phone: 968-8626) carry leather accessories. Home-made moccasins can be had at the *Algonquins* (670 Queen St. W.; phone: 368-1336); leather garments and cowboy boots are sold at *Leather Image* (617 Yonge St.; phone: 922-9657); rugged Australian-style items can be found at the *Outback* (60 Bloor St. W.; phone: 923-7048); and funky leather and suede fashions are at *Zanelle's* (288 Queen St. W.; phone: 593-0776).

Records, Tapes, and Compact Discs – The "Big Three" are *HMV* (333 Yonge St.; phone: 596-0333); *Sam the Record Man* (347 Yonge St.; no phone); and *A & A* (351 Yonge St.; no phone).

Wool – Woolen fashions and yarn can be found at *Icelandia* (134 Cumberland Ave.; phone: 927-9317). *Norma* (116 Cumberland Ave.; phone: 923-5514) carries pure wool sweaters, jackets, and suits by Canadian designer Norma Lepofsky. For Scottish woolens and knits, the best place is *Richardson's Tartan Shop* (546 Yonge St.; phone: 922-3141).

 SPORTS: Toronto is the home of baseball's American League *Blue Jays,* the National Hockey League *Maple Leafs,* and the Canadian Football League *Argonauts.* The Metro Parks Department maintains good facilities around the city for participatory sports.

Baseball – The *SkyDome* is home base for the Toronto *Blue Jays,* 277 Front St. W. (phone: 595-0077 or 341-1111).

Bicycling – There are some excellent bike paths around the Toronto parks. For folks who are really keen on biking, check *The Great Toronto Bicycling Guide,* by Elliot Kats (Great North Books; $3.95), which describes many of them. *Boardwalk Cycle* (748 Markham Rd.; phone: 431-1961) provides the wheels.

Football – The *Argonauts,* members of the Canadian Football League, play from June until early November at the *SkyDome* (phone: 595-1131 or 341-3663).

Golf – There are many pay-as-you-play courses in and around Toronto. *Lakeview* golf course (1190 Dixie Rd., three-quarters of a mile/1 km south of Queen Elizabeth Way; phone: 278-4411) is a good, narrow 18-hole course with pro shop, lockers, showers, and a snack bar. *Don Valley* golf course (4200 Yonge St., south of Hwy. 401; phone: 392-2465), a difficult municipal layout 6½ miles (10 km) from the center of downtown, has the Don River as its main hazard. This winding brook traverses the course and comes into play on at least 11 holes. *Glen Abbey* golf course (1333 Dorval Dr., Oakville, Ontario; phone: 844-1800) is the critic's choice. Designed by Jack Nicklaus, it hosts the annual *Canadian Open.* Weekend green fees are around $100 per day (cart included).

Hockey – Hockey in Toronto means large crowds every time the *Maple Leafs* defend their home ice at *Maple Leaf Gardens.* Since 1927, when the team was established, the *Leafs* have won the *Stanley Cup,* the symbol of hockey supremacy, 11 times — a record second only to that of the Montreal *Canadiens.* Tickets for *Leaf* games are not as hard to come by as they used to be; just head to the *Gardens* (60 Carlton St.; phone: 977-1641). Toronto is home to two of the top collegiate hockey teams in the country. For ticket information contact the University of Toronto (phone: 978-2011) and York University (phone: 736-2100).

Horse Racing – At *Greenwood Race Track* (1669 Queen St. E.; phone: 698-3131), thoroughbreds and standardbreds take turns on the turf. There's an enclosed grandstand and dining room. *Woodbine Race Track* (Rexdale Blvd. at Hwy. 27; phone: 675-6110) is exclusively for thoroughbred racing. Every July it is the scene of the *Queen's Plate* — the oldest continuously run stake event in North America (132 years), and the highlight of the Canadian racing season for Canadian-bred 3-year-olds. A member of Britain's royal family usually officiates during the racing ceremonies.

Jogging – In downtown Toronto, City Hall has a jogging track. In central Toronto, jog at the University of Toronto or Queens Park. The Martin Goodman Trail along the harborfront is also pleasant, as are the stretches of wooded green cutting through the city along the Humber and Don rivers.

Sailing – Boating enthusiasts have several options in the area. At Bluffer's Park Marina, located in the northeastern suburb of Scarborough, certified instructors offer lessons for all levels of sailors; they also rent sailboat and fishing vessels (7 Brimley Rd. S., Scarborough; phone: 266-7808). The *Harbourside Sailing School,* in the *Harbourfront Nautical Centre,* also provides instruction and boat rentals (275 Queen's Quay W.; phone: 947-0333). A bit farther afield, about 60 miles (275 km) northwest of the city, lie the Georgian Bay and the North Channel, which rank among the world's best areas for cruising; 25- to 35-foot sailboats are available for charter. For more information, contact *Ontario Travel* (Queen's Park; phone: 965-4008 or 800-ONTARIO) or *Ontario Sailing Association* (1220 Sheppard Ave. E., Willowdale; phone: 495-4240).

Skiing – Cross-country skiing is a way of life in Toronto, and you can do it around the Toronto islands or along the greenbelted ravines that run through the city from downtown to the *Ontario Science Centre.* Rental equipment is available at *Rudy's Sport Centre Ltd.* (1055 Eglinton Ave. W.; phone: 781-9196). The downhill picture right around the city is rather bleak — just some overcrowded mini-hills. The Collingwood area, 90 miles (144 km) north of Toronto, has the closest ski resorts, including Blue Mountain (6½ miles/11 km west of Collingwood on Blue Mt. Rd.; phone: 705-445-0231), which has 15 lifts and 29 trails.

Tennis – The Metro Parks Department (phone: 392-8184) maintains public courts in at least two parks, but the best courts are in private clubs, like the *Toronto Lawn Tennis Club,* to which you must be invited by a member. Hanlan's Point, one of the Toronto islands, has good public courts, as does Ramsden Park on Yonge Street. The *Player's Limited International Championships,* held in Toronto each summer, alternate between men's and women's events (men's tournaments are held in even-numbered years; women's in odd-numbered years). For information call 667-9777.

 THEATER: For complete listings of current performances, check the publications listed above. Toronto has a large variety of theatrical offerings, ranging from its own repertory groups to stagings of London shows by English performers. An organization called *5 Star Tickets* (phone: 596-8211) sells half-price tickets to events staged by selected professional performing arts companies on the day of performance (tickets to out-of-town events are available the day before the performance). Outside *Eaton Centre* (at Yonge and Dundas Sts.), open daily, cash only; or at *Eaton Centre* itself.

Among the most prominent of the city's more than 44 theatrical venues is the *O'Keefe Centre* (Front and Yonge Sts.; phone: 872-2262), home of the the *National Ballet of Canada,* where classical ballet and experimental contemporary works meet. The company (157 King St. E.; phone: 362-1041) is under the command of its first Canadian-born artistic director, Reid Anderson. Homegrown talent has included such dancers as Karin Kain, Veronica Tennant, Rex Harrington, and Peter Ottman. In summer the company performs at the *Ontario Place Forum* (955 Lakeshore Blvd. W.; phone: 314-9900). The *Royal Alexandra Theatre* (260 King St. W.; phone: 593-4211), called the "Royal Alex," is the place to go for Broadway, West End, and local productions; the wildly popular *Phantom of the Opera* has been playing at the *Pantages Theatre* (263 Yonge St.; phone: 362-3216) for years now. Other notable venues are the *Elgin and Winter Garden* (189 Yonge St.; phone: 968-0455), a fully restored historic theater; and the *St. Lawrence Centre for the Performing Arts* (27 Front St. E.; phone: 366-7723), for Toronto repertory groups. *Second City,* Canada's version of "Saturday Night Live" (alumni include John Candy and Rick Moranis), presents a satirical revue in a nightclub-supperclub setting at the *Old Fire Hall* (110 Lombard St.; phone: 863-1111). The *Tarragon Theatre* (30 Bridgman Ave.; phone: 531-1827) stages new Canadian plays.

For 6 weeks every summer, the *Canadian Stage Company* (*Toronto Theatre Alliance;* phone: 536-6468) presents *The Dream in High Park,* a production of a Shakespearean classic (usually *A Midsummer Night's Dream*) under the stars in a natural amphitheater of grassy slopes and trees in High Park, the city's largest recreation area. And the *Canadian Opera Company* (227 Front St. E.; phone: 363-6671) mounts a number of interesting works. Dinner theater is popular at such places as *Limelight* (2026 Yonge St.; phone: 929-9283); *Stage West* in nearby Mississauga (5400 Dixie Rd.; phone:

238-0042); *Harper's* (26 Lombard St.; phone: 863-6223); and *His Majesty's Feast* (1926 Lakeshore Blvd. W.; phone: 769-2621), a musical comedy set in King Henry VIII's time, accompanied by a lavish, period-style banquet.

. Two major theater festivals, focusing on the works of Shakespeare and Shaw, are held annually at theater centers within 2 hours of the city. The *Stratford Shakespeare Festival,* in Stratford, Ontario, 98 miles (157 km) southwest of Toronto, is one of the foremost theater centers in Canada. The main *Festival* theater performs Shakespeare's masterpieces, as well as other productions; two smaller stages — the *Avon* and the *Third* stage — present a variety of plays. The festival usually runs from May through mid-November. The *Visitors' Guide to Stratford* lists attractions, accommodations, and facilities and is available from the *Stratford Shakespeare Festival,* PO Box 520, Stratford, Ontario N5A 6V2 (or for more information, call the Toronto box office at 364-8355).

The *Shaw Festival* is presented by one of the few professional theater companies concentrating mainly on the works of George Bernard Shaw and his contemporaries. The plays are supplemented with concerts, seminars, lectures, and exhibits, all in a country setting at Niagara-on-the-Lake, 82 miles (131 km) from Toronto. The festival runs from late April through October. For information, contact the *Shaw Festival Theatre,* 200 Picton St., Box 774, Niagara-on-the-Lake, Ontario L0S 1J0 (phone: 468-2172 or 361-1544 for the Toronto box office).

 MUSIC: The *Toronto Symphony* performs in the *Roy Thomson Hall* (60 Simcoe St.; phone: 593-4828). Musical performances are also given in the Edward Johnson Building by the University of Toronto music faculty (phone: 978-3744), and at Convocation Hall, also on campus (phone: 978-2100); the *Ontario Place Forum* (955 Lakeshore Blvd. W.; phone: 314-9900); and in Nathan Phillips Square, downtown (phone: 392-7341). Classical concerts also are performed in the city's churches and schools.

 NIGHTCLUBS AND NIGHTLIFE: The city has a growing number of nightspots catering to every taste. *Bamboo* (312 Queen St. W.; phone: 593-5771) serves Thai food from noon to closing and features live reggae, salsa, and Latin music for dancing. *Berlin* (2335 Yonge St.; phone: 489-7777) combines dining and dancing, with music that ranges from salsa to Top 40 hits. The largest and liveliest discos are the *Copa* (21 Scollard St.; phone: 922-6500), *RPM* (132 Queen's Quay E.; phone: 869-1462), the *Big Bop* (651 Queen St. W.; phone: 366-6699), and *Spectrum* (2714 Danforth Ave.; phone: 699-9913). *Celebrities* (in the *Harbour Castle Westin,* 1 Harbour Sq.; phone: 869-1600) is another disco. *Beaton's* (in the *Westbury/Howard Johnson Plaza* hotel, 475 Yonge St.; phone: 924-0611) is a chic lounge and bar. The city's most impressive supper club is the *Imperial Room* (in the *Royal York* hotel, 100 Front St. W.; phone: 368-6175), where top-name entertainers perform (reservations necessary). *Barrister's Bar* (in the *Hilton International,* 145 Richmond St. W.; phone: 869-3456) is a quiet, elegant library lounge. The trendiest nightclub in which to see and be seen, however, remains *Stillife* (217 Richmond St. W.; phone: 593-6116).

Queen Street West, where such groups as *Blue Rodeo* and the *Cowboy Junkies* got their start, is the place to look for many different styles of contemporary music. Raucous performances take place at the *Black Bull* (298 Queen St. W.; phone: 593-2766) and the classic *Horseshoe Tavern* (368 Queen St. W.; phone: 598-4753). *Downtown Browne's* has the blues (49 Front St. E; phone: 367-4949), as does *Grossman's* (379 Spadina Ave.; phone: 977-7000), a down-home tavern that also features jazz. Also for jazz aficionados, there's *Chick 'N' Deli* (744 Mt. Pleasant Ave.; phone: 489-3363); *Café des Copains* (48 Wellington St. E.; phone: 869-0148); *Top O' the Senator* (253 Victoria St.; phone: 364-7517); and the *Bermuda Onion* (131 Bloor St. W.; phone: 925-1470).

Try the piano bar, *George's,* at *Bigliardi's* restaurant and mingle with hockey players after a game (463 Church St.; phone: 922-9594). *Sparkles* is a nightclub located two-thirds of the way up the CN Tower (301 Front St. W.; phone: 362-5411). Since 1977, when the *Rolling Stones* recorded at *El Mocambo* (464 Spadina Ave.; phone: 961-2558), it has been *the* place for rock in Canada. The *Lounge* at the *King Edward* hotel is a popular meeting spot (37 King St. E.; phone: 863-9700).

BEST IN TOWN

 CHECKING IN: Toronto has a proliferation of hotels to accommodate its large numbers of visitors. Even so, reservations are recommended. Choices can be made from a very wide selection. The *Hotel Association of Metropolitan Toronto* offers information about room availability and makes reservations free of charge (phone: 629-7770).

For travelers who prefer alternatives to the standard lodgings, *Executive Travel Apartments* provides fully equipped apartment units — ranging from simple studios to 3-bedroom setups — in various locations throughout the city. Some units are in modern high-rises, while others can be found in Victorian houses in more residential neighborhoods. All of the apartments are fully furnished, with full bath and kitchen. Information: *Executive Travel Apartments,* 40 St. Mary St., Toronto, Ontario, Canada M4Y 2S8 (phone: 923-1000).

Another, less expensive option is a bed and breakfast establishment. The Metro Toronto Convention and Visitors Association (phone: 368-9990) provides a complete list. One good choice is the *Hotel Association of Metropolitan Toronto* (phone: 629-7770), which offers 23 host houses, many of them refurbished Victorian homes. Most of them feature clean, large bedrooms and hearty, homemade breakfasts. In addition, most hosts can keep you apprised of what's happening around town better than any hotel concierge. Other agencies providing bed and breakfast accommodations are *Toronto Bed and Breakfast* (phone: 588-8800) and *Bed and Breakfast Accommodators* (phone: 461-7095).

Expect to pay $130 and up for a double room in the places listed as expensive; from $95 to $125 in the moderate range; and under $90 in the inexpensive category. All telephone numbers are in the 416 area code unless otherwise indicated.

Four Seasons Inn on the Park – Within 30 minutes of downtown, this "resort" on 600 acres of parkland has 568 luxurious rooms (half of them for nonsmokers), a 24-hour concierge and room service, 5 restaurants, 2 lounges, and meeting facilities for over 2,000. For those bent on fitness, there is a health club, tennis, indoor and outdoor pools, toboggans, cross-country skis, and bicycles. There also are supervised children's programs. 1100 Eglinton Ave. E. (phone: 444-2561 or 800-332-3442 in the US; fax: 446-3308). Expensive.

Four Seasons Toronto – Nicely positioned right in the heart of Yorkville, a colorful area of boutiques, galleries, sidewalk cafés, and clubs, it has 381 beautifully appointed rooms and suites. Special touches include a 24-hour concierge and room service, a health club, an indoor-outdoor pool, and a multilingual staff. There's good French dining in *Truffles* (see *Eating Out*) and continental dishes in *Le Café,* while *La Serre,* the hotel's cocktail lounge, is a nice choice for lunch. 21 Avenue Rd. (phone: 964-0411 or 800-332-3442 in the US; fax: 964-2301). Expensive.

L'Hôtel – A first class business property next to the CN Tower, it has 600 rooms and suites in a variety of styles — some specially designed for handicapped guests. Entrée Gold, the super-service-oriented "hotel within the hotel" on the eighth and ninth floors, provides separate check-in and checkout facilities, complete concierge services, continental breakfast, limousine service, cocktails, hors d'oeuvres, and complimentary local phone calls and newspapers. *Chanterelles* offers nouvelle cuisine (see *Eating Out*), and the *Orchard Café* serves continental food; for lighter fare try one of the lounges, the *Skylight,* or *Le Bar.* Other facilities include a heated pool, a whirlpool bath, saunas, squash courts, and an exercise room. 225 Front St. W. (phone: 597-1400 or 800-828-7447 in the US; fax: 597-8128). Expensive.

Inter-Continental – One of the, if not *the,* most luxurious of Toronto's lodging establishments, with 213 elegantly appointed rooms and a courtyard restaurant serving continental and French food. Its fitness center has a pool and a sauna. Within walking distance of downtown. 220 Bloor St. W. (phone: 960-5200 or 800-327-0200 in the US; fax: 960-8269). Expensive.

King Edward – Warmly referred to by locals as "the King Eddy," this place is everything a first class establishment should be — from the elegant marble-columned lobby to the spacious and tastefully furnished rooms. Its *Lounge Bar* has greeted Rockefellers and royalty; former British Prime Minister Margaret Thatcher even made her own tea in the Royal Suite. The *Café Victoria* is fine for breakfast or pre-theater dining; lunch and dinner are served at *Chiaro's.* 37 King St. E. (phone: 863-9700 or 800-225-5843 in the US; fax: 863-5232). Expensive.

Park Plaza – Situated at the crossroads of Toronto chic — Avenue Road and Bloor Street — this landmark property, now renovated, was built in the 1930s. The *Prince Arthur Lounge* has soft piano music and an intimate atmosphere as well as good food. The *Prince Arthur Dining Room* serves continental fare, as does the *Roof,* which has a spectacular view of Toronto and the islands. Banquets and professional conferences are held in the *Ballroom.* 4 Avenue Rd. (phone: 924-5471 or 800-268-4927 in the US; fax: 924-4933). Expensive.

Ramada Renaissance on Bloor – This property (formerly the *Plaza II* hotel) features 256 rooms and 18 suites, all with double beds. There's 24-hour room service and complimentary use of the squash, gym, and pool facilities of the exclusive *Bloor Park Club,* located in the same building. The glass-enclosed dining room serves good continental fare, while the lobby-level cocktail lounge offers afternoon tea. 90 Bloor St. E. (phone: 961-8000 or 800-2-RAMADA in the US; fax: 961-9581). Expensive.

SkyDome – The lodging of choice for sports aficionados — 70 of the hotel's 346 large rooms look out on the game field of the *SkyDome,* where baseball's *Blue Jays* and football's *Argonauts* play (even so, it's probably better to have an actual seat in the stadium). Each room has a mini-bar; other pluses: a state-of-the-art fitness center and a private billiards room. Its chief draw, however, continues to be the novelty of its location. Several restaurants are on the premises, including the trendy *Hard Rock Café* (see *Eating Out*), which overlooks the playing field. 45 Peter St. S. (phone: 360-7100 or 800-828-7447 in the US; fax: 341-5090). Expensive.

Sutton Place – A member of the Leading Hotels of the World group, this 280-unit property has attracted such celebrities as Al Pacino, Faye Dunaway, Paul Newman, and Kim Basinger. Guests who seek extra-special service stay in Regency Floor suites, where 24-hour butler service is provided. All guests have access to the exercise, business, and banquet facilities. Visit *Alexandra's Piano Bar,* the hotel's chic lunch spot, filled with photos of stars who have eaten there. 955 Bay St. (phone: 924-9221 or 800-268-3790 in the US; fax: 924-1778). Expensive.

Swissôtel Toronto – Located in the Trillium Terminal 3 at the international airport, this $57-million establishment has 494 rooms decorated in neo-classical style. There is a café, a lounge, and a Mediterranean-style restaurant. The sports and fitness center features a workout room, steamrooms and saunas, a swimming pool, and a whirlpool bath. At Pearson International Airport (phone: 672-7000 or 800-63-SWISS in the US; fax: 672-0889). Expensive.

Toronto Airport Marriott – This 423-room property is just 5 minutes from the airport and 20 minutes from downtown Toronto. For dining and entertainment, try the *Mikado,* a Japanese steakhouse/seafood restaurant with teppanyaki-style display cooking. The *Terrace* is a large café, and *Toucans* is an entertainment lounge. For recreation, an indoor swimming pool, a hydrotherapy pool, a weight room, and saunas are provided. 901 Dixon Rd. (phone: 674-9400 or 800-228-9290 in the US; fax: 674-8292). Expensive.

Toronto Marriott/Eaton Centre – Located in the heart of downtown, adjacent to the *Eaton Centre* complex, this new, 459-room property overlooks the 17th-century Holy Trinity Church, one of the city's oldest buildings. Several of the latest video releases are available on the color TV set in each room; there's also 24-hour room service. Also on the premises are an indoor swimming pool, a health club, and 2 restaurants — the family-oriented *Parkside* and the more upscale *J. W. Seagrills.* 525 Bay St. (phone: 597-9200 or 800-228-9290 in the US; fax: 597-9211). Expensive.

Westin Harbour Castle – This sleek twin-towered structure dominates the Toronto waterfront. Its architecture is well integrated with its surroundings, creating a luxurious and comfortable atmosphere. Its revolving *Lighthouse* restaurant affords diners panoramic views of the area, and all 978 rooms have vistas of either Lake Ontario and the islands or the city skyline. The health club has an indoor swimming pool, a whirlpool bath, a sauna, a steamroom, a gym, squash courts, and an outdoor track specially equipped to melt snow. In addition to the *Lighthouse,* the *Châteauneuf* restaurant serves French fare (see *Eating Out*), the *Poseidon* has seafood, and there are 3 lobby lounges. Free shuttle bus service between the hotel and *Eaton Centre,* City Hall, and other downtown locations. 1 Harbour Sq. (phone: 869-1600 or 800-228-3000 in the US; fax: 869-0573). Expensive.

Bradgate Arms – Ensconced in a residential downtown neighborhood, this stately hideaway has 109 rooms — all characterized by idiosyncrasies in design and decor, owing to the establishment's former incarnation as two apartment buildings. Each guestroom has a mini-refrigerator and a wet bar. The style is Old World elegance reminiscent of New York's famed *Algonquin* hotel. The restaurant, *Avenues,* boasts a formidable wine list (see *Eating Out*). 54 Foxbar Ave. (phone: 968-1331 or 800-268-7171 in the US; fax: 968-3743). Expensive to moderate.

Chestnut Park – Set just behind City Hall, on the fringes of Chinatown, and right next to the *Museum of Textiles,* this 518-room addition to the Best Western chain has a swimming pool, sauna, health club, baby-sitting service, 24-hour room service, and 8 nonsmoking floors. The restaurant, *Tapestry's,* features rare Oriental pieces from the owner's private collection (see *Eating Out*). 108 Chestnut St. (phone: 977-5000 or 800-334-8484 in the US; fax: 599-3317). Expensive to moderate.

Hilton International – This striking Canadian showpiece has 601 large, lovely rooms and is conveniently located downtown near theaters, shopping, and most of the major office buildings. There's a good selection of restaurants on the premises: The *Garden Court* has complete meals or light fare; *La Cour* has fine dining; *Trader Vic's* has Polynesian drinks and food; and *Barrister's Bar* has hearty snacks and nightly entertainment. There is a sauna and indoor and outdoor pools. 145 Richmond St. W. (phone: 869-3456 or 800-HILTONS in the US; fax: 869-3187). Expensive to moderate.

Holiday Inn on King – Conveniently located, this establishment is frequented by many business travelers who deal with the garment district on nearby Spadina Avenue. There are 425 guestrooms, 25 well-appointed suites, and an Art Deco–

style eatery called *Judy's,* whose patio serves as the venue for a popular summer luncheon buffet. Other amenities include an outdoor pool, an exercise room, a sauna, and massage facilities. 370 King St. W. (phone: 599-4000 or 800-HOLIDAY in the US; fax: 599-7394). Expensive to moderate.

Novotel Toronto Centre – Perfect for a weekend at the theater, this 266-room hotel surrounded by restaurants, bars, and sidewalk cafés is close to *O'Keefe Centre* and several other venues along Front Street. Don't be put off by its grim, gray exterior: The accommodations are bright and cheerful. The property includes a pool, a sauna, a whirlpool bath, and a health club, plus the European-style *Café Nicole.* Children under 16 — who stay for free when accompanied by a parent — receive a complimentary full buffet breakfast (a maximum of 2 children per family). 45 The Esplanade (phone: 367-8900 or 800-221-4542 in the US; fax: 360-8285). Expensive to moderate.

Prince – In the northern section of town, this 406-unit hotel provides easy access to such attractions as the *Ontario Science Centre, Canada's Wonderland,* and the Metro Toronto Zoo. It has a resort ambience, with a swimming pool, a health club, a sauna, 24-hour room service, and 3 outdoor clay-surface tennis courts. Among its dining rooms are *Katsura* — one of Toronto's finest Japanese restaurants (see *Eating Out*) — and *Le Continental;* the hotel lounge features nightly live entertainment. 900 York Mills Rd., North York (phone: 444-2511 or 800-542-8686 in the US; fax: 444-9597). Expensive to moderate.

Radisson Plaza Hotel Admiral – This lovely 157-unit place is right on the harbor; each of its 17 suites (and almost every guestroom) overlooks the water. The fourth-floor outdoor pool offers a panoramic vista of the Toronto islands and a relaxing Jacuzzi. The romantic *Commodore* dining room serves a memorable beef tenderloin (see *Eating Out*). 249 Queen's Quay W. (phone: 364-5444 or 800-387-1626 in the US; fax: 364-2975). Expensive to moderate.

Royal York – With 1,408 fully renovated guestrooms, this grande dame has been a landmark since it was built in 1929. While its rooms may be a trifle cramped, its service facilities still remain among the best in Canada. Host to royalty, prime ministers, and visiting celebrities, it also has 2 floors for conventions. The *Imperial Room* offers dinner and dancing. There is an underground gallery of stores, airline offices (airport buses are at the west door of the hotel), and restaurants such as the *Acadian Room, Dick Turpin's,* and *Benihana of Tokyo.* 100 Front St. W. (phone: 368-2511 or 800-828-7447 in the US; fax: 368-2884). Expensive to moderate.

Sheraton Centre – A city within a city, this landmark recently spruced up its 1,400 rooms, the main ballroom, and meeting areas, spending $47 million. Most of the "city" remains untouched, though, with a waterfall cascading 3 stories into the lobby, gardens and paths on the grounds, over 60 stores and boutiques, 2 theaters, and 18 restaurants and lounges, including the *Winter Palace* (see *Eating Out*). This is also home to *Good Queen Bess,* an intimate English pub literally shipped from Great Britain. The square shape of the hotel contrasts nicely with the curved structure of City Hall, to which it is linked by a footbridge. There is a sauna and an indoor-outdoor pool. 123 Queen St. W. (phone: 361-1000 or 800-325-3535 in the US; fax: 947-4854). Expensive to moderate.

Brownstone – Located on a pleasant street just 1 block from Yorkville and the shops on Bloor Street, this cozy hotel has 108 rooms. It offers 24-hour room service, a mini-bar in each room, and a complimentary newspaper every morning. There's also an intimate piano bar–restaurant, *Pralines;* for night owls, the *Chez Cappuccino* sidewalk café is just steps away (see *Eating Out*). 15 Charles St. E. (phone: 924-7381 or 800-387-8833 in the US; fax: 924-7929). Moderate.

Downtown Holiday Inn – This link in the popular chain has 717 recently renovated guestrooms. Just steps away from some of the best restaurants in Chinatown, on the premises are *Dewey Secombe,* an attractive lounge, and *Chestnut Tree,* a good eatery that serves breakfast, lunch, and dinner. There are also indoor and outdoor pools, a sauna, and a small health club. 89 Chestnut St. (phone: 977-0707 or 800-HOLIDAY in the US; fax: 977-1136). Moderate.

Westbury/Howard Johnson Plaza – These twin towers house 545 spacious, recently refurbished rooms. Each room has a color TV set that offers up to 20 of the latest video releases. *Beaton's Lounge* is open for nightly entertainment, Mondays through Saturdays, and the round-the-clock coffee shop offers light fare. 475 Yonge St. (phone: 924-0611 or 800-654-2000 in the US; fax: 924-5061). Moderate.

Bond Place – Just a block from *Eaton Centre* and near the *Pantages,* the *Elgin,* and *Winter Garden* theaters, this hotel has 286 small but functional rooms. The service is prompt and friendly, and the hotel recently refurbished its interior with a modern decor. There is a good restaurant and a cheery lounge, as well as a health club, a pool, and a sauna. Fifty-one of the units feature a queen-size bed plus a pullout couch, ideal for families. 65 Dundas St. E. (phone: 362-6061 or 800-268-9390 in the US; fax: 360-6406). Moderate to inexpensive.

Delta Chelsea Inn – An ideal place for families because some of the rooms have kitchen facilities. Renovations and expansions have made this Canada's largest hotel, with 1,586 rooms. The property is conveniently located just 2 blocks north of *Eaton Centre.* There are 2 good restaurants (with special children's menus; children under 6 eat free), a lounge, a health club, a sauna, pre-arranged free day-care in the children's creative center, and an indoor pool. 33 Gerrard St. W. (phone: 595-1975 or 800-877-1133 in the US; fax: 585-4362). Moderate to inexpensive.

Journey's End – As with all the links in this hotel chain, here are guestrooms at very reasonable prices. Amenities at most locations include fax and photocopy facilities, in-room movies, on-site parking, and a no-frills coffee shop. Children 16 years of age and under stay for free when accompanied by a parent; pets are allowed in most locations. Several locations in Toronto: Downtown, at 111 Lombard St. (phone: 367-5555; fax: 367-3470); North York, at 66 Norfinch Dr. (phone/fax: 736-4700); Bloor Street, at 280 Bloor St. W. (phone: 968-0010; fax: 968-7765); airport vicinity, at 262 Carlingview Dr. (phone: 674-8442; fax: 674-3088); and east of the airport, at 2180 Islington Ave. (phone: 240-9090 or 800-668-4200 in the US; fax: 240-9944). Moderate to inexpensive.

Primrose – The 320 guestrooms in this recent addition to the Best Western chain are surprisingly well appointed for their price range. *Café Vienna,* the dining room, offers good, solid fare; also on the premises are an outdoor pool and a sauna. There are 6 nonsmoking floors. 111 Carlton St. (phone: 977-8000 or 800-334-8484 in the US; fax: 977-6323). Moderate to inexpensive.

Victoria – Another recent Best Western acquisition, this small, 48-room property is right across the street from the famed *Shopsy's* deli (see *Eating Out*) and around the corner from the *O'Keefe Centre.* Commonly referred to as "the Old Vic," it offers few amenities save good, clean rooms, affordable rates, and a popular restaurant called the *56 Yonge* (see *Eating Out*), which serves fresh seafood and produce from nearby *St. Lawrence Market.* 56 Yonge St. (phone: 363-1666 or 800-334-8484 in the US; fax: 363-7327). Moderate to inexpensive.

Carlton Inn – This establishment is right next door to *Maple Leaf Gardens.* Most of the 536 modern rooms have a small refrigerator, and there's also a dining room, 2 pubs, a pool, and a sauna. 30 Carlton St. (phone: 977-6655 or 800-268-9076 in the US; fax: 977-0502). Inexpensive.

Selby – Recently restored to its Victorian grandeur, this 67-room property seems determined to preserve its old-fashioned prices as well. Designated a historical city landmark, the hotel sits between exclusive Rosedale Valley and downtown. There is a pleasant courtyard grill/café (summers only); guests can use the facilities of the health club across the street for a small fee. 592 Sherbourne St. (phone: 921-3142 or 800-387-4788 in the US; fax: 923-3177). Inexpensive.

EATING OUT: The postwar immigration boom coupled with Toronto's flourishing economy has stimulated a proliferation of ethnic eating places, and today the city has over 5,000 restaurants. The choice of food, which formerly ran the gamut from roast beef to Yorkshire pudding, now represents a veritable United Nations of culinary options: Chinese, French, Italian, Moroccan, Vietnamese, Indian, Greek, Japanese, Malaysian, Thai, and Caribbean, to name just a few. The quality is generally high, due to fierce competition, and while retail stores may be going through some tough economic times, the city's eateries are booming every night of the week. Expect to pay $125 and up for a dinner for two in the very expensive category, $90 to $120 in the expensive category, from $40 to $80 in the moderate category, and under $40 in the inexpensive range. Prices do not include drinks, wine, or tips. Unless otherwise specified, all restaurants are open daily. All telephone numbers are in the 416 area code unless otherwise indicated.

■ **Note:** Visitors should be aware that there is an 8% provincial tax on all restaurant bills, as well as a recently levied (and rather controversial) federal 7% GST tax. The diner is therefore paying an additional 15% even before the tip is taken into account. The tip should be based on the *pre-tax* dinner check.

Avenues – Intimate and pastel-hued, this hotel dining room is known for its attention to detail and the kitchen's imaginative entrées: succulent breast of goose with sautéed scallions and a morel truffle butter. The service is solicitous, and the wine cellar houses a selection broad enough to appeal to every palate. Reservations advised. Major credit cards accepted. In the *Bradgate Arms Hotel,* 54 Foxbar Rd. (phone: 968-1331). Very expensive.

Lotus – This is the place to which local gourmands flock for an invariably creative and excellent dining experience. Chef Susur Lee changes his menu daily; it could feature anything from poached octopus with Thai lime vinaigrette to crispy duck breast coated in a honey and hazelnut glaze — each entrée is prepared to cater to health-conscious diners. The tiny, intimate establishment seats only 30 people, and its eclectic decor includes Chinese scrolls and jars of homemade preserves. The wine list is good. Closed Sundays. Reservations necessary. Major credit cards accepted. 96 Tecumseth St. (phone: 368-7620). Very expensive.

Splendido – A recent addition to the Toronto dining scene, this spot has rapidly become a major reason to venture into this residential area of student housing and modest single-family dwellings. The 2-story front windows allow for a pleasantly sunny atmosphere that complements the bright color combinations of the dishes. The seared rack of lamb, for example, is accompanied by green mint, orange yams, and white beets. Particularly noteworthy are the restaurant's pesto creations — try the pesto pizza, cooked in an old-fashioned brick oven. The homemade desserts are some of the best in town. Closed Mondays. Reservations necessary. Major credit cards accepted. 88 Harbord St. (phone: 929-7788). Very expensive.

Truffles – This dining room only serves to enhance the already sterling reputation of its hotel, the *Four Seasons Toronto.* Dieters beware: The menu here boasts such inventive (and decadent) creations as spaghetti with black truffles and veal tenderloin with a champagne caviar sauce. The service is white-glove perfect; the wine list, extensive and on the pricey side. Reservations necessary. Major credit cards accepted. At the *Four Seasons Toronto,* 21 Yorkville Ave. (phone: 964-0411). Very expensive.

Barberian's – Just off Yonge Street, this small restaurant prides itself on its old-fashioned dinner-club ambience, and it serves food to match. Baskets of toasted bread and plates of dill pickles, olives, and vegetables magically appear on the table; you can follow those up with a huge bacon-wrapped sirloin steak and an even larger baked potato, accompanied by a seemingly endless supply of sour cream. Also of note are the late-night fondues and après-theater baked Alaska. The decor is warm and muted; the wine list extensive. Reservations advised. Major credit cards accepted. 7 Elm St. (phone: 597-0225). Expensive.

Barolo – This Cabbagetown-area spot serves generous portions of Italian specialties such as sun-dried-tomato fettuccine and scallops Barolo (the shellfish is marinated in jalapeño peppers, garlic, and other spices, then grilled and served in a white wine sauce). The shape and design of the dining area are pleasantly quirky, in keeping with the colorful neighborhood. The wine selection is excellent, and be sure to save room for dessert — from *tiramisù* to a wide range of gelati. Closed Sundays. Reservations advised. Major credit cards accepted. 193 Carlton St. (phone: 961-4747). Expensive.

Bistro 990 – It looks like a Romanesque cathedral with its heavy pillars, vaulted ceiling, and line drawings on stucco walls, but this dining room is softly lit and the kitchen is a blaze of activity, preparing French country-style dishes. Try the leg of lamb with saffron couscous. Closed Saturday lunch and Sundays. Reservations advised. Major credit cards accepted. 990 Bay St. (phone: 921-9990). Expensive.

La Bodega – Despite its Spanish name, this eatery in a Victorian mansion serves distinctly French fare, such as breast of duck with raspberry sauce and veal fillets with a cranberry *coulis*. The daily blackboard menu features specials that are designed around the fresh foodstuffs that owner Philip Wharton personally chooses every morning at the city's markets. The impressive wine list invariably includes the best lot of the season's beaujolais. The rooms adjoining the main one are elegant, and there is an outdoor patio as well. Closed Sundays. Reservations advised. Major credit cards accepted. 30 Baldwin St. (phone: 977-8600). Expensive.

Carman's – While trendier spots may come and go, this steakhouse has been a tried-and-true favorite for many years. The style is old English Tudor, and the dining area features four wood-burning fireplaces. The pièce de résistance is steak, but the rack of lamb, Dover sole, and "choose your own" lobster are excellent as well. And perhaps in homage to the owner's Greek ancestors, this is a paradise for garlic lovers. Reservations advised. Major credit cards accepted. 26 Alexander St. (phone: 924-6306). Expensive.

Centro Grill – Modern Italian decor sets the tone for this chic, crowded, and sometimes noisy place; the sounds seem to bounce off the walls as they would at a large Old World family gathering. The restaurant has remained popular for its fun atmosphere and inventive culinary combinations, such as roast lamb with a light honey–Dijon mustard crust or homemade angel hair pasta with fresh truffles and flavored olive oil. Try to get here early for a glass of wine in the relaxing piano bar. Closed Sundays. Reservations necessary. Major credit cards accepted. 2472 Yonge St. (phone: 483-2211). Expensive.

Châteauneuf – Rich burgundy tones and lovely tapestries decorate this intimate dining place in the *Westin Harbour Castle* hotel. The menu is French, and favorites such as fresh lobster medallions and crêpes filled with golden caviar and sour cream are prepared and presented with care. For dessert, try cassis or raspberry sorbet. Closed Sundays. Reservations advised. Major credit cards accepted. *Westin Harbour Castle Hotel*, 1 Harbour Sq. (phone: 869-1600). Expensive.

Cibo – The fresh, tangy mustard sauce of the veal scaloppine will more than compensate for any slight discomfort or claustrophobia in this bustling spot of elbow-to-elbow diners. The restaurant has always maintained a reputation for surprising its customers with creative nightly specials, usually involving fish or pasta. Reservations advised. Major credit cards accepted. 1055 Yonge St. (phone: 921-2166). Expensive.

Commodore – The window tables in this elegant hotel dining room afford patrons a view of yachts sailing by. House specialties include crispy duck and pheasant and a highly touted beef tenderloin glazed with roasted garlic. The service is friendly but unobtrusive, and the wine list is good. Stick with the lighter desserts. Closed Saturday lunch and Sundays. Reservations advised. Major credit cards accepted. At the *Radisson Plaza Hotel Admiral,* 249 Queen's Quay W. (phone: 364-5444). Expensive.

Joso's – The theme of this place — the female form — is all-pervasive, from the numerous paintings and statuary to the Rubenesque busts literally protruding from the walls. Located in a 2-story mansion just off Avenue Road, this establishment specializes in seafood, usually prepared imaginatively (try the crispy calamari with the spicy saffron risotto). Although the wine list is not extensive, the house wine is always a good bet. Closed Sundays. Reservations advised. Major credit cards accepted. 202 Davenport Rd. (phone: 925-1903). Expensive.

Katsura – Despite the proliferation of Japanese eateries in town, this spot is still deemed the best by many sushi devotees. Order the sushi or the teppanyaki dishes and let the cool, dark interior transport you to the Orient. There is a decent selection of light Japanese beer and very good sake; the sushi bar is a popular meeting spot for executives working in Toronto's north end. Closed Sundays. Reservations advised. Major credit cards accepted. In the *Prince Hotel,* 900 York Mills Rd., North York (phone: 444-9597). Expensive.

Metropolis – Don't be put off by its rather austere black-and-white motif: This popular spot serves up contemporary interpretations of traditional Canadian fare. Some of the specialties are cornmeal fritters with lamb sausages and East Coast shrimp and mussels steeped in wine made from Niagara grapes. And where else could one find heavy-duty maple cheesecake? Closed Sundays. Reservations advised. Major credit cards accepted. 838 Yonge St. (phone: 924-4100). Expensive.

Nami – The indoor Japanese-style grill will be the first thing to catch your eye when you enter this stylishly elegant restaurant. Torontonians long ago discovered the glories of fresh seafood, and this place prepares it perfectly. Sushi lovers gather here daily to sample the delicate raw shrimp or lobster; others prefer the seafood lightly grilled. Also outstanding is anything tempura, with a thin, exquisitely crispy batter. The wine list is limited; most patrons stick with hot sake or cold Kirin beer. Reservations advised. Major credit cards accepted. 55 Adelaide St. E. (phone: 362-7373). Expensive.

N 44° – Pronounced "North 44," the name refers to Toronto's geographical latitude. This ultra-chic spot boasts the considerable skills of chef-owner Mark McEwan, which are manifested in such culinary tours de force as corn-fried oysters with sweet pepper and jalapeño sauce and rack of lamb with rosemary crust. Desserts include homemade ice cream and sorbets; the wine list is somewhat pedestrian. Closed Sundays. Reservations necessary. Major credit cards accepted. 2537 Yonge St. (phone: 487-4897). Expensive.

Orso – Created by New York restaurateur Joe Allen and managed by the redoubtable John Maxwell, this is a converted 2-story sandblasted brick structure brought to life with pastel pinks and marbled walls. While the decor is somewhat formal, the ambience is fun and congenial, and the staff is helpful. The wafer-thin pizza, topped with mussels or mushrooms, makes a perfect starter; notable entrées include grilled swordfish with cream and mango relish or sautéed sweetbreads in a thick cream sauce with onions and mustard. The wine and beer lists are exemplary, and regulars often drop in for a cappuccino at the tiny stand-up bar. Don't miss the egg-rich *tiramisù* for dessert. Reservations advised. Major credit cards accepted. 106 John St. (phone: 596-1989). Expensive.

Scaramouche – Imaginative continental dishes featuring salmon, veal, and lamb are served in this elegant dining room in the upscale neighborhood of Forest Hills with views of the bright lights of downtown. There's also a pasta bar. A must for dessert is the bittersweet chocolate and praline truffle. Dinner only; closed Sundays. Reservations necessary. Major credit cards accepted. 1 Benvenuto Pl. (phone: 961-8011). Expensive.

Trapper's – Well worth the drive to north Toronto, this place has a Canadian-wilderness decor. Chef-owner Chris Boland has created an ever-changing native Canadian menu whose specials depend on what coast-to-coast produce, meat, and fish appear at the morning market: salmon from British Columbia, pork tenderloin from Ontario, or perhaps fiddlehead ferns from New Brunswick. Reliable repeat performers include the cheddar cheese soup and the deep-dish cobbler of apple, apricot, and pear. The wine list is good; the service amiable. Lunch and dinner during the week; dinner only on weekends. Reservations advised. Major credit cards accepted. 3479 Yonge St. (phone: 482-6211). Expensive.

Winston's – This establishment serves rich haute cuisine in a flamboyantly grand setting. The city's patricians come here to see and be seen, and visitors may have to compete with the important regulars for good tables and service. Specialties include duckling with fresh papaya, mango, rum, and wine, and Dover sole with shrimp, pine nuts, and green peppercorns. For dessert, don't pass up the Grand Marnier soufflé. Jackets and ties are mandatory for men. Closed Sundays. Reservations necessary. Major credit cards accepted. 104 Adelaide St. W. (phone: 363-1627). Expensive.

Winter Palace – Atop the 43-story *Sheraton Centre* complex, this place commands an excellent view of City Hall and Nathan Phillips Square. The interior is elegant, and the menu features French dishes with a Russian flair. Sample the *zakuska* — a dish of seven hors d'oeuvres, including caviar, partridge pâté, and smoked salmon — then follow up with the veal tenderloin or scampi Fabergé. Dining is enhanced in the summer by the multicolored lights that shimmer from the reflecting pool 43 stories below and, in winter, by the soft glow that bathes the skaters on the frozen pool in front of City Hall. There's also an extensive wine list. Closed Sundays. Reservations necessary. Major credit cards accepted. 123 Queen St. W. in *Sheraton Centre* (phone: 361-1000). Expensive.

Avocado Club – Formerly the trendy *Beaujolais,* this dining spot has dropped its prices a notch while maintaining its predecessor's high standards. Colorful murals make the huge room less impersonal, and the upholstered banquettes help to mute the noise. The menu offers diners an unusual choice between Tex-Mex and Thai dishes; the thick guacamole or the *soba* noodle salad both make excellent starters. The comprehensive wine list will suit every taste. Closed Sundays. Reservations advised on Saturdays. Major credit cards accepted. 165 John St. (phone: 598-4656). Expensive to moderate.

Boulevard Café – A Peruvian accent pervades this place, from the eclectic decor to the food. Appetizers include *tamales verdes* and salad with garlic cream. Most of the main dishes are deliciously tangy, from the spicy marinade of chicken or jumbo shrimp to the sea bass kebabs. If it's on the list of specials, the grilled chicken with yogurt marinade is a must. The Key lime pie will cool you off. No reservations, but come early for a patio seat. Major credit cards accepted. 161 Harbord St. (phone: 961-7676). Expensive to moderate.

Chanterelles – Superb food, thoughtful service, and a handsome setting off the lobby of *L'Hôtel* make this a fine dining choice. The menu includes everything from oysters and caviar to rack of lamb. There's a pre-theater dinner, but you may want to go after the performance just to try the signature cake — sinful but heavenly. Closed Sundays. Reservations advised. Major credit cards accepted. 225 Front St. W. (phone: 597-8142). Expensive to moderate.

Gatsby's – For elegant and intimate dining amidst late Victorian decor, this classy spot boasts a huge selection of continental cuisine. Closed Sundays. Reservations advised. Major credit cards accepted. 504 Church St. (phone: 925-4545). Expensive to moderate.

George Bigliardi's – Popular with the hockey crowd and high-powered business types, this elegant dining lounge serves steaks, seafood, pasta, and sausages — all with that special Italian touch. Enjoy the house cocktail, the "Midnight George," at the brass-railed bar or the piano bar. Open for dinner only. Reservations advised. Major credit cards accepted. 463 Church St., 2 blocks north of *Maple Leaf Gardens* (phone: 922-9594). Expensive to moderate.

Grano – This cozy Italian eatery serves fare with a mildly spicy kick (though the kitchen will gladly fire it up for you). Try the spaghetti and squid-ink appetizer and the grilled pink salmon with lemon and butter. The basement bakery creates wonderful bread and desserts. Closed Sundays. Reservations advised. Major credit cards accepted. 2035 Yonge St. (phone: 440-1086). Expensive to moderate.

Johnny K's – This small, trendy Beach area institution has the distinction of being one of the only places in town where vegetables are cooked *al dente*. The impeccably crafted dishes here include fresh chicken grilled with walnut oil and black linguine with shrimp and mussels. Be sure to check the dependable daily specials on the blackboards, and try to leave room for the creamy strawberry cheesecake. The window seats afford diners a view of the area's colorful "beachniks" strolling by. Reservations advised. Major credit cards accepted. 1955 Queen St. E. (phone: 698-7133). Expensive to moderate.

Old Fish Market – A casual and comfortable place where the specialties are all kinds of fresh fish and seafood. There's also an oyster bar. Reservations advised. Major credit cards accepted. 12 Market St. (phone: 363-0334). Expensive to moderate.

Ouzeri – Owner Aristedes scored an instant success with this chic and funky Greek dining spot, now considered to be the throbbing heart of Danforth Avenue. The superb fare includes a flaky, tender rabbit and onion phyllo pie and pink grilled lamb with garlic, lemon, and oregano. The extensive beer list complements the food, and retsina and ouzo are always at hand. The decor is reminiscent of a sunny Greek island. In summer, the front picture windows disappear and the street scene swells until 4 AM with festive customers. Reservations advised, though you may still have to wait for a table. Major credit cards accepted. 500A Danforth Ave. (phone: 778-0500). Expensive to moderate.

Rodney's Oyster House – Ensconced in the basement of an old office building, this tiny establishment will satisfy even the most demanding seafood connoisseur. The catch of the day — which could be one of a variety of oysters, mussels, or clams — arrives fresh by plane. Order clam or oyster chowder, and watch it made before your very eyes. The robust beer list more than compensates for the paucity of wines. Though the place gets crowded at night and at lunch during the week, it is quite relaxing on Saturday afternoons. Closed Sundays. No reservations. Major credit cards accepted. 209 Adelaide St. E. (phone: 363-8105). Expensive to moderate.

Santa Fe – One of the only Tex-Mex spots in town whose festive atmosphere does justice to its food. The main room features a long bar, usually lined with after-work margarita drinkers noshing on chili nachos. Above (in the open gallery) and below are the dining rooms, where you can sample plates of oysters, okra deep-fried in cornmeal, or hickory-smoked chicken quesadillas. Make sure to specify how spicy you want your dish. The wine list is decent, but Mexican beer is the order of the day. Closed Sundays. Major credit cards accepted. 129 Peter St. (phone: 345-9345). Expensive to moderate.

Spiaggia Trattoria – Located in the Beach district (*spiaggia* is Italian for "beach"), this tiny, usually crowded place has become a neighborhood institution. The blackboard menu changes daily, depending on what chef-owner Stephen Young has purchased at the market that morning. His pasta is inventive and delicious; the vegetables are served *al dente;* and the all-important pesto has the proper tangy taste. Try not to miss the mushroom risotto with grilled lamb sausage. The wine list is limited but exemplary. Reservations necessary. Major credit cards accepted. 2318 Queen St. E. (phone: 699-4656). Expensive to moderate.

Tapestry's – Named for its owner's penchant for fine Oriental fabrics, this dining room is filled with Asian wall hangings and other pieces from his personal collection. There is a wide range of continental fare, from the highly praised rack of lamb to the super-fresh seafood specialties. The place has its own pastry chef, so try to save room for a piece of cheesecake. A pianist at dinner adds a romantic touch. Reservations advised. Major credit cards accepted. At the *Chestnut Park Hotel,* 108 Chestnut St. (phone: 977-5000). Expensive to moderate.

Waves – Behind this little Danforth Avenue storefront can be found some of Toronto's best bouillabaisse and paella. The creative fare here, described as "New World Mediterranean," runs the gamut from "Med bread" — which comes with various toppings — to swordfish. The hand-painted tables add to the sunny ambience, and the light, pastel-colored walls serve as the perfect backdrop for the restaurant's rotating art exhibit. Reservations advised. Major credit cards accepted. 347 Danforth Ave. (phone: 466-4644). Expensive to moderate.

Windows on the SkyDome – This 650-seat restaurant offers a spectacular view of the *SkyDome*'s playing fields. Excellent prime ribs, steaks, and seafood. The international buffet is very popular. Open during all major sports events. Reservations advised. Major credit cards accepted. 300 Bremner Rd. (phone: 341-2300 or 341-2324). Expensive to moderate.

Allen's – This offshoot of New York's famed *Joe Allen,* under the same ownership and management as *Orso* (see above), attracts a wide range of types, from actors and artists to marketing managers and company presidents. It serves the best burgers in town, complemented by a huge à la carte plate of fries, and its imported-beer list is Toronto's most extensive. The big, meaty Manhattan capon wings (so called to distinguish them from Buffalo chicken wings, which are smaller and spicier) are an excellent starter; the fried chicken with cornbread and the Dijon rack of lamb are good entrées; and the banana cream pie makes a perfect dessert. In summer, try to get a seat in the fenced-in outdoor patio, where there's an open barbecue. Many regulars visit just to see which pair of outrageous eyeglass frames owner John Maxwell happens to be wearing. Reservations advised on weekends. MasterCard and Visa accepted. 143 Danforth Ave. (phone: 463-3086). Moderate.

Bamboo Club – Long regarded as the heart of the funky Queen Street West strip, this spot is also known for serving some of the city's finest Thai, Oriental, and Caribbean concoctions. The Thai noodles, or *pad thai* — a stack of thin noodles, chicken, shrimp, and blended spices, as spicy as you like — are a meal in themselves, and the Key lime pie is appropriately light and tart. Although the wine list is decent, beer seems to be the drink of choice here. There's also a great rooftop patio in the summer. This is one of Toronto's liveliest and most eclectic nightspots; get here early if you want to avoid paying a cover charge for live music. Closed Sundays. Reservations necessary. Major credit cards accepted. 312 Queen St. W. (phone: 593-5771). Moderate.

Bellair Café – Serving pasta, salads, seafood, and frozen yogurt and sorbet in a contemporary dining room, this is a popular spot for business lunches and shopping breaks. Celebrities are sometimes seen during dinner hours. Reservations advised. Major credit cards accepted. 100 Cumberland St. at Bellair (phone: 964-2222). Moderate.

Doctor's House & Livery – Located 40 minutes north of downtown Toronto, this 19th-century home has gone through several transmutations — from a doctor's house and barn to a tearoom to the restaurant and gift shop it is today. The atmosphere is very homey. The menu includes Canadian specialties like salmon cooked as you like it and duckling with sweet plums and maple syrup. The Sunday brunch features a wide range of light and heavy fare, from omelettes to prime ribs. Children's portions are available. Closed Mondays in winter. Reservations advised. Most major credit cards accepted. Nashville Rd., Kleinburg (phone: 893-1615). Moderate.

Indian Rice Factory – For those who enjoy the subtle nuances of Indian food, this restaurant (decorated in muted tones) offers some of the most enjoyable dishes in the city. Reliable staples like the delicious tandoori chicken come with homemade bread or chili pork that is so incendiary that new customers are warned about it in advance. Less adventuresome diners might try the curried chicken with aromatic spices. Reservations advised. Major credit cards accepted. 414 Dupont St. (phone: 961-3472). Moderate.

Jacques' Omelettes – This Yorkville eatery, with a French à la carte menu, is frequented by devotees of the classic French omelette. Chef Jacques Sorin prepares fresh garnishes every morning and cooks omelettes to order perfectly. The omelette niçoise is highly recommended. Closed Sundays. Reservations advised. Major credit cards accepted. 126 Cumberland Ave. (phone: 961-1893). Moderate.

Lakes – Regulars routinely fight their way through the crowd at the tiny front bar here because they know that the superb dishes created in the open kitchen are well worth the trouble. This friendly place combines the feel of a neighborhood watering hole with that of a chic dinner spot. Try the *bruschetta* (toasted bread topped with tomatoes, garlic, and cheese) or the mouth-watering chilled gazpacho (summer only) for starters; the beef filet in port sauce is a highly recommended entrée. The wine list is good, too. Closed Sundays. Reservations necessary. Major credit cards accepted. 1112 Yonge St. (phone: 966-0185). Moderate.

Old House on Church Street – Super atmosphere and delicious, huge portions are offered in this historic Toronto home. Guests may dine upstairs, or downstairs in the garden during summer months. Lamb, pasta, and seafood are all expertly prepared by the Greek chef-owner. Try the cheesecake for dessert. There's a great Sunday brunch, too. Reservations advised. Major credit cards accepted. 582 Church St. (phone: 925-5316). Moderate.

Pink Pearl – Specializing in Cantonese food, this eatery features distinguished surroundings and service; dining here is a leisurely affair. Highlights of the extensive menu include Rainbow Chopped in Crystal Fold (chopped meat and vegetables sautéed together and served with crispy noodles); Peking Supreme Beef Filet (sliced beef tenderloin sautéed with oyster sauce and served sizzling hot); and braised lobster prepared in black bean and garlic sauce. Reservations advised for dinner. Major credit cards accepted. Two locations: 120 Avenue Rd. (phone: 966-3631) and at Queen's Quay Terminal (phone: 366-9162). Moderate.

Round Window – One of Toronto's veteran fish and seafood restaurants, this no-frills establishment was a pioneer in the Danforth area. Its reputation has withstood the test of time, as the filet of sole or salmon steaks attest. The atmosphere is decidedly homey, with brisk, friendly service in the two small, cozy rooms. The clientele ranges from lingering couples to families to executives. Closed Mondays. Reservations advised. Major credit cards accepted. 729 Danforth Ave. (phone: 465-3892). Moderate.

Select Bistro – This spot on trendy Queen Street West has a genuine zinc bar, small tables set closely together, taped jazz and classical music, Canadian art posters on the walls, a first-rate wine list, and baskets of homemade bread, which are suspended on pulleys above diners' heads. The service is inconsistent, and the food varies (the fresh green and Caesar salads and garlic cheese bread are safe bets), but the atmosphere, which calls to mind a true French bistro, is the main reason for its continuing popularity. Be prepared to wait in line. Reservations advised for groups of 5 or more. Major credit cards accepted. 328 Queen St. W. (phone: 596-6405). Moderate.

Senator – Formerly a 1940s diner, it became an instant classic in 1984, when it was extensively upgraded. Located just behind the *Pantages Theatre* and *Eaton Centre,* the establishment now comprises the original diner, an upscale restaurant, and the *Top o' the Senator,* considered one of the finest jazz clubs in the dominion. The diner is renowned for its great deli sandwiches and baked goods, while the elegant dining room features dishes like rib steaks and top-quality grilled veal chops. The after-work crowd heads for the patio in the summer to enjoy the ever-changing jazz program. Reservations advised. Major credit cards accepted. 249 Victoria St. (phone: 364-7517). Moderate.

Thai Magic – And it is. This place has attracted a growing following among Rosedale residents for its daily curry dishes, *satay* and stir-fry specialties, and sumptuous appetizers, such as Thai fish cakes and spring rolls. Dinner only; closed Sundays. Reservations advised. Major credit cards accepted. 1118 Yonge St. (phone: 968-7366). Moderate.

Top of Toronto – This revolving restaurant at the top of the CN Tower has incredible views and is the critic's choice for Sunday brunch, served from 10 AM to 2 PM. Reservations advised. Major credit cards accepted. 301 Front St. W. (phone: 362-5411). Moderate.

Babbage's – A longtime staple of the Beach district, this is practically a second home for many of its residents. The downstairs pub offers good finger food, beer, and live music (weekends only), while the upstairs dining room features Chinese food and *karaoke* (singing to taped music). A pleasant watering hole for visitors taking a break from the rigors of suntanning at the beach. No reservations. Major credit cards accepted. 2282 Queen St. E. (phone: 694-8037). Moderate to inexpensive.

C'est What? – Just east of Yonge Street, this underground café attracts an eclectic after-work and late-night clientele. The fare is standard pub grub — chicken fingers, wings, and burgers — and the owners pride themselves on their microbrewery beer selection (there are 14 in all) and local wine list. Entertainment includes a panoply of board games and live music, from blues to classical. Open until 4 AM weekends and 2:30 AM during the week. No reservations. Major credit cards accepted. 67 Front St. E. (phone: 867-9791). Moderate to inexpensive.

Coyote Grill – Located in the upper shopping floors of the Queen's Quay Terminal, this Tex-Mex diner overlooks the harbor. The chicken fajitas are especially good; order them with the thick cornbread, black-bean soup, and the spicy guacamole. You can sit either by the (very) open kitchen, where you can watch food cooking on the grill, or, better yet, in a window seat, watching sailboats gliding on the water. Reservations advised for lunch. Major credit cards accepted. 207 Queen's Quay Terminal (phone: 367-2799). Moderate to inexpensive.

Ed's Warehouse – When entrepreneur Ed Mirvish bought and restored the *Royal Alexandra Theatre,* he also launched a restaurant empire, seating 1,500 guests, next door. Garish, with Tiffany lamps and plush old-time autos, this restaurant is great for beef. Jackets are a must; no blue jeans allowed. Reservations unnecessary. Major credit cards accepted. 270 King St. W. (phone: 593-6676). Moderate to inexpensive.

Filet of Sole – Fishing scenes of Peggy's Cove in Nova Scotia line the walls of this informal, top-rated seafood dining spot. The remarkably varied menu is printed twice daily. Try the shellfish platters. Near both the *Royal Alexandra Theatre* and *Roy Thomson Hall,* the place caters to theater lovers who like to linger at their tables. Open weekdays for lunch and dinner; dinner only on weekends. Reservations necessary. Major credit cards accepted. 11 Duncan St. (phone: 598-3256). Moderate to inexpensive.

Masa – The focus here is on authentic Japanese food. Customers can sit in a standard booth or dine in traditional Japanese style on tatami mats in partitioned lounges. Open weekdays for lunch and dinner; weekends, dinner only. Reservations advised on weekends. Major credit cards accepted. 195 Richmond St. W. (phone: 977-9519). Moderate to inexpensive.

Sultan's Tent – For an intriguing change, try some authentic Moroccan food in the Yorkville shopping district. The decor looks genuine: rich tapestries, low round tables, and comfortable divans and brass vases. Specialties include lamb with honey and almonds, chicken with lemon and olives, and couscous served with various meats and vegetables. For dessert try the dense combinations of honey, nuts, and layers of phyllo pastries and some strong Moroccan coffee or mint tea. Arabic music and belly dancers. Closed Sundays. Reservations advised. Major credit cards accepted. 1280 Bay St. (phone: 961-0601). Moderate to inexpensive.

Chez Cappuccino – This popular downtown place, right near Yonge Street, is notable for its convenient location, round-the-clock hours, and outdoor tables — it's a fun people watching spot. The sandwiches and salads are good, and desserts are always fresh. All kinds of coffees are served here — try a cappuccino or *café au lait.* The two cluttered little rooms resonate with recorded old-time blues music. No reservations or credit cards accepted. 3 Charles St. E. (phone: 925-6142). Inexpensive.

Church Street Café – Paintings by local artists hang on the walls, adding a bohemian touch to this informal, diner-style establishment. Continental fare includes rack of lamb, beef tenderloin medallions, and poached salmon. Reservations necessary for groups of six or more. Major credit cards accepted. 485 Church St. (phone: 925-1155). Inexpensive.

56 Yonge – Located in the *Victoria* hotel, this restaurant is much like its host establishment: good, dependable, and inexpensive. The service is casual; most regulars are on a first-name basis with the staff. The continental fare ranges from an appetizer of steamed mussels in lemon-saffron tea to a generous entrée of calf's liver, accompanied by fresh vegetables purchased at nearby *St. Lawrence Market.* Also featured is a daily CN$14.95 prix fixe dinner, which includes soup and a dessert. The somewhat limited wine list features many Canadian labels. Closed Saturday lunch and Sundays. Reservations unnecessary. Major credit cards accepted. In the *Victoria,* 56 Yonge St. (phone: 363-1666). Inexpensive.

Fitzgerald's – A quintessential neighborhood watering hole that serves possibly the best Buffalo wings in town. The downstairs bar has decent finger food and dartboards, while the elegant, quiet dining room upstairs — which has a working Franklin stove — proffers full meals of roast beef, filet of sole, and the like. On weekends, a piano player tinkles quietly upstairs while live bands play downstairs. The place features a small outdoor patio as well, open in the summer. The staff is personable; no one leaves here a stranger. Reservations unnecessary. Major credit cards accepted. 2298 Queen St. E. (phone: 691-1393). Inexpensive.

The Friendly Greek – Friendly it is, starting with Sula, who greets guests effusively as they enter her domain. The lamb souvlaki is more than generous; the village salad boasts crisp greens and pure olive oil; and the calamari is some of the best in town. Of the few wines available, stick with the Greek brands; for dessert, try a glass of ouzo along with thick black coffee and honey-soaked baklava. No reservations. Major credit cards accepted. 551 Danforth Ave. (phone: 469-8422). Inexpensive.

Groaning Board – The gimmick here is the continuous screenings of award-winning commercials from the *Cannes International Advertising Film Festival.* While you're watching, pick something from a menu of hearty meat and vegetarian dishes, soup, salad, and sandwiches and homemade desserts. Reservations advised for four or more. Major credit cards accepted. 131 Jarvis St. (phone: 363-0265). Inexpensive.

Hard Rock Café – Another link in the popular chain, this is a rock 'n' roll museum, restaurant, and guaranteed tourist attraction rolled into one. The menu is basic burgers-and-fries fare, but the food's not the main draw: People flock here to see the memorabilia (including guitars used by Elvis, Jimi Hendrix, and Stevie Ray Vaughn, some of Elton John's outrageous Captain Fantastic outfits, and one of John Lennon's early *Beatles* suits), listen to the loud background music, and soak up the atmosphere. Another plus is that it overlooks the playing field of the *SkyDome;* the restaurant sells tickets to watch baseball and football games from this vantage point (the price of the "seat" includes dinner). Reservations necessary for groups of 10 or more. Major credit cards accepted. In the *SkyDome Hotel,* 45 Peter St. S. (phone: 341-2388). Inexpensive.

Just Desserts – Virtually all manner of baked goods, from oversize butter tarts — an adaptation of the English treacle tart made with raisins, butter, brown sugar, eggs, and corn syrup — to hefty pieces of an entire realm of cheesecakes, as well as salads and quiche, are on the menu here. The desserts are the cream of the crop of the best bakeries across town. The colorful assortment contrasts nicely with the tiled black-and-white decor. Sample one of the many coffees, teas, or juices. Open until 3 AM during the week; 24 hours on Fridays and Saturdays. No reservations or credit cards accepted. 306 Davenport Rd. (phone: 922-6824). Inexpensive.

Korea House – The specialty here is succulent barbecued beef with pickled sesame leaves and cabbage. Fully licensed. Reservations unnecessary. Most major credit cards accepted. 666 Bloor St. W. (phone: 536-8666). Inexpensive.

Maverick's – Popular among Danforth locals. The meals served at this friendly urban saloon, ranging from three-egg omelettes to steaks and fries and heaping portions of pasta, are one of the city's genuine food deals. The dark wood bar has a sports theme, with several televisions hanging from the ceiling. The cheerful staff and owner Peter Tsiaris keep the place lively, especially when musician friends drop in for an impromptu Sunday night jam session. In the summer, try to get a seat on the back patio. No reservations. Major credit cards accepted. 804 Danforth Ave. (phone: 462-2605). Inexpensive.

Real Jerk – Reggae music is in the air, the corrugated tin walls are painted in bright colors, and patrons chow down Jamaican "jerk" pork and chicken entrées for less than $8. Reservations accepted for large groups only. Major credit cards accepted. 709 Queen St. E. (phone: 469-6909). Inexpensive.

Sai Woo – This culinary pioneer introduced Chinese food to Toronto back in 1954, and while countless fancier Chinese restaurants have since followed its lead, few of them serve such good, straightforward fare at such low prices. The decor is unassuming and the large dining room simple. Both Cantonese and the spicier Szechuan are served: Start with a thick egg roll or two, then try the ginger beef or the spareribs with the secret sauce. No reservations. Major credit cards accepted. In the heart of Chinatown, at 130 Dundas St. W. (phone: 977-4988). Inexpensive.

Shopsy's – Original owner Sam Shopsowitz first opened this deli generations ago, in the middle of the predominantly Jewish garment district on Spadina Avenue.

Although it now occupies a different site — across from the *O'Keefe Centre* — it still remains Toronto's quintessential delicatessen. The outdoor patio and the late hours (to accommodate the après-theater crowd) are relatively recent innovations, but the corned beef on rye, Montreal smoked meat, homemade hot dogs, thick fries, and chicken noodle soup are as delicious as they were 70 years ago. This gastronomic landmark is still the best deal in town for a sensational deli nosh. Reservations necessary at peak dining hours. Major credit cards accepted. 33 Yonge St. (phone: 365-3333). Inexpensive.

Silver Rail – It's Toronto's original tavern, the first bar in the city to serve liquor legally (in 1947). Here you'll see native Torontonians — including judges and shoppers — sipping beer at the "mile-long" bar and eating plain, simple, mashed-potatoes-and-gravy-style grub in booths. Closed Sundays. Reservations advised. Major credit cards accepted. Across from *Eaton Centre* at 225 Yonge St. (phone: 368-8697). Inexpensive.

Vines – Across the street from the *St. Lawrence Centre* and the *O'Keefe Centre,* this wine bar is an ideal place to spend an hour or two dissecting the latest play or opera. Bistro-style hot dishes and light fare — cold roast beef, pâtés, and cheese plates — complement a wide variety of international wines. A special vintage is featured daily. Closed Sundays. No reservations. Major credit cards accepted. 38 Wellington St. E. (phone: 869-0744). Inexpensive.

Young Lok – Peking and Szechuan regional food, along with a tasty Mongolian grill, are the specialties served here. The decor is reminiscent of an Oriental garden. Reservations necessary for six or more. Major credit cards accepted. 122 St. Patrick St. (phone: 593-9819). Inexpensive.

■**PEPPERONI TO GO:** Assailed with an intense craving for pizza at 2 AM? Well, even if every restaurant in town is closed and your hotel doesn't have round-the-clock room service, there is a solution: *Pizza Pizza,* a service that guarantees delivery of your order within 30 minutes, or you get it free (barring mitigating circumstances, such as inclement weather). A wide variety of toppings is offered for the thick-crust pies, from traditional pepperoni and sausage to Canadian favorites such as ham and pineapple. Take-out service is also available; there are multiple locations around the city. Orders are taken until 2:30 AM. Major credit cards accepted (phone: 967-1111).

DIVERSIONS

For the Experience

Quintessential Toronto

Toronto — the so-called Queen City, because of its loyalty to British institutions — was once a pretty dull place. Oh, it got along well enough — a few new restaurants here and there, an occasional play, a hotel refurbishment — until the summer of 1967. Torontonians who visited *Expo '67* in Montreal discovered a city only 349 miles (558 km) east of their home that was amazingly vibrant, rich in music, dancing, dining, nightlife, and general joie de vivre. To those returning to their Toronto homes everything looked drab by comparison, as plain as vanilla.

But it didn't take long for this once provincial town to learn from its eastern cousin: In the years immediately following *Expo,* Toronto city planners encouraged downtown redevelopment and banned buildings over 45 feet high; well-heeled citizens joined in, gaining a new appreciation for their red-brick Victorian homes on the tree-lined streets in the districts of Forest Hill, Rosedale, and Cabbagetown. Modern, eye-catching edifices — the *Ontario Science Centre* (1969), Ontario Place (1971), the CN Tower (1976), and *Eaton Centre* (1976) — were built. And thanks to a steady flow of immigrants that included large numbers of Italians, East Indians, Germans, Portuguese, and West Indians, the restaurant and nightlife scene changed dramatically.

Today, enjoying its ranking as one of the most livable cities in North America, Toronto is a great place to be: On a typical summer Saturday, shoppers pick through the produce of the ethnic markets, jog along the Beach boardwalk, queue up for *Blue Jays* tickets at the world-famous *SkyDome,* relax at an outdoor café along funky Queen Street West with a book and a cappuccino, and sample the bright lights and new music of Yonge Street until dawn. It goes to show that Toronto is no longer Toronto the Good, Toronto the Dull.

A DAY AT THE BEACH: At the turn of the century, many well-heeled Torontonians discovered the pleasures of summering on the banks of Lake Ontario. Accustomed to the good life, they built grand cottages along the 3-mile beach, brought their full complement of servants (and their fine china, silver, crystal, and linen), and spent July and August entertaining in style in the cool, clear, lakeside air. (The word "cottage" is misleading: Most of these summer places had at least nine rooms and a huge solarium.) Many of the cottages remain, now owned by the new generation of movers and shakers who contentedly continue the trend set by their predecessors.

Happily, the Beach (the name chosen for the area by its original status-conscious residents) is now also a popular destination for day-trippers — leisure lovers seeking an afternoon of sun and sand, a swim in the sparkling clear waters of the lake, a breeze on a windsurfing board, a sunset cruise, an evening stroll on the old-fashioned wooden boardwalk, a sumptuous seafood dinner, and perhaps a postprandial walk through the surrounding parkland before returning to life in the city. Today's Beach (residents insist on keeping the capital "B") boasts trendy shops that carry everything from funky fashion to haute couture, a variety of restaurants — you can breakfast on omelettes, lunch on hot dogs, and dine on dim sum — plus an art cinema and several hot night-spots. Offering leisure at its liveliest, the Beach has earned its place in the sun.

HANGING OUT AT HARBOURFRONT: Almost a city within the city, this place never ceases to amaze longtime residents who remember it as a desolate, barren, black hole of abandoned buildings and fenced-in factories cut off from the city by railway yards and expressways. But that was yesterday. Today locals and visitors alike can be seen at the refurbished dockside area (once an oil-soaked, broken-down wharf), trying to decide what to do first: Want to nibble on a thick deli sandwich? Try *More Glorious Food* (145 Queen's Quay W.), the best takeout around. Hire a skipper or take your own boat out into Lake Ontario? There's an updated paddle wheeler — the *Mariposa Belle* — and a three-masted schooner — the *Tristan Sandy*. Are antiques your passion? The *Harbourfront Antique Market* (390 Queen's Quay W.), a vast emporium of price-less artifacts and some fun junk, is where inveterate browsers and collectors come for their quirky jewelry, vintage books, china, furniture, and antique toys, straight out of someone's great-grandmother's attic. In all, you'll find the best in arts and crafts, boat cruises and sailing schools, ritzy shopping and fancy waterfront eateries, music and dance studios, photo studios, and art galleries happily coexisting at this waterfront haven. In summer the park at Harbourfront is at its best, with minstrels, painted clowns, and lessons in swimming and boating, windsurfing, and scuba diving. Couples and families spread blankets and picnic here, pick up a cruise around Toronto Island, or enjoy a dockside midnight stroll.

Want more? Amble the well-kept parkland toward *York Quay* (pronounced *key*), an impressive renovation of an old cold-storage warehouse that has been transformed to an Art Deco, multilevel shopping gallery. Stop to watch a piece of pottery take shape at a potters' wheel or a glass figurine being brought blazing from a kiln. Hungry? The outdoor *Water's Edge Café* (235 Queen's Quay W.) overlooks the pond, which is used for canoe lessons in summer and ice skating in winter.

In a town where everything closes on Sunday except churches and restaurants, Harbourfront's tourist area designation allows its shops to open on the Sabbath, too. Parking is hard to come by, so take the trolley car from Union Station. For a list of activities and events, contact *Harbourfront,* 410 Queen's Quay W. (phone: 416-973-4600).

KENSINGTON MARKET: If Harbourfront is the place to go on Sunday, this is Toronto's top Saturday destination. Once upon a time this ethnic market was Jewish (note the New York–style bagels here, the best in town); now it is mainly Portuguese, with a sprinkling of Ethiopian and Mexican merchants. Linguists love it: Saturday morning you can stroll through the crowded maze and never hear a word of English spoken. Come for the food, the smells, the riot of color — even the nearby houses are decked out in bright red, green, and purple. There are spicy cheeses, rich chocolates, and fresh vegetables; baskets of apples and piles of cauliflower spill onto the sidewalk as the tiny roads become the main pedestrian thoroughfare. Try a steaming bowl of soup from a little Asian noodle shop or breathe in the scents of exotic spices, interna-tional coffees, and rare teas at the *House of Spice* (190 Augusta Ave.; phone: 416-593-9724).

Grab a bun or bagel, or try the almond croissants at the *Kensington Natural Bakery* (corner of Augusta Ave. and Oxford St.); select from the variety of cheese at *Cheese from Around the World* (on Kensington Ave.); snack on olives, a natural treat from the barrels lining the sidewalks. More exotic are Caribbean delicacies such as sea moss, plantain, and goat meat; and for the health- and diet-conscious, the four fruit and vegetable shops on the corners of Augusta Avenue and Nassau Street are the best in town. Even if you're not hungry now, buy a straw basket or a grocery sack, fill it with goodies, and save it for a picnic lunch at High Park.

CUTTING IT UP ON QUEEN STREET WEST: The feel of this venue is a long way from the spirit of Queen's Park, a neighborhood of quaint redstone buildings of Old Toronto that John Updike in one short story called "brick valentines posted to a distant dowager queen." No dowager would be caught dead (or alive) here. This is a nexus for night people — musicians and music lovers, discoers and slow dancers, diners and insomniacs — all moving to their own rhythm (actually hundreds of rhythms), pulsing through the night into the wee hours of the morning. The street scene is a colorful mishmash of night owls — whether it's the punkers at the *Rivoli* (332 Queen St. W.; phone: 416-596-1908) the cowboys at the *Horseshoe Tavern* (370 Queen St. W.; phone: 416-598-4753), the bikers at the *Black Bull* (298 Queen St. W.; phone: 416-593-2766) or the more traditional crowd at the *Cameron* (408 Queen St. W.; phone: 416-364-0811) — each moves to his or her own beat.

At the center of it all is the *Bamboo Club* (312 Queen St. W.; phone: 416-593-5771) offering Thai and Indonesian specialties. In summer, visit its funky rooftop bar. Around the corner is the sleek *Stilife,* for dancing the night away in an intriguing Gothic setting (217 Richmond St. W.; phone: 416-593-6116). For those who love to linger over countless cups of coffee, the best of the cafés are *Le Select Bistro* (328 Queen St. W.; phone: 416-596-6405) and the old standard, *Peter Pan* (373 Queen St. W.; phone: 416-593-0917). Also along this most unique of Toronto streets are quirky shops with names like *Hoax* (456 Queen St. W.; phone: 416-864-9855), *Boomer* (309 Queen St. W.; phone: 416-598-0013), and *Fab* (312 Queen St. W.; phone: 416-593-5370), sporting strange and funny styles for the young and trendy. Bookstores such as *Edwards* (356 Queen St. W.; phone: 416-593-0126), the *Can-Do* (311 Queen St. W.; phone: 416-977-2351), and the *Bakka Science Fiction Shoppe* (282 Queen St. W.; phone: 416-596-8161) burn the late-night oil, as do shoe stores and upscale designer boutiques. Stroll it; sample the street's sound; experience its rhythm. Though it's an interesting place to stroll during the day, when the stars are out, there's nothing like it.

SECOND CITY: JUST FOR LAUGHS: The room is small and densely packed (in the front row your knees will brush the stage); you'll feel the buzz, the energy of the crackling wit; you'll try to listen to the gags that just keep coming but you're laughing too hard at the last joke to hear the next; your sides hurt, your eyes are tearing, but still they won't stop. For 20 seasons *Second City* has been a must-see in Toronto and it has the alumni to prove it. Some of our best-known funny folk — John Candy, Gilda Radner, and Dan Aykroyd — got their start here (and at its sister club in Chicago), mugging sight gags around the brass pole of the old fire hall at Lombard and Jarvis Streets. Some of *Second City*'s more memorable skits ("East of Eaton's" and "Shopping Down to Buffalo") rely to a degree on regional in-jokes, but don't worry: The yuks come fast and furious and most keep US audiences in mind. The cast puts on one show during the week (with nightly improv performances afterward) and two shows Fridays and Saturdays; reservations are essential.

A good value is the dinner-theater package (dinner is upstairs; just follow the brass firepole), with a basic menu ranging from roast beef to spring chicken and fresh fish. Depending on weekday or weekend, prices range from about $35 for a package or about $15 for the show alone. Information: *Second City,* 110 Lombard St. (phone: 416-862-1162).

THE FALLS, NATURALLY: Ninety miles (144 km) south of Toronto is a natural wonder of the world, surrounded by a town that gives fresh meaning to the term "honky tonk." The Niagara Falls, formed 10,000 years ago as retreating glaciers left what is called the Niagara Escarpment, were first described in Europe in 1678 by the Belgian missionary Louis Hennepin, 3 years after his arrival in Canada with French explorer René Robert Cavelier de La Salle. Located at the border of the United States and Canada, the falls and the surrounding area have a mystique of romance, and have long been a favorite of newlyweds — owing, say local historians, to a visit by Napoleon's brother and his new bride on *their* honeymoon. (Today, those wishing to tie the knot may choose from a wide choice of chapels in the area, and there are many hotels in town that cater to honeymooners.) Suitably hyped, the falls became a major tourist attraction, painted by artists, tightroped by lunatics, and shot down in barrels by people never to be seen again. Charles Dickens praised the falls in the mid-19th century: "I seemed to be lifted from the earth," he wrote. In 1885, Ontario established a provincial park to control the madness. It didn't work. Today there are helicopter trips and cable cars over the falls, tram rides along the perimeter, boat rides at the bottom, exhibits of daredevil barrels, and numerous attractions — wax museums, dolphin shows, museums devoted to Ukrainian art, museums devoted to the famous dead — that have nothing to do with the falls whatsoever. For all that, Niagara Falls remains the world's largest waterfall by volume and a sight that continues to inspire (3.6 million gallons of water flow over the 167-foot-high American Falls every 60 seconds, while more than 40 million gallons a minute crash down Horseshoe Falls, 158 feet high). So ignore the tacky sideshows and focus on the main attraction, whose thunderous power and beauty is sure to thrill even the most jaded traveler. The two best viewing towers — the 524-foot Skylon Tower and the 416-foot Minolta Tower — are on the Canadian side, on a 250-foot escarpment across from the falls. Or take a trip on one of the four boats named *Maid of the Mist* and witness the bottom of the cascade from the dry security of a raincoat provided with the price of a ticket. Finally, don't miss the show at night, when Horseshoe Falls is lighted by 4 billion candlepower in rainbow colors. Like just about everything here, the spectacle is a combination of artifice and nature — the energy for this Technicolor extravaganza is provided by the falls itself.

Toronto's Best Hotels

 Toronto has hostelries to suit a variety of tastes, from stately to hip, from large and luxurious to cozy and intimate. Whether you fancy an old-fashioned environment with ornately carved stone gargoyles and colorful stained glass or the latest chrome-and-steel architecture, Toronto offers both. Despite their differences, the city's outstanding hotels all have one thing in common: They provide attentive service and a welcoming atmosphere, just like home, only better — you don't have to make the beds here. The following are our choices of Toronto's top places to rest your head.

BRADGATE ARMS: An impressive-looking structure, it blends so nicely with its neighbors, the stately mansions and posh apartment buildings of Toronto's fashionable Forest Hill district, that it is known only to locals and a loyal list of regular guests. The 109 guestrooms are distributed between two old 6-story apartment buildings; their quirky shape adds a comfortable, home-like feel. The rooms and suites are pleasantly decorated with heavy wood furniture and antiques; some have fireplaces (non-working) and screened-in porches (though the rooms are air conditioned, fresh-air fanatics will find this a blessing on warm summer nights). The buildings are connected by a glassed-in courtyard, which lends an airy feel to the lobby fountain and greenery, while at night the adjoining piano bar supplies a romantic atmosphere for dancing. The elegant *Tapestry* restaurant offers continental fare; there's also a great Sunday brunch. Information: *Bradgate Arms,* 54 Foxbar Rd., Toronto, Ontario M4V 2G6 (phone: 416-968-1331 or 800-268-7171; fax: 416-968-3743).

DELTA CHELSEA INN: With 1,600 guestrooms, Toronto's largest property also offers a host of dining options, a fitness center and pool where you can work off those dessert calories, and even a place to park the kids — all at surprisingly reasonable rates.

Dark wood furnishings and gray, terra cotta, and deep-blue upholstery enhance the rooms. The view of the lakefront and CN Tower from the top-floor fitness center makes the treadmill seem tolerable. The *Market Garden,* a continental-style café and wine bar, and *Wittles,* with all-day dining and a bountiful buffet, are good dining choices. The *Chelsea Bun* has a fine reputation for its piano bar and entertainment lounge (check out the Sunday afternoon jazz gatherings), and the new *Elm Street Bar* is another good after-hours watering hole. The summer season heralds the opening of the 200-seat *Chelsea Garden Terrace.* The patio also features outdoor jazz and quiet combos on weekend evenings during the summer. Only steps from Yonge Street and 2 blocks north of *Eaton Centre,* it offers special theater packages that allow you to book your room and purchase tickets for *Phantom of the Opera* at the same time. Children will enjoy their own creative center, with games and toys and special movie showings. Information: *Delta Chelsea Inn,* 33 Gerrard St. W., Toronto, Ontario M5G 1Z4 (phone: 416-595-1975 or 800-877-1133; fax: 416-585-4362).

FOUR SEASONS: The flagship property of the internationally renowned chain boasts a guest/employee ratio of almost 1 to 1! Touting the best location in town for leisure- or business-minded guests, it's in the heart of the city's chicest shopping area, surrounded by designer boutiques, galleries, and outdoor cafés, yet only a 10-minute drive to the financial district. Its 243 large, recently renovated guestrooms have their own dressing rooms and marble bathrooms; the 142 suites have separate sitting rooms, balconies, and private Jacuzzis. Other amenities include round-the-clock room service, a concierge, a health club, an indoor/outdoor pool, a sauna, and a Jacuzzi. The hotel also caters to the business traveler with personal computers, cellular phones, an executive secretary, and 18 meeting rooms. Eighteen floors are reserved for nonsmoking guests. There also are several fine restaurants, including the highly rated *Truffles* (see *Toronto's Top Restaurants*), the less formal *Studio Café,* and *La Serre* lounge. Information: *Four Seasons Hotel,* 21 Avenue Rd., Toronto, Ontario M5R 2G1 (phone: 416-964-0411 or 800-332-3442 in the US; fax: 416-446-3308).

INTER-CONTINENTAL TORONTO: The newest luxury property in town, this link in the well-known chain is located across from the *Royal Ontario Museum* and *Varsity Stadium;* die-hard sports fans can actually watch a soccer game from the privacy of their rooms (if they're above the 4th floor facing the stadium). The quiet atrium lobby, decorated with cherry-wood paneling and a ceiling mural, provides an immediate respite from the hustle and bustle of Bloor Street. Each of the 201 rooms and 12 suites is elegantly decorated with rich fabric wall coverings, shiny brass fixtures, and marble baths. (For even greater luxury, the McMaster Suite features a separate dining room, a library, and a sitting room with a fireplace and a baby grand piano.) *Signatures,* the hotel's main restaurant, offers several delicacies for diners who aren't watching their weight — sweet corn and lobster chowder, shrimp tempura, or Muscovit duck breast with sun-dried cherries and black olive chutney. (The restaurant also features a very popular Sunday brunch; be sure to make reservations early.) There's also a fitness center and a lap pool. Information: *Hotel Inter-Continental,* 220 Bloor St. W., Toronto, Ontario M5S 1T8 (phone: 416-960-5200 or 800-327-0200 in the US; fax: 416-960-8269).

RADISSON PLAZA HOTEL ADMIRAL: Originally opened by Toronto restaurateur Walter Oster, this lakefront property recently came under the umbrella of the Radisson hotel group. But rest assured, the character of the place has not changed. The decor of the 157 rooms and 17 suites reflects a nautical theme in soothing blue and green, with brass fixtures and mahogany sea chests. An open promenade deck on the fifth floor is the perfect place to sit and watch the yachts gliding through the waters of Lake Ontario. If you get too warm, you can take a quick dip in the pool, only steps away from your deckside lounge chair; if you're not warm enough, there's a sauna (which — though no one seems to know why — is named Stephanie). Dining options include the *Commodore Dining Room,* whose view of the Toronto Islands complements the continental fare; the *Galley* restaurant, with more modest fare; and the *Bosun's Bar,* a good spot for an after-dinner snack. The hotel is conveniently located near Harbourfront, and just steps out the front door is a huge entertainment complex with dining, dancing, and bars. Also, the *Harbourfront Antique Market* is just across the street. Parking at the *Admiral* is underground (be sure to get your ticket stamped at the desk) and the trolley line, which hooks up to all connections at Union Station, now runs in front of the hotel. Information: *Radisson Plaza Hotel Admiral,* 249 Queen's Quay W., Toronto, Ontario M5J 2N5 (phone: 416-364-5444 or 800-387-1626 in the US; fax: 416-364-2975).

ROYAL YORK: An underground tunnel connects this property, the grande dame of Toronto hotels, to Union Station across the street. The *Canadian Pacific Railroad* built the property in 1929 as a haven for cross-country train travelers. Even if you're not staying here, do as the natives do and stop in for some people watching in the lobby. A recently begun (and ongoing) $100-million renovation includes repolishing the marble panels in the lobby and redecorating the 1,210 rooms and 198 suites with flowered wallpaper and antique reproductions. There are a total of 12 restaurants and bars, including the elegant *Imperial Room;* the *Gazebo,* set in an airy garden; and *Benihana of Tokyo,* a link in the international chain of Japanese steakhouses. Other amenities include a pool and health club. Information: *Royal York Hotel,* 100 Front St. W., Toronto, Ontario M5J 1E3 (phone: 416-368-2511 or 800-828-7447; fax: 416-368-2884).

SUTTON PLACE/HOTEL KEMPINSKI: A member of the Leading Hotels of the World group, this property combines modern service with Old World opulence. It's a popular haunt for celebrities; you may catch a glimpse of such luminaries as Kim Basinger, Paul Newman, and Faye Dunaway in the corner of *Alexandra's Lounge* or *Sans Souci.* While the exterior is rather unassuming, the lobby is decorated with marble, sparkling chandeliers, antique furniture, and Persian rugs. The 208 guestrooms and 72 suites feature amenities such as mini-bars, color TV sets, and VCRs. There is also 24-hour room service, a beauty salon, and a barbershop. The award-winning *Sans Souci* dining room serves continental fare and boasts an extensive wine cellar. Information: *Sutton Place/Hotel Kempinski,* 955 Bay St., Toronto, Ontario M5S 2A2 (phone: 416-924-9221 or 800-268-3790; fax: 416-924-1778).

Toronto's Top Restaurants

The influx during the last half century of immigrants to Toronto has had a positive effect on the city's culinary scene. No longer the kind of place where roast beef and mashed potatoes constitute haute cuisine, there are now virtually hundreds of restaurants offering continental, French, Chinese, Greek, Italian, and Japanese dishes (to name just a few). This gastronomic explosion has created a dazzling (and sometimes confusing) array of choices. The places we list below have different atmospheres, menus, and price ranges, but each combines excellent food with good service — the hallmarks of a satisfying dining experience.

ALLEN'S: Proprietor John Maxwell created this eatery, an offshoot of *Joe Allen's* in New York, as a friendly neighborhood saloon. The long, blue-walled room has a dark wooden bar in front and tables and booths in back, and an old jukebox plays pop tunes — from Big Band numbers to rock hits from the 1950s and 1960s. Photographs of Broadway and Hollywood stars and Maxwell's collection of vintage Jaguars (cars, not cats) add to the quirky decor. Though the menu changes weekly, typical items are crab burgers, rack of lamb, Manhattan capon wings (a meatier and less spicy version of Buffalo chicken wings), and sirloin steaks with caramelized onions. Another good choice is the burger with chunky fries on the side (it's not listed on the menu, but just ask). During the spring and summer, the restaurant offers dining on its back patio and a special menu featuring barbecued chicken, shrimp, lobster, and pork. Information: *Allen's,* 143 Danforth Ave. (phone: 416-463-3086).

LA BODEGA: One of the best French restaurants in the city (in spite of its Spanish name), it is set in a stately Victorian mansion. The decor evokes old-fashioned charm: lace curtains, antique furnishings, and tapestries. The menu features crispy breast of duck with raspberry sauce and fresh seafood, and the lengthy wine list includes several of each year's best beaujolais. In the background, French folk songs and classical music complete the mood. In summer, there is dining on the patio at tables sheltered by large, bright umbrellas. Information: *La Bodega,* 30 Baldwin St. (phone: 416-977-1287).

ORSO: Another John Maxwell dining place (see *Allen's,* above), this Italian establishment is housed in a renovated 2-story 19th-century building. The decor is simple and elegant, with cool pastels, dark wooden floors, and marble walls; the plates and bowls are hand-crafted and imported from Italy. A good starter is pizza with a wafer-thin crust (try the mussels and mushroom combo), and the choice of entrées includes rack of lamb, salmon with pasta, and grilled swordfish with cream and mango relish. For dessert, choose between delicate Italian ices or a rich mascarpone mousse coated with thick marsala. There are also 2 small bars on each floor that serve wine by the glass, imported beers, and a great cup of cappuccino, as well as a variety of grappa, the Italian liqueur known as "firewater." Dining on one of the two outdoor patios is a pleasant way to spend a warm summer evening. Information: *Orso,* 106 John St. (phone: 416-596-1989).

OUZERI: Eating here is like going to a block party: Aristedes, the owner, has created a bustling social atmosphere to complement his menu of Greek specialties. In summer, the large picture windows disappear and the crowd spills out onto the sidewalk, talking, sipping, and nibbling until the wee hours (4 AM). Entrées include rabbit and onion pie wrapped in a phyllo crust; grilled lamb with garlic, lemon, and oregano; and calamari fried in olive oil. The wine list features several good Greek vintages, plus retsina and ouzo. At lunch during the week, the restaurant presents a Greek version of dim sum; carts are rolled through the room bearing such delicacies as tender octopus chunks. Information: *Ouzeri,* 500 Danforth Ave. (phone: 416-778-0500).

SCARAMOUCHE: Named for a character in the commedia dell'arte, there are paintings of Scaramouche and other members of the "cast" lining the walls at this romantic, candlelit restaurant. The menu changes weekly in the main dining room, which serves continental dishes and Italian specialties; the adjoining pasta bar provides lighter Mediterranean fare. Sample entrées include calamari, sautéed and served with shiitake mushrooms and sweet red peppers; mussel soup laced with saffron; salmon and trout (both smoked on the premises); and tender veal chops accompanied by sweet morels and Jerusalem artichokes. The wine list concentrates on French and Italian labels, with an occasional American vintage. For dessert, try the fresh strawberries, apples, and peaches wrapped in puff pastry. It's not the easiest place to find due to its location on a little side street just off Avenue Road (ask for directions in advance or find a knowledgeable cab driver), but you'll find the dining experience worth the effort. Information: *Scaramouche,* 1 Benvenuto Pl. (phone: 416-961-8011).

SHOPSY'S: The quintessential Toronto deli, it started out as a rather seedy dive in the heart of the Jewish garment district on Spadina Avenue. Over the years, it attracted a large, loyal clientele. When the restaurant moved to a more uptown location a few years ago, fans worried that the quality of the food would suffer, but the menu has remained the same: great hot dogs, huge sandwiches spilling over with corned beef or Montreal smoked meat, potato pancakes, knishes, creamy potato salad, and bagels with cream cheese and lox. Its setting — directly across from the *O'Keefe Centre* and the *St. Lawrence Centre* — makes this a popular pre- and post-theater stop; in summertime, there's also outdoor seating along Front Street — great for people watching. Information: *Shopsy's,* 33 Yonge St. (phone: 416-365-3333).

SPIAGGIA TRATTORIA: Tucked away at the end of Queen Street East, this little blue room, with its house-party atmosphere, is always crowded — definitely not the place for an intimate supper. But the menu of Italian specialties — carrot, ginger, and orange soup; spinach and herb linguine served with sautéed shrimp and scallops in a fresh basil and tomato sauce; osso buco; or cioppino (a delicate seafood stew) — is well worth waiting for. The wine list features labels from smaller vineyards in Italy and France, while the beers are from Canadian breweries. Information: *Spiaggia Trattoria,* 2318 Queen St. E. (phone: 416-699-4656).

TRAPPER'S: The name evokes images of the simpler, wilderness-oriented days of Canada's past and owner-chef Chris Boland has successfully reproduced that era's hearty fare using fresh local produce, meat, game, and fish. You can watch your order being prepared in the open kitchen at the back of this boxy little restaurant designed in muted earth tones. Choose from such traditional Canadian dishes as chicken and liver pâté with port preserve or Ontario pork loin, stuffed with fettuccine, ripe olives, scallions, and aged Canadian cheddar and served with gooseberry sauce. If you've never had cheddar cheese soup, this is the place to sample it. The lengthy wine list includes almost 300 vintages, both domestic and imported. Dessert offerings (if you still have room) include dark-rum chocolate truffle cake or a deep-dish cobbler of apples, pears, and apricots served with ice cream. Information: *Trapper's,* 3479 Yonge St. (phone: 416-482-6211).

TRUFFLES: For several years, the dining room at the *Four Seasons* hotel has garnered accolades for its fine continental fare and romantic atmosphere. The elegant decor features antique tapestries, oil paintings, and chairs upholstered in gray-blue velvet brocade. Linen-covered tables are set with porcelain, crystal, silver, and fresh flowers. The menu, overseen by executive chef Susan Weaver, offers rich, sumptuous dishes (calorie-counters should beware): Maine lobster sautéed with corn and onions, roast rack of lamb, Atlantic salmon with leeks and beluga caviar, and spaghettini with black truffles. The wine list features more than 200 vintages from France, Italy, Canada, the US, South America, Australia, and Spain. To top off the meal, you can choose from among such decadent desserts as chocolate macaroon and banana cake, Grand Marnier soufflé with vanilla sauce, and a pineapple milkshake complete with a chocolate straw. Information: *Truffles at the Four Seasons Hotel,* 21 Yorkville Ave. (phone: 416-964-0411).

For the Body

Great Golf

 A sure sign of spring is the sound of "fore!" in the air. In Toronto, this is often heard in practice sessions in backyards throughout the city, as anxious duffers sharpen their strokes even while the last traces of frost are still on the ground. Despite its long and bone-chilling winters, Toronto is a golfing town. Although many of the best courses, such as the *King Valley Golf Club* and the *Aurora Highlands Country Club,* are now private, members-only affairs, there are several public courses in the area that offer a challenging venue for the visiting golfer.

CALEDON COUNTRY CLUB: The 6,140-yard course here is part of a public resort offering other sports facilities, such as tennis courts and an outdoor pool. The par 71, 18-hole venue is set on scenic, challenging terrain in the hills of Caledon, 40 miles (64 km) northwest of the city. The greens fees on weekdays are CN$30 before 3 PM and CN$25 afterward; on weekends, the fees are CN$35 before 3 PM and CN$25 afterward. It's worth noting that the greens can be quite fast — three putts per hole is not uncommon. Information: *Caledon Country Club,* 2121 Olde Baseline Rd., Inglewood, Ontario L0N 1K0 (phone: 416-798-4830).

DON VALLEY GOLF COURSE: Actually 6½ miles (10 km) from the center of downtown Toronto, this difficult municipal course has the Don River as its main hazard. This winding brook traverses the course and comes into play on at least 11 holes. Greens fees are CN$20 during the day and CN$16 after 5:30 PM. Information: *Don Valley Golf Course,* 4200 Yonge St., Willowdale, Ontario M2P 1N9 (phone: 416-392-2465).

GLEN ABBEY: Site of the annual *Canadian Open,* this 7,112-yard, 18-hole Jack Nicklaus–designed course has hosted many of the sport's greats and offers an exciting challenge to the experienced golfer. (It may prove too difficult and frustrating for novices, however, in spite of the club's excellent instruction program.) Greens fees are CN$90 on weekdays and CN$95 on weekends and holidays. Also on the grounds are the *Canadian Golf Hall of Fame* and a museum of golf memorabilia. Located on Dorval Drive in Oakville, about 15 miles (24 km) from midtown. Information: *Glen Abbey,* 1333 Dorval Dr., Oakville, Ontario L6J 4Z3 (phone: 416-844-1811).

LAKEVIEW: The 98-year-old course here hosted the *Canadian Open* in 1923 and 1932. Despite its short length (6,039 yards), this par 71 venue in Mississauga (12 miles/30 km west of downtown Toronto) presents 18 challenging holes, featuring narrow fairways and undulating greens. There's also a creek that passes through the course and comes into play on 8 holes. The greens fee is CN$20. Information: *Lakeview Golf Club,* 1190 Dixie Rd. S., Mississauga, Ontario L5E 2P4 (phone: 416-278-4900).

RICHMOND HILL: Built in 1991, this short (6,004-yard) 18-holer throws a surprising number of hazards at the unwary golfer — about 70 sand traps, streams, ponds, and very narrow fairways that require accurate shots. It's a tough par 70 — worth a visit even though it isn't particularly scenic. Greens fees are CN$35 on weekdays and CN$42 on weekends. Located in Richmond Hill, just outside the city, at the intersection of Highway 7 and Bathurst Street. Information: *Richmond Hill,* 8755 Bathurst St., Richmond Hill, Ontario L4C 4X7 (phone: 416-889-4653).

Taking to the Waters: Sailing and Yachting

Every year, as spring blossoms into summer, white sails are hoisted by the hundreds in the waters along Toronto's Harbourfront area. Sailing Lake Ontario is a popular activity among city dwellers and various clubs dot the coastline from Oakville in the west to Port Hope in the east, with the majority located along the city's shoreline. Most of these, such as the tony *Royal Canadian Yacht Club,* are strictly private. But never fear: Toronto has facilities for tars of all types — tony and otherwise — that offer boat and equipment rentals; some also conduct classes. And for more serious sailors, the opportunity to cruise along Ontario's Georgian Bay and North Channel or the Thousand Islands and the Bay of Quinte are virtually irresistible.

BLUFFER'S PARK MARINA: Located northeast of the city at the base of the Scarborough Bluffs on a 400-acre site of scenic parkland and beaches, the area's newest marina has more than 500 berths and offers sailing lessons (with instructors certified by the *Canadian Yachting Association*) geared to both novice and advanced sailors. Sailboats for pleasure cruising and larger boats for fishing excursions are available for rent. The facility is especially convenient to the eastern side of the city, but it is only a short drive from downtown and nowhere near as crowded as the various Harbourfront operations. To get here, take Lakeshore Boulevard East to *Greenwood Racetrack* (it becomes Woodbine Avenue here). Take Woodbine north to St. Clair Avenue; turn right, then continue to Brimley Road. Information: *Bluffer's Park Marina,* 7 Brimley Rd. S., Scarborough, Ontario M1M 3W3 (phone: 416-266-4556 for rentals; 416-267-8379 for sailing school).

HARBOURSIDE SAILING SCHOOL: A harborside company (incorporating *Executive Sailing Charters*) providing instruction and boat rentals. Courses range from a 30-hour basic sailing course to an advanced 16-day workshop on offshore cruising. Craft available for charter include yachts and powerboats as well as sailboats. Located in the *Harbourfront Nautical Centre,* in the middle of Harbourfront, just west of the *Radisson Plaza* hotel. Information: *Harbourside Sailing School,* 283 Queen's Quay W., Toronto, Ontario M5V 1A2 (phone: 416-947-0333).

ONTARIO'S GEORGIAN BAY AND NORTH CHANNEL: For fine vacation cruising, a Toronto sailor is apt to travel to Lake Huron's spectacular Georgian Bay, which lies about 60 miles (96 km) northwest of Toronto across the neck of land that separates the city from the lake. The vast, bay- and cove-notched, island-dotted expanse of water known as the North Channel — contained to the south by hundred-mile-long Manitoulin Island and to the north by the Ontario mainland — ranks among the prime cruising areas of the world. You can sun yourself on a lonely rock, pick blueberries the size of grapes, fish, swim, explore long fjord-like bays, and spend your nights anchored in the leeward side of an island or tied up in a tiny cove where it's just you, the water, and the stars. Or you can dock at one of the many resorts and marinas concentrated around Killarney, on the mainland, and Little Current, on Manitoulin Island, for a good meal and some friendly conversation. Powerboating has always been popular, but sailing is taking over, due to the cost of gas; a few 25- to 35-foot sailboats are available for charter.

Information: *Ontario Ministry of Tourism and Recreation,* 77 Bloor St. W., 9th Fl., Toronto, Ontario M7A 2R9 (phone: 800-ONTARIO or 416-314-0944); and *Ontario Sailing Association,* 1220 Sheppard Ave. E., Willowdale, Ontario M2K 2X1 (phone: 416-495-4240).

THOUSAND ISLANDS AND THE BAY OF QUINTE: This province has its fair share of lakes and waterways, from the Great Lakes north to Hudson Bay. Toronto citizens are such wildly enthusiastic sailors, in fact, and the harbor is so full on weekends that some locals assert they'd rather contend with a highway. But for vacation cruising, one of the prime destinations is this area at the eastern end of Lake Ontario, where the lake flows into the St. Lawrence River. The Thousand Islands — over 1,700 pink granite or limestone outcroppings ranged between Kingston and Brockville — offer good fishing, fine swimming, and delightful scenery. St. Lawrence Islands National Park provides mooring, camping, picnic facilities, and interpretive programs throughout the islands (see listing later in this section). The Bay of Quinte — long, narrow, and irregular — ranks among the province's prettiest backwaters, and some people prefer it to the Thousand Islands nearby because of the virtual absence of commercial and power-cruising traffic. The bay, in the heart of historic Prince Edward County, is flanked by prosperous farmlands, wooded slopes, limestone escarpments, sandy beaches, and several of Ontario's oldest towns; occasionally, you'll sense yourself in the heart of the Canadian North. To get to the Bay of Quinte from the west, you can either travel around the Isthmus of Murray or, like most boaters, traverse the straight-as-an-arrow, 7-mile (11-km) Murray Canal, near Trenton — a lovely trip. The bay is also the southern terminus of the Trent-Severn Waterway, a 240-mile (380-km) inland waterway connecting Lake Ontario to Georgian Bay through the heart of central Ontario. Most services can be found in Kingston. Information: *Eastern Ontario Travel Association,* 209 Ontario St., Kingston, Ontario K7L 2Z1 (phone: 613-549-3682); *Ontario Ministry of Tourism and Recreation,* 77 Bloor St. W., 9th Fl., Toronto, Ontario M7A 2R9 (phone: 800-ONTARIO from the continental US and Canada, except the Yukon); *St. Lawrence Islands National Park,* Box 469, RR3, Mallorytown, Ontario K0E 1R0 (phone: 613-923-5261); *Venture Yacht Charters,* Portsmouth Olympic Harbour, 53 Yonge St., Kingston, Ontario K7M 1E4 (phone: 613-549-1007); the *Portsmouth Olympic Harbour,* 53 Yonge St., Kingston, Ontario K7M 1E4 (phone: 613-544-9842); and the *Murray Canal,* c/o the Trent-Severn Waterway, PO Box 567, Peterborough, Ontario K9J 6Z6 (phone: 705-742-9267).

Biking in Toronto

 The streets of "Muddy York" (as Toronto was once known) were originally designed for horse and buggy, and later for automobile traffic. But though the lowly bicycle was completely overlooked as a possible means of transportation at the time, several areas of the city provide pleasant, scenic trails.

Bike rental shops can be found throughout Toronto. Some of the best are *Toronto Island Bicycle Rental* (on Centre Island; phone: 416-365-7901); *Boardwalk Cycle* (748 Markham Rd.; phone: 416-431-1961); *High Park Cycle and Sports* (1168 Bloor St. W.; phone: 416-532-7300); and *McBride Cycle* near Harbourfront (180 Queen's Quay W.; phone: 416-367-5651). For more information about local trails and places to rent equipment, check out *The Great Toronto Bicycling Guide,* by Elliot Katz (Great North Books; $3.95).

HIGH PARK: The largest recreation area in the city, this 400-acre park just west of downtown is easily accessible by subway (bikes are allowed on the subway, except at rush hour). Its bike trails meander through the park, where you can stop to visit the historic Colborne Lodge, feed yaks and llamas at the small zoo, row a boat on Grenadier Pond, or take in an afternoon concert at the bandstand. It's also possible to connect with the 12-mile (20-km) Martin Goodman Trail, which leads to the lakeshore beaches of Sunnyside Park. (Note, however, that High Park is especially popular — and crowded — on summer weekends.)

MARTIN GOODMAN TRAIL: Spanning the full length of Toronto's lakefront — from the far eastern end of the Beach district to the Humber River, and past the Sunnyside beaches in the west — the recently repaved 12-mile (20-km) trail is one of the most pleasant bike paths in the city. The shoreline trail, named for late *Toronto Star* editor Martin Goodman, extends along Lake Ontario past such local sites of interest as Fort York and the *Marine Museum,* through Harbourfront, and beneath the shadow of the CN Tower. Note that the portions of the trail near the east and west beaches have become very popular with local cyclists, so you may have a lot of company as you pedal.

ROSEDALE VALLEY: Situated in mid-Toronto, this 9-mile (14-km) trail, which winds through the wooded area of the Rosedale Valley and along the Don River, affords an opportunity to sample the countryside without ever leaving the city (or even losing sight of it). Start on Yonge Street just north of Bloor at the Rosedale subway stop. The bike path, located on the right side of the road, spirals downward into the Don Valley ravine. The trail leads under the Bloor Viaduct, the bustling bridge where Bloor Street becomes Danforth Avenue, and wends its way alongside the Don River. Once under the bridge, you have a choice: Follow the river north to the beautiful displays of colorful plants at Edwards Gardens (about 5 miles/8 km away); continue south to Cherry Beach; or hook up with the Martin Goodman Trail and ride along the shores of Lake Ontario.

TORONTO ISLANDS: To get to these dots of land, a picturesque spot for biking, take a ferry from dockside at Queens Quay behind the *Harbour Castle Westin.* The closest subway stop is Union Station on Front Street, and the ferry docks are just a few minutes' walk (don't try riding your bike here, as traffic is usually very heavy). The islands are linked by bridges, so you can easily ride from one to another. The trails are decidedly informal: Some are paved, while others are hard-packed dirt; in most areas you can choose to ride along the grass as well. A good, well-defined route is on the semicircular trail from Ward's Island to Hanlan's Point, but the islands are made for casual wanderings, alongside trees, bushes, and waterways, stopping for a snack at a refreshment stand or relaxing on a bench along the way. You also can cook your lunch at one of the many stone barbecue pits.

For the Mind

Memorable Museums

 As the cultural and cosmopolitan center of Canada, Toronto and its environs have an impressive number of museums covering a wide variety of subjects. Here visitors can study landscapes of northern Canada painted by the legendary "Group of Seven," experiment with electricity, explore the area's history — or even visit a hockey hall of fame. Each is worthy of note; some will inspire you to return for another look. Your stay in Toronto will be enriched by a visit to one or all of them.

ART GALLERY OF ONTARIO: This white concrete structure houses the Henry Moore Sculpture Centre, with the world's largest public collection of Moore's work (300 pieces, including 5 large bronzes and 40 major original plasters, as well as drawings, woodcuts, and etchings). Also here is the Moore Gallery, an impressive room designed by the sculptor himself, in which natural light through the ceiling illuminates 15 large sculptures, all plaster casts or original plasters. Other highlights of the permanent collection are works by Tintoretto, Augustus John, Renoir, Rubens, and other Old Masters, Impressionists, and early 20th-century artists. Over half of the permanent collection is devoted to works of Canadian artists, including the Group of Seven landscape painters and contemporary artists. One of the most important art collections in the country, it is the heart (or at least the memory) of the art world of English Canada. The museum recently completed an extensive expansion and renovation, refurbishing its 20 galleries and adding another 30; the additional space will house contemporary works of Canadian and international painters, sculpture, drawings, and Inuit artwork. Connected to the gallery by an underground walkway is the Grange, the oldest remaining brick house in Toronto (ca. 1817), which has been restored to its original polish as a 19th-century gentleman's home. Closed Mondays. Admission charge. Information: *Art Gallery of Ontario,* 317 Dundas St. W. (phone: 416-977-0414).

HOCKEY HALL OF FAME AND MUSEUM: For the serious hockey fan, a visit to this historical museum is a must. The *Stanley Cup,* the oldest of North America's professional sports trophies, is housed here (the NHL team that wins the cup each year gets to hold it for a month). So are most of the sport's other famous trophies — *Challenge Cup, Canada Cup,* and all of the National Hockey League's major trophies. Officially endorsed by the NHL, the CAHA, and the International Ice Hockey Federation, the *Hockey Hall of Fame* has sections devoted to famous goalies, the skates and sticks of well-known players, and other celebrated paraphernalia of the sport; a number of audiovisual presentations and regular programs are also part of the show. The museum is temporarily closed while it moves to a new downtown location at the corner of Front and Yonge Streets; it is scheduled to reopen early this summer. Information: *Hockey Hall of Fame and Museum,* Exhibition Pl. (phone: 416-595-1345).

MARINE MUSEUM OF UPPER CANADA: On the grounds of the 115-year-old *Canadian National Exhibition,* this historic museum is the last surviving structure of seven buildings that were erected in 1841 to replace the original Fort York. A tribute to Toronto's port, from its origins with the fur trade to its modern-day traffic of ocean freighters, Great Lakes steamers, and reconstructed paddle wheelers, the museum houses displays of model ships, marine artwork, and an audiovisual presentation of the maritime history of the Great Lakes. There is also a statue of Torontonian Ned Hanlan, the world rowing champion in 1880, as well as the dockside steam tug named after him. Open daily except *Christmas, Boxing Day* (December 26), and *New Year's Day.* Admission charge. Information: *Marine Museum of Upper Canada,* Lakeshore Blvd., Stanley Barracks, Exhibition Pl. (phone: 416-392-6827).

McMICHAEL CANADIAN ART COLLECTION: Though located some 25 miles (40 km) north of the city, this art gallery is well worth the drive. Donated to the province of Ontario in 1965 by Robert McMichael, a local businessman, and his wife Signe, the collection features Canadian landscape paintings. Among the pieces are many works of the Group of Seven, who immortalized Canada's northern wilderness in their paintings and profoundly influenced Canadian art. The building is almost a work of art in itself: Built of hand-hewn logs and fieldstone (encompassing the McMichaels' original log-cabin residence), it is set on a lovely 100-acre parcel of land overlooking the Humber River Valley. Other items on display include sculptures and prints by Inuit and Northwest Coast Indian artists. There is also a gift shop selling prints of the exhibits, art and history books, and postcards. You can bring a picnic to enjoy on the grounds, but there is also a good restaurant on the premises that serves lunchtime fare. Open daily from May to October; closed Mondays the rest of the year. Admission charge. To get there, take Highway 401 west to Highway 400 north, then take Major Mackenzie Drive west into Kleinburg and follow the signs to the museum. Information: *McMichael Art Collection,* Islington Ave., Kleinburg (phone: 416-893-1121).

ONTARIO SCIENCE CENTRE: Ontario's contribution to Canada's centennial celebration, this spectacular facility was built in 1967 at a cost of $30 million. Each year since then it has attracted over 1.5 million visitors from all over the world. Designed by architect Raymond Moriyama, the museum is extremely well integrated with its site on the Don River ravine. The structure is comprised of several buildings on different levels. Visitors enter the museum at the street level and work their way down on glass-enclosed escalators that offer views of the lush, wooded valley. The focus here is on modern science (only a fifth of the exhibits are historical) and the emphasis is on interaction. Each of the many exhibits, which include the Food/Earth Hall, Exploring Space, the Hall of Communication, the Hall of Life, the Hall of Transportation, the Science Arcade, and the Hall of the Atom, provides visitors with plenty of opportunities to participate. You can generate electricity with a bicycle, play "hangman" with a computer, make a machine talk, and test your fitness, reflexes, or perception. Demonstrations, films, and theater performances also are offered regularly. There are no guided tours (although knowledgeable staff members are around to offer assistance if needed), so visitors may set their own pace, plotting a course with the help of the *Science Centre*'s map. There are far too many things to see and do in one visit, so pick a few exhibits that interest you, and take your time pushing buttons, cranking cranks, playing games, and learning more about science, technology, and the world. Open daily. Admission charge. Information: *Ontario Science Centre,* 770 Don Mills Rd. (phone: 416-429-4100).

ROYAL ONTARIO MUSEUM: Affectionately known as the *ROM,* this is Canada's largest public museum — made even larger after an $83-million renovation and expansion project. With its unique combination of departments in art, archaeology and science (20 in all), it offers visitors a veritable feast of exhibits from which to choose. Among the highlights is the internationally acclaimed 800-piece Chinese collection, which includes art and artifacts displayed in period room settings, and the only Chinese tomb in the Western world. There also are impressive collections of textiles and weapons, and Egyptian mummies and other artifacts. Among the popular science exhibits are a gallery of dinosaur skeletons, the Life Sciences Gallery with its living insects, and the bat cave, which also features live specimens of the creepy creatures. Recent additions include the European Gallery, the Gallery of Birds, and the Ethnology Gallery of the Native Peoples of North America. The adjacent *McLaughlin Planetarium* has interactive displays, computer games, and laser and other shows. Two other *ROM* buildings are a short walk from the main museum: the *Sigmund Samuel Building* is devoted to the decorative arts of Canada, and the *George E. Gardiner Museum* has an extensive collection of ceramic art. The *ROM* gift shop sells interesting items from around the world. Located not far from the financial hub of Canada on Bay Street and close to lavish shopping in Yorkville, the museum is a rich preserve of civilization in the midst of a city that lives furiously in the present. The main museum and the *Samuel Building* are closed Mondays between *Labour Day* and *Victoria Day;* the *Gardiner Museum* and planetarium are closed Mondays year-round; the entire complex is closed on *Christmas* and *New Year's Day.* Admission charge. Information: *Royal Ontario Museum,* 100 Queen's Park (phone: 416-586-5549).

Historic Houses

Toronto is passionately committed to preserving its heritage, as is evidenced by its historical society, which has fought vigorously to balance the chrome and steel of modern architecture with the rough-hewn stone and mortar buildings of past generations. And local developers have been challenged to create innovative designs that successfully achieve this balance. For instance, *Eaton Centre,* the ultramodern shopping gallery, was designed around the city's oldest church, the Church of the Holy Trinity (built in 1845), and Scadding House, the 1857 home of Henry Scadding, an early Toronto historian. Historic sites abound throughout the city; they can be recognized by the brass plaques that explain their significance. Listed below are a few places to get you started on a tour through Toronto's past.

CASA LOMA: The high turrets of this huge mansion can be seen for miles around, poking through treetops in the northern part of the city. Sir Henry Pellatt, a pioneer in the use of hydroelectric power in Canada, built this 98-room house between 1911 and 1914 to accommodate his extensive collection of antique furniture and art. Fascinated with medieval architecture, Pellatt spent years (and about CN$5 million) gathering the finest materials and furnishings to create his European-style castle: Scottish stonemasons built the walls of the structure; oak paneling was imported from Great Britain and marble from Italy. The mansion features a secret staircase, a conservatory, a wine cellar, 25 fireplaces, and 15 bathrooms. Outside, vast horse stables made of mahogany and marble (and complete with carpeting on the floor) are connected to the house by an 800-foot tunnel. Eventually, Sir Henry fell on hard times, and *Casa Loma* was appropriated by the city for back taxes and neglected for many years. Then, in 1937, the *Kiwanis Club* and the *Garden Club of Toronto* restored the house and grounds to their former glory. On Saturday nights during the summer, there's ballroom dancing in the conservatory. Open daily. Admission charge includes a guided tour, but you can take a self-guided tour if you prefer. Located 2 blocks north of the Spadina subway stop. Information: *Casa Loma,* 1 Austin Terr. (phone: 416-923-1711).

COLBORNE LODGE: When architect John George Howard built his home in 1837, he and his wife were alone in the wilderness, miles from the small city of Toronto. Today the cottage stands in the middle of High Park, which Howard donated to the city in 1873. It is a splendid example of an 18th-century Regency-style cottage, with a verandah along three sides affording spectacular views of both Lake Ontario to the south and Grenadier Pond to the west. The house was designed with both summer and winter kitchens, a wine cellar, and one of the first examples of indoor plumbing in North America. The staff, outfitted in authentic period costumes, will show you the antique furnishings and early Canadian art, including some watercolors by Howard himself. Open daily. Admission charge. The lodge is a pleasant 15-minute walk through the park from the High Park station along the Bloor subway line. Information: *Colborne Lodge,* Colborne Lodge Dr., High Park (phone: 416-392-6916).

FORT YORK: This site marks the founding of Toronto in 1793, when a small garrison was constructed to protect the entrance to Toronto Bay. It was invaded and temporarily occupied by American troops in 1812; the next year, British forces marched on Washington and sacked the city in retaliation. During this invasion, the president's mansion was almost totally destroyed; it was rebuilt quickly and painted white, giving birth to its nickname, "the White House." Today, the defensive walls of Fort York encompass gunpowder magazines, soldiers' barracks, and the more comfortable officers' quarters. There are various other restored structures on the site and tours are given by staff dressed in authentic guards' uniforms. Open daily. Admission charge. Information: *Fort York,* Garrison Rd. off Fleet St., near Exhibition Pl. (phone: 416-392-6907).

MACKENZIE HOUSE: Built in 1857, this house was given to Scotsman William Lyon Mackenzie, who was Toronto's first mayor (1834–1835), by his followers. Originally dedicated to the formation of a fair and equitable Canadian political system, which he supported in his own newspaper, the *Colonial Advocate,* Mackenzie's views became more extreme; he instigated the Upper Canada Rebellion of 1837, an uprising of 750 laborers and farmers against the government. The rebellion was quickly squelched; Mackenzie fled to the US, but was granted amnesty 12 years later and permitted to return. (His followers were not so lucky: They were either executed or sent to prison camps.) This gaslit row house in downtown Toronto has not changed since Mackenzie lived here; the furniture, napery, kitchen utensils, and even the costumes of the staff are authentic to the 1850s. There is also a reconstructed print shop, the place where the Scottish political leader produced his inflammatory daily pamphlets. Open daily. Admission charge. Located in the heart of downtown, just steps north of Queen Street. Information: *Mackenzie House,* 82 Bond St. (phone: 416-392-6915).

SPADINA: The name of this house, just east of *Casa Loma,* is an Indian word for "hill." Built in 1866 for financier James Austin, the 50-room house — unlike others of the period — is spacious and open, reminiscent of an Italian villa. Four generations of Austins have lived on the estate, and the eclectic collection of Victorian, Edwardian, and Art Nouveau furniture reflects that history. The Palm Room and the billiards parlor have been faithfully maintained in a style authentic to the late 19th century. Nature lovers will also appreciate the fine gardens, restored by the *Garden Club of Toronto* and planted with over 300 varieties of plants and shrubs. Open daily. Admission charge. Located 2 blocks north of the Spadina subway station. Information: *Spadina,* 285 Spadina Rd. (phone: 416-392-6910).

Performing Arts: Theater, Music, and Dance

 Time was when Torontonians were accustomed to staying home at night — the moon came out, they went inside. As recently as 30 years ago there were only two theaters in Toronto. It was the development of fine local groups such as the *National Ballet of Canada,* the *Canadian Opera Company,* and the *Second City* comedy troupe that lured steadily growing legions of people out of their homes for an evening's entertainment, and the rest, as they say, is history. The afore-mentioned companies, as well as Broadway and West End road productions and innovative works by up-and-coming local artists, can be found treading the boards at the following major theaters.

ELGIN AND WINTER GARDEN: These two venues occupy the same building and, not surprisingly, they are often lumped together in the minds of local residents: The 1,000-seat *Winter Garden* is stacked atop the 1,500-seat *Elgin*. Both were designed by architect Thomas Lamb; the lower theater, completed in 1913, has an elegant, stately appearance, while the upper one, completed in 1914, is more avant-garde, with land-scape murals on the walls and pillars that resemble trees. Both stages now host large-scale touring productions from Broadway and London's West End. Daily public tours of both theaters are available. Information: *Elgin and Winter Garden,* 189 Yonge St. (phone: 416-594-0755).

MASSEY HALL: Named for Hart Massey, of Canada's famed Massey clan (Ray-mond, the late Hollywood actor, and Vincent, a former Governor-General of Canada, are other members), who built it in 1894. This cavernous, 2,765-seat, 3-level music hall boasts perfect acoustics throughout. (Some seats have restricted vision, though, so it's a good idea to check with the box office before purchasing tickets.) Formerly home of the *Toronto Symphony* before they moved to *Roy Thomson Hall,* today it hosts concerts by well-known performers of music ranging from classical and jazz to rock and blues. Canadian singer Gordon Lightfoot's week-long series of concerts here continues to be an annual rite of spring in the city. Located on Victoria Street, around the corner from Yonge Street and *Eaton Centre.* Information: *Massey Hall,* 178 Victoria St. (phone: 416-363-7301).

O'KEEFE CENTRE: Home of the *National Ballet of Canada* and the *Canadian Opera Company,* the center also hosts visiting Broadway shows and concerts by a wide range of popular artists. Located at the edge of the Esplanade, a street of many restaurants and pubs, it's easy to find a place to have dinner before or after the show. Information: *O'Keefe Centre,* 1 Front St. E. (phone: 416-872-2262).

OLD FIRE HALL: *Second City,* an offbeat comedy troupe à la "Saturday Night Live," presents its satirical sketches 7 nights a week here. The building, which was in fact once a fire station (it dates from 1867), is now a 200-seat theater and restaurant. An offshoot of the original Chicago-based comedy company, *Second City* has been presenting its particular brand of biting and topical humor in Toronto since 1974. Well-known comedians Dan Aykroyd, John Candy, and Martin Short, among others, got started here. Information: *The Old Fire Hall,* 110 Lombard St. (phone: 416-863-1111).

PREMIER DANCE THEATRE: Eberhard Zeidler, the architect behind the construc-tion of *Eaton Centre,* built this space exclusively for dance; one special feature of the design is that no one in the audience is more than 50 feet from the stage. More than 80 companies have performed here since its opening, including *Les Ballets Jazz de Montréal,* the *Alvin Ailey American Dance Theater, DanceBrazil,* and Israel's *Batsheva Dance Company.* There is also an annual series of dance works sponsored by the Canadian Imperial Bank of Commerce. Information: *Premier Dance Theatre,* Queen's Quay Terminal (phone: 416-973-4000).

ROYAL ALEXANDRA THEATRE: Acquired and restored to Edwardian splendor by Toronto store owner and entrepreneur Ed Mirvish in 1963, this theater stages shows from New York and London, as well as local productions. Don't expect anything experimental, but it's Broadway-quality theater. Information: *Royal Alexandra Theatre,* 260 King St. W. (phone: 416-593-4211).

ROY THOMSON HALL: Home of the *Toronto Symphony Orchestra,* this unique round structure, which opened in 1982, is clad in diamond-shaped glass panels that glisten in the sunlight and allow the lights of evening performances to shine through at night. The design, by Canadian architect Arthur Erickson, is considered daring to some, inspiring to others. The acoustics — controlled by state-of-the-art technology — are excellent. Information: *Roy Thomson Hall,* 60 Simcoe St. (phone: 416-593-4828).

THEATER FESTIVALS

If you're a fan of first class theater, keep in mind that two internationally renowned theater festivals are held every year throughout the spring, summer, and fall season within 2 hours of downtown Toronto. Focusing on two of the undisputed masters of playwrighting, William Shakespeare and George Bernard Shaw, these events provide a unique opportunity to experience the best of the boards; they are definitely worth a special trip.

SHAW FESTIVAL, Niagara-on-the-Lake: With some help from an energetic citizenry instrumental in restoring the many old buildings and homes of this historic Upper Canada capital, George Bernard Shaw has done for Niagara-on-the-Lake (located 82 miles/131 km from Toronto) what Shakespeare did for Stratford. Every year, from late April through October, three separate theaters are given over to productions of ten plays by the celebrated playwright (author of *Pygmalion, Major Barbara,* and *Arms and the Man,* among others) and his contemporaries. Anything written during Shaw's lifetime (1856–1950) may be performed. What began as a small community of devoted actors has become one of the most successful professional theaters in North America. Information: *Shaw Festival,* PO Box 774, Niagara-on-the-Lake, Ontario L0S 1J0 (phone: 416-468-2172).

STRATFORD FESTIVAL, Stratford: This event, held in Stratford (98 miles/157 km from Toronto) from May through mid-November, produces some of the best theater in the world. Originally known for its star-studded productions of Shakespeare, the festival now presents a fine program that also includes plays by other classical writers, world premieres, musicals, and contemporary classics. Alec Guinness and Irene Worth performed here in the festival's early years; its fame has since attracted actors like Maggie Smith and Peter Ustinov. Guest celebrity lectures and other related events also are part of the program. A trio of performing halls houses productions running in repertory throughout the season — there's so much theater that you could stay for days and still not see everything. The *Festival Theatre,* with a thrust stage that has 2,262 seats within 66 feet of it, presents four or five plays per season; the *Avon Theatre,* with a traditional proscenium arch stage, features contemporary works and classics; the *Tom Patterson Theatre* (another thrust) spotlights the work of the *Young Company.* Information: *Stratford Festival,* PO Box 520, Stratford, Ontario N5A 6V2 (phone: 519-271-4040).

A Shutterbug's Toronto

Toronto is a vibrant, lively city with a wealth of photogenic characteristics: historic old buildings standing brick-to-chrome beside the latest trends in architectural design; the famous CN Tower silhouetted along the city skyline; residents from diverse ethnic groups; and the natural beauty of High Park, Grenadier Pond, and Lake Ontario. The hustle and bustle of commercial activity downtown, sailboats cruising in the harbor, and the *Caravan* festival are only a few of Toronto's photographic possibilities. Even a beginner can achieve remarkable results with a surprisingly basic set of lenses and filters. Equipment is, in fact, only as valuable as the imagination that puts it into use.

Don't be afraid to experiment. Use what knowledge you have to explore new possibilities. Don't limit yourself with preconceived ideas of what's hackneyed or corny. The fact that the CN Tower has been photographed hundreds of times before doesn't make it any less worthy of your attention.

In Toronto, as elsewhere, spontaneity is one of the keys to good photography. Whether it's a sudden shaft of light bursting through the clouds and hitting the sailboats skimming the waters of the harbor or merchants carting in their produce as the light of dawn creeps up on the *St. Lawrence Market,* don't hesitate to shoot if the moment is right. If photography is indeed capturing a moment and making it timeless, success lies in judging just when a moment worth capturing occurs.

A good picture reveals an eye for detail, whether it's a matter of lighting, positioning your subject, or taking time to frame a picture carefully. The better your grasp of the importance of details, the better your results will be photographically.

Patience is often necessary. Don't shoot a view of the Flatiron Building highlighted against the sunset gold of the Royal Bank Tower if a cloud suddenly dims the building's glow. A hot-dog vendor pushes his cart in front of Mackenzie House as you're setting up the shot? Reframe your image to eliminate the obvious distraction. People walking toward a scene that would benefit from their presence? Wait until they're in position before you shoot. After the fact, many of the flaws will be self-evident. The trick is to be aware of the ideal and have the patience to allow it to happen. If you are part of a group, you may well have to trail behind a bit in order to shoot properly. Not only is group activity distracting, but bunches of people hovering nearby tend to stifle spontaneity and overwhelm potential subjects.

The camera provides an opportunity, not only to capture Toronto's charm, but to interpret it. What it takes is a sensitivity to the surroundings, a knowledge of the capabilities of your equipment, and a willingness to see things in new ways.

LANDSCAPES, LAKEFRONTS, AND CITYSCAPES: Toronto's busy streets, lakefront vistas, and historic buildings are compelling photographic subjects. Getting the full sweep of the city's visual effect can be vital to a good photograph.

Color and form are the obvious ingredients here, and how you frame a picture can be as important as getting the proper exposure. Study the shapes, angles, and colors that make up the scene and create a composition that uses them to best advantage.

Lighting is a vital component in landscapes. Take advantage of the richer colors of early morning and late afternoon whenever possible. The overhead light of midday is often harsh and without the shadowing that can add to the drama of a scene. This is where a polarizer is used to best effect. Most polarizing filters come with a mark on the rotating ring. If you can aim at your subject and point that marker at the sun, the sun's rays are likely to be right for the polarizer to work properly. If not, stick to your skylight filter, underexposing slightly if the scene is particularly bright. Most light meters respond to an overall light balance, with the result that bright areas may appear burned out.

Although a standard 50mm to 55mm lens may work well in some landscape situations, most will benefit from a 20mm to 28mm wide-angle. The Childrens' Village at Ontario Place, with city skyscrapers looming in the distance, fits beautifully into a wide-angle format, allowing not only the overview, but the opportunity to include other points of interest in the foreground.

To isolate specific elements of any scene, use your telephoto lens. This is the best way to photograph a sailboat on the harbor or capture a musician playing in the street in front of *Eaton Centre.* The successful use of a telephoto means developing your eye for detail.

PEOPLE: As with taking pictures of people anywhere, there are going to be times in Toronto when a camera is an intrusion. Your approach is the key: Consider your own reaction under similar circumstances, and you have an idea of what would make others comfortable enough to be willing subjects. People are often sensitive to suddenly having a camera pointed at them, and a polite request, while getting you a share of refusals, will also provide a chance to shoot some wonderful portraits that capture the spirit of the city as surely as the scenery does. For candid shots, an excellent lens is a zoom telephoto in the 70mm to 210mm range; it allows you to remain unobtrusive while the telephoto lens draws the subject closer. And for portraits, a telephoto lens can be effectively used as close as 2 or 3 feet.

For authenticity and variety, select a place likely to produce interesting subjects. The Harbourfront area is an obvious spot for visitors, but if it's local color you're after, visit the city's crowded Chinatown, sit at an outdoor café in Yorkville and watch the parade of shoppers, or stroll around Queen Street West, where leather-jacketed bikers mingle with business executives in suit and tie. Aim for shots that tell what's different about Toronto. In portraiture, there are several factors to keep in mind. Morning or afternoon light will add richness to skin tones. To avoid the harsh facial shadows cast by direct sunlight, shoot in the shade or in an area where the light is diffused. The only filter to use is a skylight.

SUNSETS: The beautiful red glow of the setting sun glinting off the water of Lake Ontario is well worth the effort of capturing it on film.

When shooting sunsets, keep in mind that the brightness will distort meter readings. When composing a shot directly into the sun, frame the picture in the viewfinder so that only half of the sun is included. Read the meter, set, and shoot. Whenever there is this kind of unusual lighting, shoot a few frames in half-step increments, both over and under the meter reading. Bracketing, as this is called, can provide a range of images, the best of which may well be other than the one shot at the meter's recommended setting.

Use any lens for sunsets. A wide-angle is good when the sky is filled with color-streaked clouds, when the sun is partially hidden, or when you're close to an object that silhouettes dramatically against the sky.

Telephoto lenses also produce wonderful silhouettes, either with the sun as a backdrop or against the palette of a brilliant sunset sky. Bracket again here. For the best silhouettes, wait 10 to 15 minutes after sunset. Unless using a very fast film, a tripod is recommended.

Red and orange filters are often used to accentuate a sunset's picture potential. Orange will help turn even a gray sky into something approaching a photogenic finale to the day and can provide particularly beautiful shots linking the sky with the sun reflected on the water. If the sunset is already bold in hue, the orange may overwhelm the natural colors. A red filter will produce dramatic, highly unrealistic results.

NIGHT: If you think that picture possibilities end at sunset, you're presuming that night photography is the exclusive domain of the professional. If you've got a tripod, all you'll need is a cable release to attach to your camera to assure a steady exposure (which is often timed in minutes rather than fractions of a second).

For most nighttime situations, a strobe does the trick, but beware: Flash units are often used improperly. You can't take a view of *Casa Loma* with a flash. It may reach out 30 to 50 feet, but that's it. On the other hand, a flash used too close to your subject may result in overexposure, resulting in a "blown out" effect. With most cameras, strobes will work with a maximum shutter speed of 1/125 or 1/150 of a second. If you set the exposure properly and shoot within range, you should come up with pretty sharp results.

CLOSE-UPS: Whether of people or of details of architecture, close-ups can add another dimension to your photography. There are a number of shooting options, one of which is to use a 70mm or a 210mm lens at its closest focusable distance. Unless you're working in bright sunlight, a tripod will be worthwhile. If you are very near your subject and there is a good deal of reflective light, it may pay to underexpose a bit in relation to the meter reading.

If you do not have a telephoto lens, you can still shoot close-ups using a set of magnification filters. Filter packs of one-, two-, and three-time magnification are available, converting your lens into a close-up lens. Even better is a special macro lens designed for close-up photography.

In Toronto, a good photograph may be just around the corner. Keep your eyes peeled and your camera ready. The following are some good places to start looking.

A SHORT PHOTOGRAPHIC TOUR

FLATIRON BUILDING: Looking west from the corner of Front and Church Streets, the Flatiron Building (orginally called the Gooderham Building) seems to spearhead the point of a triangle. The dramatic juxtaposition of this 1891 red-brick building with the modern glass-and-chrome A. E. LePage Building directly behind it creates an interesting perspective on old and new Toronto.

QUEEN'S QUAY TERMINAL AND HARBOURFRONT: This area provides a good opportunity to blend Toronto's colorful ethnic mix with its lovely natural scenery. Out on the harbor are sailboats, paddle wheelers, and yachts, and the Toronto Islands loom in the background. You can get excellent portraits of people lingering over coffee at a sidewalk café, children playing, clowns blowing up brightly colored balloons, and artists creating hand-crafted pottery in the fiery kilns of the *York Quay Centre.*

BEACH DISTRICT: A stretch of Queen Street East that runs from *Greenwood Racetrack* on Woodbine Avenue to the bottom of Victoria Park Avenue, the Beach district presents myriad photographic possibilities. Standing near the water's edge facing west, you can get a shot of a wide strip of sand bordered by an old wooden boardwalk with the CN Tower looming above it all. This is a good place to shoot the old-fashioned trolley cars as they dispense their passengers along the route. Also, look for an interesting angle on the huge hillside mansions overlooking the beach.

CN TOWER: The outdoor observation deck of the 1,122-foot CN Tower is a great place to capture an aerial view of the entire city. You can see the many aspects of Toronto simultaneously: the green parks, the harborfront, the Toronto Islands, and urban buildings melding into green countryside. Not to mention that the tower itself makes a good subject — and it can be photographed from almost anywhere in the city.

KENSINGTON MARKET: Here is all of Toronto's ethnic mix jam-packed into one place. More than the usual amount of patience may be needed to capture the perfect shot, as this marketplace is always crowded, but the spectacle of Portuguese, Jewish, Caribbean, and Italian vendors hawking their wares to passersby creates colorful and varied street scenes.

CHURCH OF THE HOLY TRINITY: Toronto's truce between modern urban development and historical preservation is encapsulated in the juxtaposition of this 1845 church and *Eaton Centre,* which is built around it. A good view can be obtained by looking through the west windows on one of the shopping gallery's upper levels.

TORONTO ISLANDS: These islands are an excellent vantage point from which to shoot the Toronto skyline. The sight is especially impressive when the sun casts subdued lighting on the city and reflects off the Royal Bank Tower. On the islands themselves, the impressive *Royal Canadian Yacht Club,* a vast white Southern-style mansion complete with pillars and porticos, is also a worthy subject.

DIRECTIONS

Introduction

Toronto is a pleasant city, a likable city, a solid kind of Anglo-Saxon city, not wildly exciting, but full of interesting bits and pieces, odd vistas and quirky little historical sidelights. Considering that it started out as an Indian village (called Taheyagon) where the occasional amusement was a rollicking 3-day drunk during which French traders engaged in a debauch called "Ganuary," running naked through the village with kegs of brandy under their arms, it's all turned out pretty well. It's quieter now, but at least you don't have to worry about French traders, and the high cost of brandy keeps debauchery to a minimum.

Actor Peter Ustinov described his native Toronto as "New York run by the Swiss," and no wonder: A major financial center, it has a diverse ethnic population, its streets are kept clean, things run on time, people line up politely for buses and such, and though they're not exactly folksy, Torontonians don't have the hard veneer that crusts some residents of other large North American cities. And, as in many old European capitals, there are trees everywhere. Just look down on the canopy of green from the 150-story observation deck of the CN Tower, which not only offers a God's-eye view of Toronto, but on a clear day lets you see the spray rising above Niagara Falls, some 90 miles (144 km) to the southwest across Lake Ontario.

Toronto is an ideal city for walkers. Armed with a good map outlining its streets and avenues and its bus, subway, and streetcar lines, you should have no problem finding your way. If you do, just ask; most locals will be more than happy to help you. Which is another reason so many visitors like the place. And be sure to ask about the underground network of corridors with their shops, restaurants, and bars that runs beneath the downtown core (the better to escape the rains of summer and the icy streets of winter). Bounded by Front, Yonge, York, and Queen Streets, the underground city is tied in to all the major buildings in the area, as well as to Union Station to the south and the giant *Eaton Centre* complex to the north. With its vast corridors seemingly running off in all directions, the underground can be a bit confusing at first — but the clear signposting and directional guides will set you on the straight and narrow.

US visitors will find many British touches in Toronto — from its wealth of tearooms to its spelling of words. Here it's centre, not center, harbour, not harbor — a blend of the best of both worlds. With its British heritage adapted to the American experience, here you'll find traditional London-style fish and chips aplenty, but with ketchup sharing space on the table with vinegar and bewigged barristers and queen's counsels matching wits with Lower 48–bred lawyers. It's a cultural mish-mash, but happily, it seems to work quite well.

Unlike European capitals, there is no grandeur here, no sweeping prospects or grand boulevards. While it has the soaring CN Tower dominating its skyline and the golden sheen of Royal Bank Plaza gracing its financial district, Toronto's roots lie in the narrow, potholed lanes of Muddy York; many of its downtown streets are simply commercial and Yonge Street, its main thoroughfare, is not only lacking in grandeur but has long stretches that are downright tawdry. And though the one street with some sweep and style — wide and handsome University Avenue between Front and College Streets — boasts a boulevard, statues, and even fountains, it also plays host to eight lanes of traffic.

But all that said, there are fascinations hidden away in the city for the curious who want to stroll and peer and pry its nooks and crannies and relax along its abundant green spaces. Follow these routes; they'll give you a sense of history and show you a Toronto that's a little Swiss, more than a touch British, and delightfully Canadian.

Walk 1: University of Toronto

Right in the heart of the bustling city, just yards from the traffic of University Avenue, lies the University of Toronto (the U of T to locals), an area of tree-shaded walks, sun-dappled squares, and some prime examples of 19th-century architecture. It was here that the first heart pacemaker was developed, Pablum was created, insulin was isolated, and cobalt therapy was developed for the treatment of cancer. It was here, too, that Marshall McLuhan announced the "Medium is the Message" and developed his global village concept; Donald Sutherland and Kate Reid went on to stage and screen success; Glenn Gould to the great concert halls; Norman Jewison and Arthur Hiller to their Hollywood directors' chairs. Canadian novelist Robertson Davies — now in residence at the university's Massey College as a founding master and senior fellow emeritus — used the university as a setting for his *Rebel Angels,* a tour de force of Jungian magic and mystery.

One of two universities within Metropolitan Toronto (the other is York; once an affiliate of the U of T, it is located in the northern part of the city), the institution is almost a city in itself. Bounded by Bay Street to the east, Spadina Avenue to the west, College Street to the south, and Bloor Street to the north, the university's 250 buildings — covering some 1.5 acres all around the Provincial Parliament Building in Queen's Park — are home to 52,000 students and 11,500 faculty and staff. Also within this area are the *Royal Ontario Museum (ROM)* and its *McLaughlin Planetarium,* both of which add a cultural accent to this leisurely 2½-hour walk. If you plan to stop in at the museum complex (and you should), add several hours more, because there is so much to see that a visit here can wreak havoc with your schedule. (Better yet, save the museum and planetarium for another day.)

Before starting out, a little history. The university is not a monolithic whole but a collection of 12 colleges, all of which get along nicely today, but many of which quarreled bitterly during the last century.

The first school, King's College, an Anglican institution founded by the government in 1843, immediately ran into cross fire from followers of other religions who objected to the Anglicans being favored by government funding. The battle was so fierce that after 6 years the government secularized the college (later renamed University College). But this in turn incensed the Anglicans, the social and political elite of the new city of Toronto, and, spurred by John Strachan, Canada's first Anglican bishop, they financed and opened their own college — Trinity — in 1851. For their part, the Methodists had Victoria College (founded in 1841), the Presbyterians had Knox College (founded in 1843), and the Roman Catholics would open St. Michael's Col-

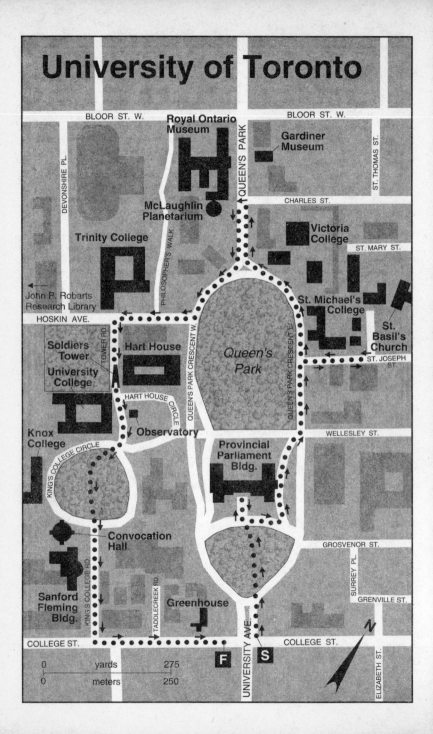

lege in 1852. All of which made for spirited competition, or, more accurately, acrimony in the schoolrooms and on the playing fields of the city's institutions of higher learning. And by the 1880s even the most theologically partisan could see that whatever their religious beliefs, the schools could achieve more by working together than they could fighting their separate battles. And so in 1887 the five colleges plus Wycliffe College, which the Anglicans had opened in 1877, joined in a federation known as the University of Toronto. After WWII four more colleges were added to the downtown St. George campus — Innis, Massey, Wordsworth, and New — and the Scarborough and Erindale campuses were created outside the city limits. Today all are open to anyone who can meet the admission standards.

This walk starts at the northeast corner of University Avenue and College Street (exit the subway at the Queen's Park station) at the Sir Frederick Banting and Charles Best Department of Medical Research (112 College St.), built 9 years after the two had isolated insulin and used it in the treatment of diabetes. Catercorner across University is the concave, modernistic Ontario Hydro Building (in Ontario, power companies are known as hydro companies, a reminder of the age when water generated all the electricity in the province) and beyond it a monumental Romanesque-Revival building erected in 1891 by Canadian architect E.J. Lennon to house, of all things, a police station. Today it plays a much more academic role as part of the Ontario College of Art. It's worth a look because you'll see other notable Lennon works — the Old City Hall at Bay and Queen Streets, the stately *King Edward* hotel on King Street, and the baronial vastness of Casa Loma (see *Special Places* in THE CITY).

Walk north, crossing at the lights (traffic is very heavy here) to the grassy space in front of the pink sandstone bulk of the Provincial Parliament Building, which stands like a 19th-century squire, four-square and hardy on its patch of green while the University Avenue traffic growls and rumbles as it splits and flows around both sides of the oval park. John Updike characterized the building as a "brick valentine to a distant dowager queen" and it has a bluff dignity that recalls the age of the queen empress, a statue of whom can be found in the park; here, too, is a statue of Sir John A. Macdonald, one of Canada's first prime ministers. A visionary who believed in building a Canada that would stretch from sea to sea, Macdonald's reputation also extended to his escapades, his wit and humor, and his fondness for the bottle, which was legendary. The building itself, seat of the provincial government (roughly similar to a state legislature), was designed in 1886 in the Romanesque style by US architect Richard Waite, who ruffled some local feathers not only because he was from south of the border but because he was on the selection panel that decided he should get the job.

Inside the Parliament Building it's all mahogany and marble, plush chambers and portraits of long-dead politicians, with a brief description of Ontario's history and a collection of early Canadian art. Visitor information is available just inside the entrance and there are tours of the building (for schedules, contact the Queen's Park Information Office at 416-325-7500). Try to visit when you can watch some of the 130 honorable Members of Provincial Parliament — or MPPs — in action.

Exit by the front doors and turn left to follow the sidewalk around the building to Wellesley Street, where you can see two cannons captured by the British from the French in 1758 at the Battle of Louisbourg, which set the stage for the capture of Quebec by James Wolfe the next year. Nearby (at 90 Wellesley) is the mansion that cookies built: the former home of William Christie, who came from Scotland in the mid-1880s and was so successful in the bakery business that the city named a street after him.

From Wellesley walk north on Queen's Park Crescent East, glancing over at the green acres of Queen's Park itself, where students sprawl on the lawns and joggers puff past. The statue of a man on horseback is Edward VII (Victoria's somewhat wayward son), who opened the park in 1860. He and his steed once stood in Edward Park in New Delhi, India, but had to beat a hasty, if somewhat cumbersome, retreat when independence rolled around. So the Canadians took him in and gave him a place to sit and watch the world go by.

Continue along Queen's Park Crescent East to St. Joseph Street, the site of St. Michael's College and Gothic-style St. Basil's Church, built in 1858. And be sure to note the large, late 19th-century homes on Elmsley Place, running north from St. Joseph's Street. They were privately owned until the early part of this century, when they were bought by the college to serve as student residences.

Walk back along St. Joseph's and turn right up Queen's Park Crescent East to the top of Queen's Park. To the left, at the north end of the park, is a cenotaph to Canadian soldiers and to the right is Victoria College, the first such school in the British Empire not under the control of the Church of England to receive a royal charter. It was, in fact, built by the Methodists, but in 1925 it became affiliated with the United Church of Canada, an amalgamation of several Protestant sects.

Continue north at Queen's Park to the intersection of Charles Street, but before crossing the street at the traffic lights, look north to see on the left the dome-shape *McLaughlin Planetarium* (100 Queen's Park; phone: 416-586-5736) and, immediately to the north, the vast bulk of the *Royal Ontario Museum* (*ROM;* 100 Queen's Park; phone: 416-586-5549). Also part of the musuem, though in separate buildings, are the *Sigmund Samuel Canadian Collection* to the south of the main complex (14 Queen's Park Cr. W.; phone: 416-586-5524) and the *George R. Gardiner Museum of Ceramic Art* across the street from the *ROM* (111 Queen's Park; phone: 416-586-8080).

Admission to one museum will get you into them all (though there is no admission charge for the *Canadian Collection*) and you should see them all, particularly the *ROM,* one of the world's largest museums (with some 6 million items within its walls). Here is the only Ming tomb in the world, the finest Chinese collection outside that country, dinosaur skeletons, Plains Indian displays, Egyptian relics, a Bat Cave where special effects bring thousands of the creatures to life, and the chilling adventures offered by the live tarantulas, scorpions, and giant hissing cockroaches of the Life Sciences Gallery. Don't pass up the night sky of the planetarium, the pioneer crafts and toys in the *Sigmund Samuel,* or the 2,000 pottery treasures of the *Gardiner* — everything from mystic dragons to high-heeled ceramic pumps.

Certainly you can't see them all in the middle of a walk (you'd never get it done), but note the buildings and plan a return visit.

Cross at Charles Street to the west side of Queen's Park, where the university's Faculty of Law lies hidden behind the wrought-iron fence. If you are interested in Art Nouveau, visit the hall inside the faculty building to admire its painted ceiling; return to the street and walk south, pass the Sigmund Samuel Building (mentioned above), and turn right onto Hoskin Avenue. On the right is Philosopher's Walk, a pleasant path leading north to Bloor Street, and at 6 Hoskin Avenue is Gothic-looking Trinity College, the Anglican institution built after the original King's College was secularized. Of particular note is the chapel: Designed by Sir Giles Gilbert Scott and completed in 1955, it is considered one of the most important examples of Gothic Revival architecture on the continent.

Cross Hoskin Avenue at the lights; walk down Tower Road, turn right to catch a glimpse of the John P. Robarts Research Library, a monstrous concrete-and-glass building whose main claim to fame is that it houses 2.6 million volumes in the humanities and social sciences and has room for 2.1 million more. As for the university as a whole, its libraries house some 7 million volumes.

Walk down Tower Road past the playing field on the right to the tower rising above the archway. Known as Soldiers Tower, it was completed in 1924 to honor alumni who had died in battle; its 51 carillon bells are played during convocations and on other special occasions. Once through the archway turn left to walk to Hart House Circle. The building in front of you is Hart House, built in collegiate Gothic style in 1919 as an undergraduate men's center, complete with banquet hall (the Great Hall), rooms for games, reading, music, and lectures, plus a swimming pool, a chapel, a library, and a theater. Also inside are a modest art gallery that displays pieces from Hart House's Canadiana collection (7 Hart House Cir.; phone: 416-978-8398),and a non-denominational chapel with a fanciful Art Deco–inspired mural.

Hart House was named after Hart Massey (1823–96), and its construction was overseen by his grandson, Vincent Massey (1867–1967). The first native-born governor-general of Canada, Vincent lectured in modern history at the U of T before being appointed as the queen's representative to Canada. In 1870, his grandfather moved the family business, Massey Manufacturing Company (later Massey-Ferguson Ltd.), a farm implement manufacturer, to Toronto; since that time few families have been as important to the cultural history of Toronto (if not to English Canada) as the Masseys: The *Massey Music Hall,* near *Eaton Centre,* was presented to the city in 1894 by Hart (before the modern music hall on King Street West was called *Roy Thomson Hall* it was known locally as the *New Massey Music Hall*); in 1951, the Massey Commission, chaired by Vincent, formed the basis of the modern Canadian Broadcasting Corporation (CBC) and the National Film Board of Canada (NFB); and Massey College, a residential college for senior scholars and graduate students at the U of T, was funded by the family, as are the "Massey Lectures," a longtime CBC Radio series that has included among its presenters Martin Luther King, Northrop Frye, and Carlos Fuentes. Hart's other grandson and Vincent's brother, the actor Raymond Massey

(1896–1983) is better known to some as TV's Dr. Gillespie, the mentor to Dr. Kildare (Richard Chamberlain), and to others as Broadway's and Hollywood's Abe Lincoln. In Broadway's 1938 production of *Abe Lincoln in Illinois* it was said that by casting Massey in the role of Lincoln producers "took the face off the penny and put it into the hearts of millions of Americans."

The oldest building on campus is the former observatory on Hart House Circle, which was designed by Frederick William Cumberland, who also designed St. James Cathedral on James Street, the central portion of Osgoode Hall on Queen Street, and the medieval-looking fortress of learning that is University College, just a hop and a skip from the observatory and the next stop on this walk. To see it to best advantage, turn right onto King's College Circle from Hart House Circle and walk to the center of the field. After almost a century and a half, the first building constructed for the newly created University of Toronto is still the most commanding. And the most startling, for it has an eclectic mix of styles from Romanesque to medieval and back with no rhyme or reason, and the windows, doors, and pillars on one side do not match those on the other. Some said it was a deliberate attempt to ensure that the architectural style could not be said to favor any particular religion. Others blamed the various ethnic backgrounds of the tradesmen and construction workers involved in the building project. Or perhaps our usually humorless Victorian forebears were for once having fun.

The college was almost demolished by a fire in 1890, but escaped with its exterior intact and re-opened after repairs in 1892. The cone-shape Croft Chapter House to the left was one of the few buildings to escape severe damage in the fire. But it has another claim to fame as the scene of a reputed murder back in the last century, with two different tales coming to the same bad end. One version notes the deep gash of an axe in the wood of the front door and says two stonemasons working on the building began fighting there over a woman they both loved; one killed the other with a blow from the axe and dumped the body into the main tower, where it lay until it was discovered after another fire in 1910. The other story says that a stonemason named Ivan Reznikoff became enraged when a friend pointed out to him that a Greek workman was using his face as the model for a gargoyle. When Reznikoff discovered the Greek was also trying to steal his girlfriend, he attacked him while they were working on the roof. But the other man was quicker: He stabbed Reznikoff and dropped his body down the unfinished tower well, where his remains were discovered some 30 years later. They've been reburied in the northwest corner of the quadrangle, but students say they have seen and heard Reznikoff haunting the building still. At any rate, if you'd care to check, a gargoyle said to be modeled after Ivan can be seen just above eye-level on the exterior, west of the main entrance.

On the second floor of the building to the left of Croft Chapter House is the office of the Alumni and Community Relations Department, a good place to visit for more information. Walking tours are offered through this office Mondays to Fridays at 10:30 AM and 1 to 2:30 PM from June through August. Groups should book ahead (21 King's College Cir.; phone: 416-978-5000).

To the left as you face University College is Knox College (23 King's College Cir.), whose cloistered courtyard will give you a good feel for the life of a scholar, or so say Hollywood folk. Knox College has been used as a set in such movies as *Paper Chase* and *Dead Ringer,* and in several Perry Mason made-for-TV movies.

To the left again is Convocation Hall (31 King's College Cir.); past Convocation Road on the right, where King's College Circle becomes King's College Road, is the Sir Sanford Fleming Building (10 King's College Rd.), named after an engineer who left his mark on the world, designing the first made-in-Canada stamp (the 3-pence beaver), finding the route for the national railway through the Rockies, then in retirement laying the foundation of international standard time. The building, completed in 1907, 8 years before he died, now houses (what else?) the engineering department.

From there keep going south until you reach College Street; turn left to walk back to the Queen's Park subway station. But before you duck down the well-swept steps stop off at the 60-year-old greenhouse next to the university's Botany Building to wander among the tropical plants — everything from jicama vines to banana trees.

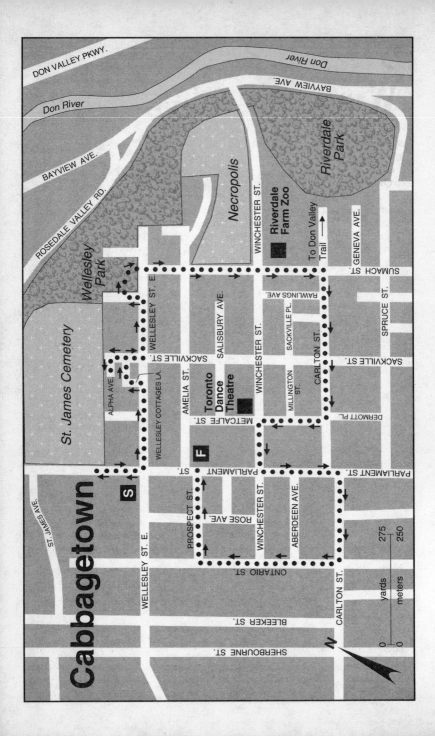

Walk 2: Cabbagetown

In this city of lively neighborhoods, each with its own distinct personality, the one with the least romantic-sounding name is probably the most appealing. Once described as North America's largest Anglo-Saxon slum, Cabbagetown (no one is quite sure of the origins of the name) has stubbornly retained the best of the old and selectively embraced the new. A Depression-era development of Victorian-style homes and cottages, it was threatened with extinction after World War II, as developers sought to raze the 19th-century dwellings and erect blocks of high-rises in their stead. Many of the homes had been leveled before Cabbagetowners stepped forward en masse to put an end to the architectural carnage. They succeeded and, happily, most of the buildings remain intact.

An area roughly 20-plus blocks square, bounded by Wellesley Street on the north, Gerrard Street on the south, the Don River on the east, and Parliament Street on the west, Cabbagetown was originally called The Don, after the river that runs past it. Later, in an attempt to gentrify the working class neighborhood, the name was upgraded to Don Vale. Most locals figure that the area's present name was inspired by the skunk cabbages found growing in profusion in the Don River Valley, or by the odor that permeated the halls of local boarding houses in those days, or by the fact that the Irish immigrants who once lived here planted the front lawns of their homes with cabbages — or perhaps all three. Regardless of the name's origins, today's Cabbagetowners give the lowly vegetable a place of honor on their green-and-white neighborhood flags, many of which you'll see proudly displayed on office buildings, shops, and homes along this 2-hour, architecturally rich walk.

The design of the homes — mostly row houses — in this working class area is of particular interest for its inventiveness and style. Though many of the homes have only a 16-foot frontage (that was the standard length of timber used for building at the time), they evolved in a grand mix of styles — from Greek Revival to Victorian Gothic. As varied as the origins of its architecture, so, too, were Cabbagetown's residents, hailing from Scotland, Ireland, Great Britain, and Central Europe.

Now a trendy place that attracts young couples drawn by the relatively low rents and the challenge of sandblasting and restoring the existing homes to their century-old state, Cabbagetown stands as a small 19th-century enclave in a city of cavernous streets and towering buildings.

This walk begins at the corner of Wellesley and Parliament Streets (take the subway to the Wellesley station on Yonge Street and transfer to a Wellesley Street bus to Parliament Street). As you exit the bus, cross Parliament to the east side and turn left (north) to St. James Cemetery, just up the street. By far the larger of the two cemeteries of the same name in the city (the other is on the grounds of St. James Cathedral at King and Jarvis Streets;

also see *Walk 5: St. Lawrence Market*), it's shaded by century-old trees and offers a prime example of Old English Gothic architecture: the 1858 Chapel of St. James-the-Less (even the name smacks of Old England), with its hammer-beam ceiling, marbled chancel, and massive Tiffany stained glass windows.

Leaving the cemetery, turn left and walk south to Wellesley again; turn left at the corner and walk to 314 Wellesley, typical of the imaginative bent of local builders, with its designs of an owl and serpent in the protruding stonework, the exaggerated peak of its gables, and the varied sizes of its windows (Nos. 316 and 334 Wellesley are other examples of this style).

Continue east to Wellesley Cottages Lane and turn left to see the lath-and-stucco houses, built in 1887 to house local laborers. At the end of the lane, turn right and walk east to Sackville Street, then left onto Alpha Avenue, a cul-de-sac of mansard-roofed cottages.

Backtrack to Sackville Street and walk south to Wellesley Street again; turn left and left again at the lane near 402 Wellesley; the Owl House (390 Wellesley St. E.), named for the terra cotta figure under one of the windows, was the turn-of-the-century family home of Canadian illustrator C.W. Jeffreys, whose most famous drawing, of militant farmers marching into battle in the short-lived rebellion of 1837, can be viewed by prior arrangement at the *National Archives* in Ottawa. At the end of the street is Wellesley Park, a small area of grass and trees, which once was the site of the area's only factory, a glue and blacking business owned by P.R. Lamb and Company. Cross the park and turn right onto Sumach Street; here are several attractive groupings of houses from the 19th century with mansard roofs, gables, bay windows, and red and yellow brickwork.

Glue wasn't the only contribution to the area made by the Lamb family: It was Lamb's son who founded the nearby Riverdale Farm Zoo (at Sumach and Winchester). Boasting a 19th-century barn, period implements, as well as a noisy population of pigs, cows, sheep, and chickens, it also offers occasional arts and crafts programs for children and daily demonstrations by potters and painters. This is a working farm, and although children are discouraged from petting or feeding the animals, they can help with the daily chores. Open daily from 9 AM to 4 PM; no admission charge. 201 Winchester St. (phone: 416-392-6794).

North of the farm is Cabbagetown's second cemetery, the Necropolis, or City of the Dead, where many of Canada's famous (and infamous) are interred. Among those buried here are George Brown, founder of the *Globe* (forerunner of Toronto's daily *Globe and Mail*); William Lyon Mackenzie, the fiery radical who led the brief Upper Canada Rebellion of 1837 (when the rebellion failed Mackenzie fled to the US; he returned some years later to such popularity that Torontonians built a home for him, now a museum) and two of his unluckier confederates who were captured and executed; and Edward (Ned) Hanlan, the world's foremost oarsman in the 1880s (a point on the Toronto Islands is named after him). Built in 1872, the cemetery's Gothic chapel is also worth a look.

At this point lift your spirits by backtracking to Winchester Street to *Nick's Café* (116 Winchester St.; no phone), a Cabbagetown favorite for ice cream or just a cup of coffee or tea. Then walk south on Sumach Street for 2 blocks to No. 384, an odd-looking Victorian house decked out in multicolored pastels. Its seeming jumble of architectural styles, exaggerated pointed roofs, and other oddities have earned it the name Witch's House. You'll understand why when you see it. Just to the left is No. 384½, a charming cottage with a bright red British mailbox (direct from London) on its picket fence.

Continue south to Carlton Street; if you go to the left you can follow the Don Valley Trail, one of many walks that snake through Toronto's ravines and valleys. This detour — 4 miles (6 km) long, twisting its way south to the lakefront at Cherry Street, about 2 miles (3 km) east of Yonge Street — is for hardier walkers. Another way to explore the area is along its excellent bike trail.

If you decide against the Valley Trail hike or bike ride, return to the corner of Carlton and Sumach, turn left, and walk to 314 Carlton, a small brick house built in 1875 by Benjamin Brick, a developer who built a number of houses in this style along Carlton Street; many of these 1-story brick structures have now been transformed into offices and small stores. Brick is also responsible for the ornate gilded plaster ceiling inside at No. 308. (The owner's house is included in the Cabbagetown Tour of Homes, described below.) Here, too, set back from the street down long paved lanes, are some of the best examples in town of restored carriage houses (such as No. 303); No. 295 was once the residence of Hugh Neilson, a telephone company executive who in 1878 was one of the first people in town to have a private telephone. The homes on this part of Carlton Street, replete with gabled roofs, stone- and brickwork variations, and decorative touches of stained glass, are some of the finest and largest examples of Victorian architecture in the district. As with the rest of Cabbagetown, most of these homes have undergone extensive interior renovations.

Continue west on Carlton to Metcalfe Street. The former church building on the northeast corner of Metcalfe and Winchester is now home to the *Toronto Dance Theatre,* which performs regularly at Harbourfront when not touring the US or Europe. Three well-known modern dancers, Peter Randazzo, David Earle, and Patricia Beatty, members of Martha Graham's original group, trained here back in 1968.

From here walk west on Winchester Street to Parliament Street; turn left, walk south to Carlton, and cross at the traffic light. On the southwest corner of the intersection, note the branch (ca. 1905) of the Canadian Imperial Bank of Commerce; at the time its bay-windowed second floor was rented out to bring in additional income.

Walk west on Carlton to see several fine examples of changing styles and colors of brick, with yellow used to highlight red (No. 219) or red to highlight yellow (Nos. 226 and 228). At 226 are the *Tapas Bar* and *El Cid* restaurant, two Spanish drinking and dining spots, the first a downstairs bar and the other a more traditional eatery on the main floor (phone: 416-323-9651 for both).

A little farther west, at Ontario and Carlton Streets, turn right and go north to take a look at 481 and 483 Ontario Street, two 1877 Gothic-style Victorian houses, and, across the street, a row of 1877 yellow-brick homes built in the popular bay and gable style. The group of modern buildings on the west side of the street is subsidized and co-op housing, a compromise made by residents to developers' attempts to turn the neighborhood into an area of high-rise apartment buildings.

Continue north on Ontario Street for 1 block to Winchester Street for a look at Nos. 7 through 11, examples of the Queen Anne style, and, farther along, Nos. 13 and 15, which have the mansard roofs of the Second Empire style. Farther north, 56 Rose Avenue stands out in this predominantly Victorian-style neighborhood: An 1858 house built by a local contractor, its hipped-roof main building and mansard tower at the rear are reminiscent of an Italian villa.

Turn right at Prospect Street, a short block that intersects Rose Avenue, and walk 1 block to Parliament Street. If hunger strikes you can stop for coffee and a Nanaimo bar (a Canadian snack of chocolate-covered nuts and graham wafers) at *Lennie's Whole Foods* (489 Parliament St.; phone: 416-967-5196), near the corner of Prospect and Parliament Streets.

For those who've worked up bigger appetites, the best cafés along Parliament are *Poor William* (No. 505; phone: 416-924-7575) and *Now* (No. 533; phone: 416-961-7357); or dine *à la française* at *La Plume* (No. 557; phone: 416-921-0769) or around the corner on Carlton Street at *Brasserie Les Artistes* (243 Carlton St.; phone: 416-963-9433). For a local celebrity haunt, visit *Ben Wicks* (424 Carlton St.; phone: 416-961-9425), named after a local cartoonist and writer. Other area restaurants offer Italian, Japanese, French, and American (hamburgers, French fries, and the like) fare. Shoppers will find the neighborhood rife with stores and boutiques carrying everything from fine antiques to funky fashions — mostly of the "pre-loved," or used, variety. And if you visit around *Christmas,* join the celebrations with radio and television personalities at the annual open house of the Cabbagetown studios of the Canadian Broadcasting Corporation (No. 509; phone: 416-977-6222).

The best time to visit, though, may be the second week of September, when some residents open their homes to tours during the annual Cabbagetown Tour of Homes. You can get information on tours and other special events by calling the *Cabbagetown Community Arts Centre* (454 Parliament St.; phone: 416-925-7222).

Walk 3: The Financial District

A stroll through Toronto's financial district provides a quick lesson in the vagaries of 20th-century architecture, as the financial booms of the 1920s, the 1960s, and 1980s each left a legacy of construction from those periods. The Jazz Age, for instance, brought a handful of exuberant Art Deco masterpieces — structures like the Canadian Permanent Building, whose lobby could pass for a set in a Fred Astaire–Ginger Rogers movie.

With the 1960s came a phase of Miesian minimalism, inaugurated by (and typified by) the stark black towers of the Toronto-Dominion Centre. Following that trend, the financial community over the next decade impetuously threw up a series of streamlined glass-and-concrete towers that ate up every possible square foot of increasingly rare property. The booming 1980s saw a turn away from that increasingly cold and sterile style, however, as builders were constrained by city regulations to devote a portion of their property to publicly accessible open space. Megalithic building/plaza/atrium complexes, with street-level space typically given over to sculptures, art exhibits, pedestrian squares, and vest-pocket parks, sprang up, gradually tempering the harshness of the ascetic-looking structures dating from the 1960s and transforming the downtown area into a modern and airy district. Indeed, this part of town now abounds in glitz and glitter, sun-filled atriums and soaring towers, and plazas and courtyards.

The nerve center of Toronto's financial district is at the corner of King and Bay Streets, the location of the offices of Canada's five chartered banks, the Toronto Stock Exchange (the second-largest in North America, after New York City's), and innumerable major firms. The area exudes a decidedly Wall Street ambience, as men in dark blue suits stride purposefully along, briefcases swinging, and visitors crane their necks to peer at towering skyscrapers.

There's more to the heart of Toronto than meets the eye, however, for underneath the bustling streets is another city filled with shops, movie houses, bars, and restaurants (where other blue-suited men stride just as purposefully down the corridors en route to expense-account lunches). There are 5 miles (8 km) of streets in this underground city, a sprawling labyrinth covering 10 city blocks stretching from *Eaton Centre* to Union Station and connecting every major building in the area. In the free-spending 1980s, these costly corridors were dubbed the "Cashacombs," where a thousand or so high-fashion emporia vied for the attention of winners of boardroom battles and stock-exchange coups. This subterranean city is accessible through the lower level of almost any building in the area or from several subway stations — Dundas, Queen, King, Union, Osgoode, St. Andrew, or St. Patrick. The

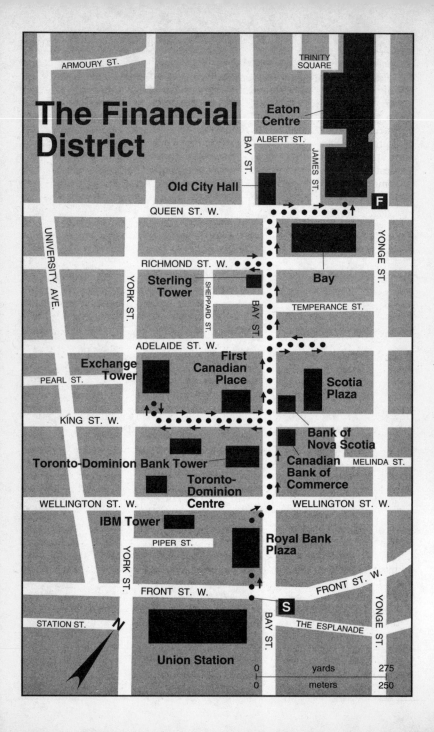

entrances, as well as the corridors, are fairly well marked, and there are passageways linking all the major buildings.

This 2-hour walking tour begins near Union Station, at the southwest corner of Front and Bay Streets. Across the street is the glistening Royal Bank Plaza, a brilliant monument to the success of Toronto's financial community. Constructed in 1977, the building was definitely a few years ahead of its time, as it practically flaunts the architectural equivalent of conspicuous consumption: Its glass façade shimmers with more than 2,000 ounces of gold dust (honest!). The effect, albeit pleasing, has come to be regarded by some critics as somewhat gratuitous, especially in the 1980s, when banks were charging double-digit interest rates — a period during which one Canadian politician was prompted to quip, "I would rather have corn flakes on my breakfast table than gold flakes on my window."

Inside the plaza is a 12-story glass atrium filled with greenery. Hanging above the entire space is a glittering, 100-foot sculpture constructed of aluminum tubes of varying lengths; below the sculpture is a bubbling fountain and a mall, one of the many entrances to Toronto's catacombs.

Leave the plaza from the north tower and turn right onto Bay Street. From this spot, if you look to the left (north), the clock tower of Toronto's 1899 Old City Hall is clearly visible. Cross Wellington Street to 234 Bay Street, the site of the Toronto Stock Exchange from 1937 to 1983. Note the stone Art Deco relief above the steel doors depicting the activities of some of the companies that traded here. It's up to the viewer to determine the artist's attitude toward the exchange's habitués — the elderly gentleman decked out in top hat and tails (fourth from the right) appears to be reaching into the pocket of the workman ahead of him. Many Canadians still refer to "Bay Street" when discussing the financial world, even though the new stock exchange is located on King Street West.

King Street is just up Bay Street, and at the intersection of the two thoroughfares are the headquarters of four major banks. On the northeast corner is the Bank of Nova Scotia (44 King St. W.), which was designed in 1929 (but not completed until 1951) and abounds with Art Deco motifs and architectural hallmarks, such as bas-relief stone carvings relating the history of the bank. Right beside it is the modern version, the recently completed 69-story *Scotia Plaza,* whose exterior is sheathed in 19 acres of Swedish red granite. The concrete underneath the granite, if used to pave a sidewalk, would stretch all the way from Toronto to Montreal (about 550 miles). Besides offices and shops, the plaza houses the *Camberley Club* — a hotel that caters primarily to business travelers — and the *BMW Gallery,* which specializes in modern art (21 Adelaide St. E.; phone: 416-365-1088).

The original Canadian Bank of Commerce building, begun in 1929 and completed 2 years later, sits across the street on the southeast corner of King and Bay Streets. Inside are paintings relating Canada's transportation history — an unexpectedly rich subject, given the country's perennial battle against the elements, from raging rivers to driving snows. The solidity of the structure's 34 stories stands out even amid newer, taller structures — a fact that becomes apparent when you exit through the back to Commerce Court, at the foot of the new Bank of Commerce (now called the Canadian Imperial

Bank of Commerce, or the CIBC). The court is actually a complex of three office buildings dating from 1972, with the smallest, 5-story one faced with reflective stainless steel (the other two are sandstone). In keeping with public-friendly city regulations, the huge outdoor Commerce Court at the base of the towers is open to all: This is where employees flock during sunny weather to eat lunch.

The complex of black obelisks on the southwest corner of Bay and King Streets is the Toronto-Dominion Centre, designed by minimalist Mies van der Rohe. When the first towers went up in the late 1960s, they were hailed by critics as evidence of Toronto's emergence as a world class, modern city. When other high-rises of a similar style rose in the downtown core, however, those same critics howled, saying the city had gone too far in allowing the downtown area to become a bland (albeit multicolored — gold, silver, and bone white) strip of upended rectangular boxes.

The most recent addition to the Toronto-Dominion Centre is the IBM Tower on the south side of Wellington Street, west of Bay Street. Note the bronze sculptured cows grazing on the lawn near the tower, adding an incongruously bucolic flavor to this decidedly urban landscape of concrete and steel. And, possibly in another effort to offset the impersonal ambience of the complex, the tower's mezzanine exhibits a collection of Inuit art (open weekdays from 8 AM to 6 PM; weekends from 10 AM to 4 PM; no admission charge; phone: 416-869-1144). In the summer, the grounds are the venue for a variety of concerts. For the second-best bird's-eye view of the city and Lake Ontario (CN Tower claims the best), ride up to the observation deck on the 54th floor of the Toronto-Dominion Bank Tower, on the southwest corner of Bay and King.

On the northwest corner of the intersection looms the white, marble-clad First Canadian Place, the tallest office building in Toronto (72 stories). Housed here are the offices of Canada's first chartered bank, the Bank of Montreal; linked to it by a glass-enclosed walkway and pedestrian park is the Exchange Tower, home of the Toronto Stock Exchange. Enter the main floor lobby and take the escalator up to the Exchange Visitors' Center. Here, behind the glass of the observation balcony, the young Turks of Canadian trading flash hand signals and wave papers, communicating in the peculiar international language of the stock market. The almost neon-bright colored jacket each trader wears represents his or her company affiliation. Open to the public (no admission charge), the Exchange offers lessons on the world of bulls and bears, free 45-minute daily tours (Tuesdays to Fridays at 2 PM), and a video presentation that explains the Exchange's trading process. The visitors' center is open weekdays from 9 AM to 4:30 PM (2 First Canadian Pl.; phone: 416-947-4670).

From here, backtrack to Bay Street, turn left, and walk north. On the east side of Bay Street is a small, anachronistic stone building (No. 303), the home of the *National Club*. The place's unassuming aspect belies its importance in Canadian history: It was here, in 1868, that members of the Canada First group first convened. While the club itself lasted fewer than 10 years, its discussions and pronouncements laid the foundation for the country's two major political parties — the Progressive Conservatives and the Liberals —

as well as Canada's first sustained literary movement (which included such writers as Charles Mair and Bliss Carman). The *National Club,* founded in the 1870s as an outgrowth of Canada First, now claims more than 1,000 members, and is one of the country's most influential luncheon clubs.

Continue north to the Canadian Permanent Building (320 Bay St.), a graceful testimony to the influence the European Art Deco movement had on Toronto's architecture. Don't miss the carved stone phoenixes on the building's exterior corners, and make sure to check out the inside of the elegant marble-walled lobby, if only to see the detail on the ornate brass elevator doors — especially the one adorned with a wise old owl.

Turn right at the corner of Bay and Adelaide Streets and walk to the 16-story Concourse Building (100 Adelaide). Completed in 1928, this Art Deco landmark has a tile mosaic over the main entrance depicting flight, shipping, agriculture, and industry. The mosaic was designed by J.E.H. MacDonald, a member of the Group of Seven art movement.

Backtrack to Bay Street and continue north. This area will soon sport a new look, as it is the proposed site of the *Bay-Adelaide Centre,* a massive retail and office tower mega-complex scheduled for completion by the end of 1994. Stop in for a nosh and coffee at *Sammy's Bay Street Exchange* (330 Bay St.; phone: 416-361-3133), located in an atrium between two old financial buildings. Continue north on Bay Street past Temperance Street, a name perfectly suited to the starchy, stiff-collared Toronto of yore. (The street was so named because the land was donated to the city with the long-since-expired stipulation that neither liquor nor tobacco — nor snuff — be sold here.) Just before Richmond Street is the 20-story Sterling Tower (No. 372), a 1929 structure with stone gargoyles and dragons gracing its Gothic-looking façade. At the corner of Bay and Richmond Streets, turn left and walk down a few doors to the Graphic Arts Building (73 Richmond St.). Built in 1913, it was designed to resemble a Greek temple; note the six stone columns in front.

Return to Bay Street and turn left (north) toward the looming clock tower of Old City Hall. On the southeast corner of Queen and Bay Streets is the *Bay* (401 Bay St.; phone: 416-861-9111), the retail giant formerly known as the *Hudson's Bay Company,* back when it dealt in furs. On the ninth floor of the 1894 building is the *Thomson Gallery,* one of the most interesting (and little-known) art showplaces in the city. It's owned by communication-empire bigwig Kenneth Thomson, Lord Thomson of Fleet (he inherited his title from his father, a native Canadian who had to establish himself as a citizen of Great Britain in order to be designated a lord). The gallery contains a priceless collection of Canadian paintings by such artists as Cornelius Kreighoff, Paul Kane, and Paul Peel. The gallery and its specialty store, which carries prints and reproductions, are open Mondays through Saturdays from 11 AM to 5 PM; admission charge (phone: 416-861-4571).

From there, cross Queen Street to *Eaton Centre,* a gargantuan shopping complex stretching for several blocks. Beneath its gigantic glass-and-steel arched roof are more than 300 of Toronto's finest shops and restaurants. And even if you don't feel like shopping, it's a surprisingly restful place filled with natural light, trees, plants, and fountains — the perfect spot to end your tour of Toronto's financial district.

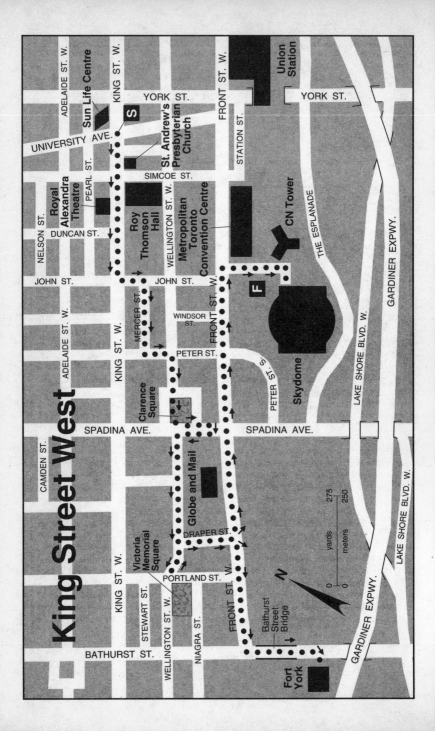

Walk 4: King Street West

Change comes easily and fleetingly to this area just west of University Avenue. In the past decade, old buildings and vacant lots have been replaced at a rapid rate by such mega-attractions as *SkyDome,* the world's most impressive domed stadium and the first to boast a retractable roof; *Roy Thomson Hall,* an internationally acclaimed music auditorium; and North America's newest (and yet-to-be-named) theater in 30 years, set to open this June with *Miss Saigon* as its first production. Major buildings, such as the Metropolitan Toronto Convention Centre, and the national headquarters and central radio and television studios of the Canadian Broadcasting Corporation, have also become part of the city's changing skyline. And more office and retail developments are on the drawing board.

Once called "New Town" because new parliament buildings were built here in 1829 and a new lieutenant-governor's house in 1866, the area flourished for a time when stately University Avenue was the route of choice for pedestrians and horse-drawn carriages. But in subsequent years, the neighborhood changed: Commerce abandoned King Street for Yonge Street, which offered a direct transportation link between the factories, warehouses, lumberyards, and grain elevators near the lakeshore and the towns and villages to the north; the lieutenant-governor's residence was transferred to Chorley Park in fashionable Rosedale; and the Parliament moved to Queen's Park Circle. All that remained of this "New Town" soon after the turn of the century were a few tree-lined neighborhoods of conservative-looking houses, lone august buildings dating from the late 1880s, and a motley sampling of commercial and industrial structures. How times have changed.

For this 1½-hour walk, exit the subway at the St. Andrew stop at the corner of King Street and University Avenue. Go to the southwest corner and look up at the mirrored twin towers of the Sun Life Centre on King Street's north side. Completed in 1984, the center's towers were allowed to rise beyond the 3-story limit of the time because its builders struck a deal with the financially troubled St. Andrew's Presbyterian Church across the street — trading a substantial donation from Sun Life for a civic blessing. Hallelujah!

Flanked on the east by a nondescript office building, the 1875 church stands between Simcoe Street and University Avenue and is all but hidden from view until you suddenly come upon it. It was designed by English-born architect William Storm in the Scottish baronial style — it even includes Old Country turrets. The distinctive stones on the left corner of the roof depict a builder's tools of the trade. In its early days, the church's parishioners included a small population of locals, guests from the nearby hotel, and government workers.

When the government moved and this section of Toronto failed to win popularity as a residential neighborhood, the church came to depend on its congregants making pilgrimages from other neighborhoods each Sunday. The Sun Life money came in handy, too.

At one time, this corner of King and Simcoe Streets was known as Toronto's four corners of wisdom. In addition to the church (salvation) on the southeast corner, a hotel and bar (damnation) stood to the northeast, Upper Canada College, a private boys' school (education), was on the northwest, and the Parliament Building (legislation) was on the fourth corner. Only the church remains today.

There's a lot less discord these days on the southwest corner where the laws were once made. *Roy Thomson Hall,* home of the *Toronto Mendelssohn Choir* and the *Toronto Symphony,* now occupies the site and brings in artists from all over the world. Named for the former Lord Thomson of Fleet (1894–1976), who built a far-flung media empire in North America and Britain, the 2,800-seat building is shaped like an inverted bowl with glass sheathing and is said to be one of the most acoustically perfect halls ever built. Free guided tours are conducted daily except Sundays at 12:30 PM, except when there is a performance; call ahead to confirm (60 Simcoe St.; phone: 416-593-4822).

On the south side of the street just west of *Roy Thomson Hall* are the new futuristic-looking headquarters of the Municipality of Metropolitan Toronto, the collective governing body of the City of Toronto and the surrounding municipalities of Mississauga, Etobicoke, Scarborough, North York, and East York.

Across from the concert hall on the north side of King Street are several restaurants catering to office workers as well as to the concert and theater crowds who frequent this area. There also are some noteworthy sites on this side of the street — go a few steps west on King Street for a look at No. 212, a 19th-century building with pressed terra cotta detailing around its windows.

Another worthwhile stop is the splendid *Royal Alexandra Theatre* (No. 260; phone: 416-593-4211), a 1907 Beaux Arts building called the "Royal Alex" by locals. One of the best-loved landmarks in the city, it owes its existence to one man: Ed Mirvish of *Honest Ed's* discount store on Bloor Street, who bought and refurbished the theater in 1963 and restored its sumptuous interior and Victorian façade. (He did the same for the historic and venerable *Old Vic* theater in London.) Mirvish's interest in the performing arts also extends to brand-new structures — he is responsible for building Toronto's (and North America's) newest and yet-to-be-named theater (on King St.).

Aside from the theater, Mirvish's various enterprises include the *Museum of the Absurd* (270 King St. W.; no phone), *Ed's Warehouse,* a roast-beef and ribs place (270 King St. W.; phone: 416-593-6676), and *Old Ed's* restaurant complex of Italian, Chinese, and Canadian food (west of the *Royal Alex* at No. 276; phone: 416-872-3333), with hearty and tasty fare at reasonable prices. And be it theater, museum, or restaurant, the atmosphere in all of Mirvish's places — the garish opulence of red velvet, Tiffany lamps, stained glass windows (with religious scenes in the *Cathedral Bar*), statues of Neptune, and Royal Doulton chamber pots — has made him one of Toronto's most beloved characters.

But if *Ed's* is not to your dining or visual tastes, there are several other restaurants nearby: the *Duncan Street Grill,* a steak and seafood specialty house on the north-south road that abuts King Street at the *Royal Alex* (20 Duncan St.; phone: 416-977-8997); *Japanese Tidal Wave* (100 Simcoe St.; phone: 416-597-0016); and two seafood places — *Filet of Sole* (11 Duncan St., upper floor; phone: 416-598-3256) and *Whistling Oyster* (11 Duncan St., lower floor; phone: 416-598-7707). For more casual fare — chicken wings and beer — join the queue at the *Loose Moose* (220 Adelaide St. W.; phone: 416-971-5252).

Walk west away from the *Royal Alex* to the northeast corner of John and King Streets, the site of the 1829 York Hospital, Toronto's first. Farther along King are several good-to-excellent dining spots serving French, Italian, and Japanese fare, and the new *Holiday Inn on King.*

Cross the street and turn left to walk south on John Street toward the CN Tower. Stop at the corner of Mercer and John Streets and look south on John to see the east entrance of the *SkyDome* stadium (we will see more of it at the end of this tour). One block to the left is the new $580-million (and still counting) headquarters of the Canadian Broadcasting Corporation. The massive blue and red concrete-and-glass complex is only part of the $1-billion development in the immediate area, which will also include two office towers, retail space, a hotel, and a 1-acre public park. Turn right at Mercer Street and walk to No. 24, one of the oldest buildings in the area (1859) and the only brick structure from that time.

Continue west on Mercer, turn left onto Peter Street, and walk a half block to Wellington Street. (From the end of Peter Street you can see the west entrance to the *SkyDome* and its beckoning sculpture of exuberant fans jutting from the outer walls.) At Wellington Street look east for one of the best views of the bank core, including the glittering Royal Bank Plaza and Commerce Court. Continue west on Wellington to a small area of park benches and trees where the street veers to the right; there is a row of Second Empire houses built in 1880 as part of a gentrification plan for the area. They were renovated in the 1960s and now contain private businesses and residences.

Walk to the northwest corner of the park for a look at the historical plaque erected to commemorate the birthplace of the first Canadian to win Britain's coveted Victoria Cross. Alexander Dunn received the honor for valor during the infamous Charge of the Light Brigade at Balaclava in 1854. Though he survived the famous, ill-fated charge, Dunn was killed while hunting wild game in Abyssinia.

Wellington makes an abrupt turn here; there is no pedestrian crossing at Spadina so walk south to the corner of Front Street, cross with the lights, and then turn right. Walk north again to the broader continuation of Wellington, which was built on a grand scale by late 19th-century planners on the assumption that the area would develop into a prestigious residential neighborhood. That didn't happen, but the vestiges of this hope can be seen in some of the buildings on the north side of the street, particularly Nos. 376, 374, 422, and 424, each with a carved stone lion's head out front.

Farther west on Wellington Street is Victoria Memorial Square. At the center of this small park is a monument commemorating the soldiers who died (some are buried here) defending the town of York from US troops during the War of 1812–1815. Some of the original gravestones survive and are still legible.

Head east on Wellington, and turn right to walk south on Draper Street, a little-known Toronto gem. The small but cozy houses lining this short street, complete with its mom 'n' pop variety store, date from the 1880s; most of them have been faithfully restored. The Second Empire mansards of the houses on the left side of the street contrast nicely with the bay and gable houses on the right. Note the historical plaques by the front doors, a gift of Toronto's 150th anniversary committee of 1984. At the end of the street you can see in the distance the remains of grain elevators and parts of the Harbourfront area.

To visit historic Fort York (see *Memorable Museums* in DIVERSIONS) with its re-creations of early life in "Muddy York," turn right, continue along Front Street, turn left at Bathurst Street, then cross over the Bathurst Street Bridge and follow the signs to the fort. If you choose not to stop there, a left turn on Front Street leads back toward the city center and the CN Tower. In the distance is the shining gold tower of Royal Bank Plaza. At 440 Front Street is the *Globe and Mail,* one of Toronto's newspapers. The stainless steel Art Deco doors were taken from the paper's original King Street office when the company moved to its present location in 1962.

When the CN Tower was first proposed, some Torontonians railed against constructing the concrete obelisk, saying that the tower would scar the city's skyscape, that it was too fanciful, too risky, and likely to fall. But all fears were allayed when the tower became the city's most popular tourist attraction.

And, in fact, as you continue east you'll understand the growth that the graceful 1,815-foot-high CN Tower has wrought: the cluster of office buildings on the north side of Front Street, the Metropolitan Toronto Convention Centre on the south, with CN's exclusive *l'Hotel* adjoining (see *Toronto's Best Hotels* in DIVERSIONS), and even *SkyDome,* which might not have come into existence if the tower had not been there. Before the tower was built (1973–76), the western parts of King and Front Streets were, much like the Harbourfront area, abandoned and unsightly. Now, the only remaining large undeveloped plot is the railway land south of Front Street.

Exactly what will be built on the 80-odd acres west of the *SkyDome* will depend on the outcome of a long-standing dispute between City Hall and the *Canadian National Railway,* the owner of the rail lands and the tower. There is agreement, however, that the land will contain office towers and as many as 5,000 affordable housing units.

Going to the 150-story observation deck of CN Tower is as much a must for visitors to the area as a day trip to nearby Niagara Falls. Elevator "pilots" whisk passengers up to the top in glass-enclosed cars in less than a minute (although the wait to get on the elevator may take an hour during peak summer weeks). Once there, you can eat in the revolving restaurant, sip a libation in the lounge, or, in the evening, dance in the world's highest nightclub. But most people make the trip just for the view; admission charge (phone: 416-360-8500).

From the tower walk west toward the gold-colored sculpture of baseball fans (a sort of Mt. Rushmore for bleacher bums) on the northeast façade of the *SkyDome*. Called *The Audience,* this painted fiberglass monument to the faithful fan was installed in 1989 by Toronto artist Michael Snow, who also created the wonderful flock of Canada geese hovering beneath the arched glass roof of *Eaton Centre.*

The *SkyDome,* called simply *The Dome* by Torontonians, is perhaps the best-known sports and facilities center built in the past decade. A multipurpose stadium, it also houses the *SkyDome* hotel and four restaurants (not including the *McDonalds* fast-food outlets found throughout the place) and hosts car rallies, moto-cross events, auto shows, cricket matches, exhibitions, and concerts. But the pièce de résistance is the stadium's fully retractable roof, the first of its kind in the world; in 20 minutes the 8-acre interior can be covered or exposed to the elements, to the delight of the fans of baseball's American League *Blue Jays* and the Canadian Football League's *Argos,* both of whom play their home games here. If the stadium is not in use, you can take an hour-long guided tour, which includes a film presentation and a behind-the-scenes look (*SkyDome,* Front and Peter Sts.; phone: 416-341-3663, 416-360-7100 for the *SkyDome* hotel).

From here you can stretch your tour — and your legs — to include the Harbourfront area by walking past the *SkyDome* along the pedestrian walkway between the stadium and the tower. Or follow the signs and take the covered and heated Skywalk to Union Station and public transit, an especially nice way to end this tour if the weather makes walking outside difficult.

Or if you haven't already done so, you can use the CN Tower as an observation post from which to survey the city and the walk you've just concluded. If it's a clear day, you'll see the mist rising above Niagara Falls, across the water some 60 miles away.

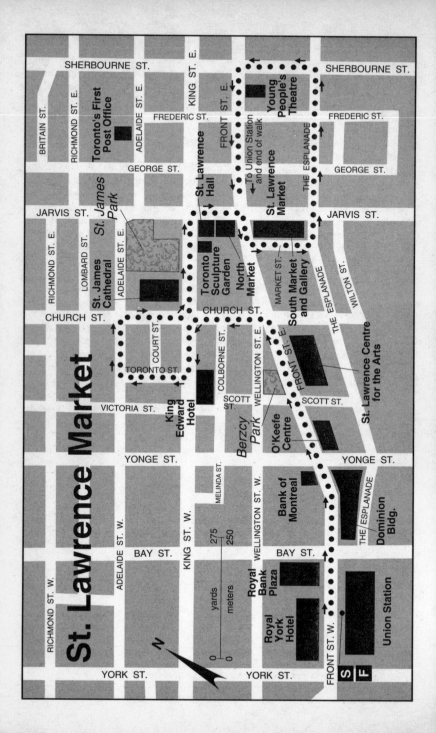

Walk 5: St. Lawrence Market

If the financial center at Bay and King Streets represents the new Toronto of international commerce and wealth, the *St. Lawrence Market* district heralds the early years of the city's history. This area was originally the infamous "Muddy York," of which it was said you could lose your boots in two steps and your trousers in four. In 1824, a representative of the queen described the site as "better calculated for a frog pond or beaver meadow than for the residence of human beings."

But despite its swampy surroundings, York (which was named for the Duke of York) was designated the provincial capital in 1797, four years after it was founded by Lieutenant-Governor John Graves Simcoe. At the time of Simcoe's arrival, the capital was Niagara-on-the-Lake, near the US border, and he wanted to find a location that would be easier to defend against an invasion from the south. York was chosen because of its seclusion and the protection offered to shipping by the Toronto Islands, which at that time were connected to the mainland. History validated Simcoe's choice; even though American forces did manage to capture Fort York during the War of 1812, it was too far from the US border for them to retain possession, and it reverted to the British.

Over the years, York flourished, growing from a marshy little village into a significant city (with a marshy center), home to soldiers, to government bureaucrats and their families, and to the shopkeepers who served them. It was divided into five political wards, each of which had a market named for a saint. The *St. Lawrence Market* was the most prominent because the government was nearby. But the area's stock fell somewhat when York was incorporated into the city of Toronto in 1834: With new growth of industry and commerce, the well-to-do citizenry moved to other, more fashionable parts of the city. The provincial Parliament and civic government soon followed, establishing themselves west of Yonge Street, where they function today. Few people remained behind, and the area became known only for the remnants of history that still clung to the collection of abandoned and neglected buildings.

Some 75 years passed before the *St. Lawrence Market* began to show signs of a resurgence. As historical preservation and architectural restoration became fashionable, the market became an obvious choice for development and renovation. Offices and stores sprang up here and there in the district, and it has become a center for performing-arts venues, restaurants, nightclubs, upscale shops, and luxury condominium complexes.

Bounded by Yonge Street to the west, the Esplanade to the south, Adelaide

Street to the north, and Sherbourne Street to the east, the *St. Lawrence Market* district is an elegant mix of new and old, chic and quaint. By day, the area bustles with office workers; at night and on weekends the streets resonate with the chatter and clatter of theatergoers, nightlife owls, window shoppers, and families out to stock the kitchen cupboard. The two indoor markets held on Saturday mornings are especially popular because of the mountains of fresh produce offered at attractively low prices. For many Torontonians this market excursion is a weekly ritual.

This walking tour will take from 2 to 3 hours, depending on your mood and pace. It starts at cavernous Union Station on Front Street, where Toronto's urban subway, commuter *GO* railway, and cross-country trains converge.

Officially opened by the Prince of Wales in 1927, Union Station is a monumental example of Classical Revival architecture that takes up an entire city block from York Street to Bay Street. It was built by Canadian architect John Lyle, noted for his strong, simple style (he also designed the *Royal Alexandra Theatre*). From the lower concourse, climb the stairs to the Great Hall, which is 250 feet long and 84 feet wide and has an 88-foot barrel ceiling. On clear days the room is awash in natural sunlight, which streams through the 4-story arched windows at either end. Carved in stone near the ceiling are the names of area cities, towns, and villages once served by the station. In front of the building is a statue of a man holding a globe, a 1985 gift from Toronto's Italian community to then Prime Minister Pierre Trudeau. He gave it back to the city as a symbol of Canada's multiculturalism.

Leave the station via the central exit, which opens onto Front Street; the *Royal York,* Toronto's landmark hotel, is on the north side of the street. The 27-story building, built in 1929 and designed in a symmetrical Beaux Arts version of the Romanesque style, was once the largest structure in the British Commonwealth. Owned by *Canadian Pacific* (which also owns the station), it has over 1,400 rooms, numerous restaurants and lounges, and remains one of the foremost hotels in the Commonwealth, popular with world leaders, royalty, and celebrities.

From Union Station, walk to the right along the curved stretch of Front Street, noting the gold-colored Royal Bank Plaza on the left (see *Walk 3: Financial District*). At the corner of Bay and Front Streets take another look at the gigantic front pillars of the mammoth station. Union Station and the curved Dominion Building (on the south side of Front Street, ahead of you when you continue the walk) have a similar design. The effect was achieved on purpose when the Dominion Building was erected in 1935 as a customs house. The Quarter-Mile Sweep, as the 2-block stretch of massive curved buildings is called, has been complemented by a recently built, tree-lined center lane.

Cross Bay Street and continue to Yonge Street, which is listed in the *Guinness Book of World Records* as the longest street in the world (about 1,142 miles/1,827 km from its start in Toronto to its end at the border of Manitoba and the US). On the northwest corner of Front and Yonge stands the former Bank of Montreal building. The exterior of this 1886 structure is a paean to economic enterprise, with detailed statues portraying Commerce,

Music, and Architecture on the south, and Industry, Science, Literature, and the Arts on the east. Some less lofty interests are represented here, too: The façade is somewhat marred by pockmarks that, according to local lore, were caused by a bank robbery decades ago. The building, complete with bullet holes, has been preserved as part of the massive BCE Place development, headquarters of Bell Canada Enterprises, and it is set to become the new home of the *Hockey Hall of Fame,* scheduled to reopen this summer. Spanning the length of the block from Bay to Yonge Streets is a 4-story galleria with shops and restaurants, including *Marche,* an informal buffet-style eatery serving soups, salads, fresh seafood, breads, and pastries (42 Yonge St.; phone: 416-366-8986).

Just across the way, on the southeast corner of Yonge and Front Streets, is the modern-looking *O'Keefe Centre,* home of the *Canadian Opera Company* and the *National Ballet of Canada* (1 Front St. E.; phone: 416-393-7469). The 3,200-seat performance center was completed in 1960 by the O'Keefe Brewing Company Ltd., and is now owned and operated by the Municipality of Metropolitan Toronto. Its first production, the 1960 world premiere of *Camelot,* which featured Richard Burton, Julie Andrews, and Canadian-born Robert Goulet, marked Toronto as a noteworthy theatrical center.

The *St. Lawrence Centre for the Arts* (next door) was built to celebrate Canada's centennial in 1967; today this weighty cement edifice is home to the *Canadian Stage Company, Theatre Plus,* and many musical ensembles. It also plays host to educational forums, public speakers, and musical events (27 Front St. E.; phone: 416-366-7723). Along this stretch of Front Street is a variety of shops and boutiques, including *Frida's* (No. 39; phone: 416-366-3169), with the best in Ontario-made crafts, from old-time bonnets to snazzy sweaters, and *Mountain Equipment Co-op* (No. 35; phone: 416-363-0122), the place for suede and leather backpacks for the urban hiker.

Across the street on the north side of Front is Berzcy Park, a small area of benches and trees named after William Berzcy, a prominent painter and one of the first German immigrants to live in the area (he was lured here in 1794 by the promise of 6,000 acres of land, which he never received). The park's construction was part of the first modern revitalization program on the waterfront, which included *Ontario Place,* Harbourfront, the CN Tower, and the *SkyDome.* In June, Berzcy Park is one of the locations for the annual *du Maurier Ltd. Downtown Jazz Festival,* with music offered by a variety of groups, from classical to jazz (phone: 416-363-8717).

Take a close look at the wall at the east end of the park. It appears that a massive piece of canvas is peeling away from a 4-story building, but it's an optical illusion. The fanciful trompe l'oeil mural was painted by Toronto artist Derek Besant in 1980; he used the edifice's windows to create the deception. No other mural in this city of murals (including Charlie Pachter's *Queen on a Moose*) attracts as much attention; this building is one of the most photographed in Toronto.

Continue east along Front Street to Church Street. Here, three streets — Church, Front, and Wellington — converge and present an example of the city's widely divergent architecture. Turn right on Wellington Street and walk a short distance farther east, then look back at the Flatiron Building nestled on a pie-shape lot. The building, erected in 1892 by the Gooderham Brewery as its corporate headquarters, is mirrored in the modern office complex behind it; still farther away, the CN Tower looms on the skyline. The juxtaposition of these three structures captures the contrast between modern innovation and historic preservation that characterizes Toronto.

Return to the corner of Church and Front Streets and walk north on Church to King Street. On the northeast corner was the site of the city's first church — the Church of England of St. James, built in 1807. The original wooden church was pulled down and replaced with a wood-and-stone building in 1831. That church, destroyed by fire, was rebuilt in 1839, and it suffered another blaze 10 years later. St. James Cathedral, the current structure, was begun in 1850 by Frederick William Cumberland (who also designed University College), and was completed in 1853. The Gothic Revival cathedral's 306-foot spire, built by architect Henry Langley and finished in 1874, is the tallest in Canada and the second-tallest in North America (only St. Patrick's Cathedral in New York City is taller). The interior is also worth a look for the Tiffany window in the Lady Chapel and the many relics of Toronto's early establishment.

Not far from the entrance of the cathedral, on the left, you'll find the 1817 gravestone of John Rideout, an early member of its congregation who was the last York resident to be killed in a public duel. Rideout and his adversary, Sam Jarvis, after whom the street east of here is named, were arguing about money when Rideout challenged Jarvis to a duel with pistols. According to the story, Rideout cheated a bit by firing at the count of nine instead of ten, but he missed high and wide. Jarvis's bullet hit its target dead center, and the unlucky Rideout was "consigned to an early grave," as the tombstone records.

From the church, turn left to the Victorian gardens of the city-owned St. James Park to the east. On a summer day, a concert might be going on at the band shell here. Directly across from the park, on the south side of King Street, is the Toronto Sculpture Garden. Works by Canadian and international artists are displayed here on a rotating basis, and the exhibits can include anything from scrap-metal abstracts to waterfalls.

Continue west on King Street (named after King George III, the offending monarch during the Revolutionary War) for 2 blocks; at the corner of King and Victoria Streets stands the stately *King Edward* hotel. Locally known as the "King Eddy," it enjoyed a reputation as one of the city's most prestigious hostelries at the turn of the century, but its star had tarnished over the years until Forte, the British hotel group, purchased it in 1981 and restored it to its former elegance. If you need a break at this point, drop into the *Consort Bar* for a quiet libation or enjoy afternoon tea (served daily; jacket preferred) from 3 to 5 PM (37 King St. E.; phone: 416-863-9700).

Backtrack to the corner of King and Toronto Streets and turn left up Toronto, heading north. Once Toronto's seventh post office, the building at No. 10 resembles a classic Roman temple. Farther north, at No. 17, is an 1876 building in the Renaissance style which has housed the Consumers Gas Company of Toronto for more than 100 years.

At Adelaide Street, 1 block farther north, turn right to the former York

Country Magistrates Court (No. 57). The courthouse, another work by Frederick William Cumberland, was restored in 1982 as *Adelaide Court,* a complex housing several small theaters, bars, and restaurants. Two participants in the Upper Canada Rebellion of 1837, led by William Lyon Mackenzie, were executed behind the building. They were later buried in a single grave in Cabbagetown. (Mackenzie himself escaped execution by fleeing to the US, but he returned under amnesty 12 years later.) Near the intersection of Adelaide and Church Streets is *Nami* (55 Adelaide St. E.; phone: 416-362-7373), a good spot for sushi and tempura.

Walk right on Church to King Street, then head left, past St. James Cathedral and the Sculpture Gardens. At the corner of King and Jarvis Streets is *St. Lawrence Hall,* known simply as *Town Hall* (157 King St. E.). During its heyday, this 1850 Renaissance building with its Corinthian façade and cupola was the social and cultural center of Toronto; John A. Macdonald, Canada's first prime minister, held political meetings here.

Town Hall sits on the site of the building that housed the first council offices of the village of York (which fortunately had moved to the present location of the nearby *St. Lawrence Market* before the building was destroyed by fire in 1849). At the turn of the century, the building contained a stage where such artists as Tom Thumb and Jenny Lind (the "Swedish Nightingale") performed, as well as municipal office space, a market, shops, and a large banquet room. Restored in 1967 as part of the city's official centennial celebration, the hall has resumed its role as a center for social and cultural gatherings; the *National Ballet of Canada* houses its main administrative offices here.

This area is a good spot for a lunch or dinner break, as there are several restaurants. Among the best, at the corner of Jarvis and Adelaide, is the *Bombay Palace* (71 Jarvis St.; phone: 416-368-8048), which specializes in East Indian dishes and curries. A short block farther north, at Lombard and Jarvis Streets, is the *Old Fire Hall,* an 1867 fire station which is now home to the renowned *Second City* comedy club and restaurant (110 Lombard St.; phone: 416-863-1111; see *Quintessential Toronto* in DIVERSIONS). This Toronto incarnation of the original Chicago comedy revue is where such well-known comedians as John Candy, Rick Moranis, Dan Aykroyd, and Martin Short got their start.

At George and Adelaide is Toronto's first post office, built in 1833 and now a museum containing period exhibits and postal souvenirs. It's open from 10 AM to 4 PM; no admission charge. 260 Adelaide St. E. (phone: 416-865-1833).

Backtrack to the entrance of *St. Lawrence Hall* at King and Jarvis Streets and head south on Jarvis, until you reach the *St. Lawrence Market. South Market,* the larger of the two regions that comprise the heart of this district, contains 12 permanent stalls of city vendors; *North Market* is where area farmers sell their produce every Saturday morning, starting as early as 5 AM. Though you certainly shouldn't miss the opportunity to browse through the fresh fruits and vegetables if the Saturday food fest is in session, *South Market,* open from Tuesdays through Saturdays, is the real attraction; it's an ideal place to catch a glimpse of Torontonians going about their daily business.

Take time out to sample the wares: piping-hot homemade bread, cakes, cookies, pies, muffins, and croissants; freshly ground coffee; a wide selection of cheese; and fresh-pressed cider (in season). You'll also find fish and meat galore, but for a true taste of Canada, try peameal bacon on a bun (also known as "back bacon" or, in the US, "Canadian bacon") from one of the market's several delis. Or venture down to the building's cavernous lower level, past stalls offering colorful and fragrant flowers, and browse among the clothing and craft shops.

The *St. Lawrence Market* is the latest incarnation of several previous markets on this site. The first City Hall, a 3-tiered building of red brick and white stone, was constructed here in 1845; council offices were on the second floor, but it also held a meat market, shops, stalls, and a police station in the basement. After City Hall moved to Bay and Queen Streets in 1899, the building underwent extensive changes, including the removal of its clock tower and cupola. Stone pillars and the lintel stand as remnants of the original 1845 entranceway, and a plaque at the door describes the varied history of this place.

On the second floor of the building, which was renovated in 1977, is the *Market Gallery* (95 Front St. E.; phone: 416-392-7604), a showcase for historical exhibits of old photos, archives, and artifacts. Open Wednesdays through Saturdays from 10 AM to 4 PM, and from noon to 4 PM on Sundays. Admission charge.

Leave from the Front Street exit of *South Market* and walk left to the corner of Front and Market Streets. Then take a left and continue down Market Street toward the Esplanade, a popular commercial strip that runs east and west from Jarvis to Yonge Streets. In this popular nightclub area are such heavily frequented clubs as *Brandy's* (58 The Esplanade; phone: 416-364-6671), *Scotland Yard* (56 The Esplanade; phone: 416-364-6572), and *Muddy York's* (5 Church St., at The Esplanade; phone: 416-364-5788).

Though this stretch is known for its nightlife, it also has some daytime attractions that are fun for kids. The *Old Spaghetti Factory* (54 The Esplanade; phone: 416-864-9761) offers a special children's menu, video games, a carousel, and a full-size Toronto streetcar; next door is the *Organ Grinder* (58 The Esplanade; phone: 416-364-6517), a burgers-and-fries eatery with a multitude of musical instruments, including its namesake organ, available for playing. The atmosphere is fun, rollicking — and very loud.

Walk along the Esplanade (away from Yonge Street); turn left on Sherbourne Street, and turn left again onto Front Street. Here is the *Young People's Theatre,* an internationally known troupe devoted exclusively to children's theater. The group commissions short works from Canadian playwrights and performs them at schools throughout Ontario. The century-old building was originally a depot for horse-drawn streetcars (165 Front St. E.; phone: 416-864-9732).

Completing the circle, continue in the same direction along Front Street to Union Station.

Index